Aspects and Prospects of Teacher Education

Aspects and Prospects of Teacher Education

Dr. Sabita Mishra

BLACK EAGLE BOOKS
Dublin, USA | Bhubaneswar, India

Black Eagle Books
USA address:
7464 Wisdom Lane
Dublin, OH 43016

India address:
E/312, Trident Galaxy, Kalinga Nagar,
Bhubaneswar-751003, Odisha, India

E-mail: info@blackeaglebooks.org
Website: www.blackeaglebooks.org

First International Edition Published by
Black Eagle Books, 2023

ASPECTS AND PROSPECTS OF TEACHER EDUCATION
by **Dr. Sabita Mishra**

Copyright © Dr. Sabita Mishra

All rights reserved. No part of this publication may be reproduced, stored in a retrieval system, or transmitted, in any form or by any means, electronic, mechanical, photocopying, recording or otherwise without the prior permission of the publisher.

Cover & Interior Design: Ezy's Publication

ISBN- 978-1-64560-362-7 (Paperback)
Library of Congress Control Number: 2023932348

Printed in the United States of America

Foreword

In this book, Dr. Sabita Mishra discusses the Aspects and Prospects of Teacher Education. She portrays her own experience as a teacher by throwing light on the issues faced by a teacher for which one needs to orient oneself for a balanced teaching atmosphere. The book consists of 17 chapters, focusing on different aspects of teacher education, such as issues and challenges in teaching and quality management, she also discusses how information and communication technology can be integrated in education.

As a teacher's personality directly influences the personality of students, discussion has been made on integration of peace and value orientation, life-skills, creativity and stress management in teacher education. Besides, the book focuses on leadership role of the teacher, teacher education for sustainable development and the role of teacher in the formation of a bright future of the nation. From research point of view, innovative pedagogy is also discussed. All chapters are very well designed and elaborated from different perspectives of teacher education. The book can be very helpful in developing the quality and value of the teacher for a healthy society.

Kalyanamalini Sahoo
Faculty member, University of Lille, France

Preface

Teacher education in India has a long history. Since the ancient period, it has been a major part of the education system. Teacher is the real social architect who can really shape the destiny of the nation. Emphasizing the importance of teacher, the National Policy on Education (1986) states, 'the status of the teacher reflects the socio-cultural ethos of the society; it is said that no people can rise above the level of its teachers'. This statement indicates the vital role of the teacher in shaping the fate of the nation and rebuilding the society by educating the young minds.

The teacher education is facing a number of issues and challenges. In the present context the expectation of the community from the teacher has been multiplied, teacher –student relationship is far more complex and the government is formulating new policies and finding new norms and standards for teachers. This compels the teachers to play a dynamic role and equip themselves with the latest knowledge and skills to meet the emerging challenges.

Over the last half a century and particularly in the recent decades teaching learning has been undergoing drastic changes. The process of teaching-learning is tuned with innovation and emphasis has shifted from teacher-centred, lecture-based instructions to student-centred interactive learning environments. Teacher has to generate new knowledge among students by employing a variety of technology tools and innovative pedagogies in teaching to satisfy diverse needs of different categories of students effectively.

Inclusive education is an innovative step towards quality education and assists in developing each child fully and helps in universalisation of education. Teachers are required to be trained in inclusive practices. Quality education largely depends upon the quality of teacher and the quality of teacher can be enhanced through continuous professional development programmes. Life skills education has major role in shaping teacher's personality. Training of life skills education will surely enable the teachers to play their multifarious roles in school, home and society most effectively. The role of teacher for sustainable development of the nation is complex and nuanced. Teachers are considered to be the change agents to put into action the sustainable development goals.

Present society needs effective, reflective, and creative teachers who can participate in the improvement of the whole educational process. Future teachers need to be value oriented, enlightened, and empowered to lead communities and nations in their march towards better and higher quality of life. The teachers having a futuristic vision can only lead the society towards an egalitarian one.

Keeping in view the above points, the present book has been conceptualized. The book consists of seventeen chapters covering various aspects and prospects of teacher education. I hope this book will serve as reference book and fulfil the needs of the students, teachers, policy makers and researchers in the field of education.

    I am indebted to my family members for their continuous inspiration and support for writing this book. I express my sincere thanks to the publisher Black Eagle Books for his timely support to publish this book.

Dr. Sabita Mishra

CONTENTS

Chapter: 1
    Concept of Teacher Education — 13

Chapter: 2
    Issues and Challenges in Teacher Education — 33

Chapter: 3
    Teacher Effectiveness and Reflective Practice in Teaching — 45

Chapter: 4
    Quality Management in Teacher Education — 72

Chapter: 5
    Information and Communication Technology Integration in Teacher Education — 88

Chapter: 6
    Innovative Pedagogy and Teacher Education — 104

Chapter: 7
    Teacher Education and Inclusive Practice — 122

Chapter: 8
    Professional Development of Teacher — 147

Chapter: 9
    Life Skills Education for Teacher — 164

Chapter: 10
    Creativity and Teacher — 183

Chapter: 11
    Leadership Role of Teacher — 198

Chapter: 12
    Value-oriented Teacher Education — 217

Chapter: 13
    Integration of Peace in Teacher Education — 234

Chapter: 14
    Stress Management and Teacher — 249

Chapter: 15
    Views of Great Educationists for Teacher — 266

Chapter: 16
    Teacher Education for Sustainable Development — 282

Chapter: 17
    Role of Teacher for Future of the Nation — 299

References — 311

Chapter-1

Concept of Teacher Education

Teacher education is an integral component of the education system. It is a discipline which educates future generations. It develops both teachers and teacher educators. Since ancient times, almost in all societies of the world, teachers have shown right path to people to come out from the darkness of ignorance, false beliefs etc. Teaching is not only a profession but also the drive to build a responsible society. It is believed that a nation can flourish if it has good teacher. Teachers work on the grass root level of the society from where they can ensure a great nation. Therefore, the National Education Policy has made some recommendations to improve teacher education (NEP, 2020).

Meaning of Teacher Education

According to Goods Dictionary of Education Teacher education means "all formal and informal activities and experiences that help to qualify a person to assume the responsibilities as a member of the educational profession or to discharge his responsibilities more effectively". Teacher education now includes every aspects of the student-teacher's personality. The students are the future of the country, so only a trained and skilful teacher makes them best and help them to be the future of the country. Teacher is like a pot maker. As the pot maker, makes a well-shaped pot, similarly, the teacher also makes a perfect student with the help of providing guidance and teaching. Only a skilful and trained teacher has the capacity to provide proper guidance and teaching. So, the teacher education is the only thing which helps the teacher to be skilful and trained.

The National Council for Teacher Education (NCTE) has defined Teacher education as "a programme of education, research and training of persons to teach from pre-primary to higher education level. Teacher education is a programme that is related to the development of teacher proficiency and competence that would enable and empower the teacher to meet the requirements of the profession and face the challenges there in". It encompasses skills, sound pedagogical theories and professional skills.

Teacher education is vital in creating a pool of school teachers that will shape the next generation. Teacher preparation is an activity that requires multidisciplinary perspectives and knowledge, formation of dispositions and values, and development of practice under the best mentors. Teachers must be grounded in Indian values, languages, knowledge, ethos, and traditions including tribal traditions, while also being well-versed in the latest advances in education and pedagogy (NEP, 2020).

Teacher education is the process of providing teachers with the skills and knowledge necessary to teach effectively in a classroom environment. It includes the policies and procedures designed to equip teachers with the knowledge, attitudes, behaviours and skills they require to perform their tasks effectively in the classroom. Teacher education as such is an institutionalized educational procedure that is aimed at the purposefully organised preparation or further education of teachers who are engaged directly or indirectly in educational activities. Teacher education aims at helping the teacher in understanding the nature, abilities, aptitudes, developmental level, individual differences, emotion, instincts, sentiments, ambitions of the child and assists them in making better adjustments.

History of Teacher Education

Teacher education is as old as the human civilization. Teacher education in India has a long history. Since the ancient period it has been a major part of the educational system. Gurukula system of education during Vedic period was somewhat modified and enriched under the influence of Buddhist Vihara-based system. This continued till 11th century A.D. The arrival of the Muslims witnessed the rise of Maktabs. This also continued during British period.

19th century is regarded as landmark in teacher education course as various teacher education institutions were established to facilitate learning. In 1906-1956, the program of teacher preparation was called teacher training. After independence the first step in this direction was setting up of the University Education Commission (1948) which made valuable suggestions regarding pre-service and in-service education of teachers and linking the programme of teacher preparation with the university system. In 1953 the Secondary Education Commission examined the conditions of school education with specific suggestions about the preparation of teachers. The Education Commission (1964-66) gave a comprehensive report, which served as a basis for establishing a uniform national structure of education covering all stages and aspects of education. It laid stress on the importance of practice teaching and in-service education. It recommended allocation of more funds for teacher preparation, better salaries and improved service conditions for teachers and teacher educators to attract competent people to the profession. Based on these recommendations the National Policy on Education (NPE, 1968) was made. In 1974, NCTE was set up by Government of India to bring development in teacher education. Many universities and state governments revised the courses of teacher education. The Ministry of Education document "Challenge of Education-A Policy Perspective" (1985) has mentioned, "Teacher performance is the most crucial input in the field of education, but lamented that much of teacher education was irrelevant, that selection procedures and recruitment systems were inappropriate and the teaching was still the last choice in the job market". It laid emphasis on aptitude for teaching in the entrants on reorganization of the teacher education programme and on in-service education.

The National Education Policy (1986) has similarly said, "The status of the teacher reflects the socio-cultural ethos of a society; it is said that no people can rise above the level of its teachers. The government and the community should endeavour to create conditions which will help to motivate and inspire teachers in constructive and creative lines. Teachers should have the freedom to innovate to devise appropriate methods of communication and activities relevant to the needs and capabilities of the concerns of the community".

National Policy on Education (1986) recommended enrichment programme for both pre-service and in-service teachers, computer education and new as well as alternative models of teacher preparation. During the last two decades, the teacher education curricula have received severe criticism. There is hardly any difference between the performance of trained and untrained teachers because of outdated teacher education curricula. Reconstruction of teacher education curricula is the need of the hour. It has to be transformed from information based to experience based. Over the last half a century and particularly, in the recent decades, teaching learning has been undergoing great changes. There has been a shift towards student centric classrooms with teacher's role more as facilitator of learning rather than an autocratic master. Teacher education institutions have been proliferating and mushrooming all over the country until the arrival of National Council for Teacher Education (NCTE). NCTE insisted on mandatory norms and standards for these institutions. As a result of the intervention of NCTE, many institutions were developed their standards and brought improvement in the salary of teacher.

The NCTE was established in 1995 under the NCTE Act, with a view to achieving planned and co-ordinated development of teacher education system throughout the country, the regulations and proper maintenance of norms and standards in the teacher education system and the matters connected there with. To improve the quality of teacher education NCTE has entered into Memorandum of Understanding (MOU) with NAAC in 2002 for accreditation of teacher education institutions. Indeed, the NAAC has done a commendable job in introducing the culture of uniform educational standards as well as tools for testing these standards. NAAC has accredited more than 200 teacher education institutions in India with the assigned grade C+ to A+.

Teacher education system in India is a biggest system globally and is expanding. During 2002-2003, there were around 5.5 million teachers in India. The enrolment in teacher education institution was more than 2, 00,000 every year. There were around 2,000 teacher education institutions during 2002-03. There are different types of teacher education courses running in these institutions. At present, there are 16917 teacher education institutions in India, and these institutions are offering a total number of 24199 courses (NCTE, 2020). The total number of teachers in 2019-20 was 9.68 million, an increase of more than 250,000 over total teachers in 2018-19, the annual government estimate showed. This growth in teachers' number is a positive sign as it increases the pupil-teacher ratio.

Studies in the field of teacher education reveal that the quality of pre-service and in-service teacher education programmes in India are deteriorating and the professional commitment and overall competence of teachers leave much to be desired. Therefore, everything necessarilyhas to be done to ensure that teacher education institution in India produce teachers of high quality and calibre, conscious initiatives are necessary to influence the quality of teacher education at various levels.

Characteristics of Teacher Education

Some of the characteristics of teacher education are given below:

- Teacher education is a continuous process and its pre-service and in-service components are complimentary to each other. According to the International Encyclopaedia of Teaching and Teacher Education (1987), "Teacher education can be considered in three phases: Pre-service, Induction and In-service. The three phases are considered as parts of a continuous process".
- Teacher education is based on the theory that "Teachers are made, not born" in contrary to the

assumption, "Teachers are born, not made". Since teaching is considered as an art and a science, the teacher has to acquire not only knowledge, but also skills that are called "tricks of the trade".

- Teacher education is broad and comprehensive. Besides pre-service and in-service programmes for teachers, it is meant to be involved in various community programmes and extension activities viz. adult education and non-formal education programmes, literacy and development activities of the society.
- It is ever evolving and dynamic. In order to prepare teachers who are competent to face the challenges of the dynamic society, teacher education has to keep abreast of recent developments and trends.
- The crux of the entire process of teacher education lies in its curriculum, design, structure, organization and transaction modes, as well as the extent of its appropriateness.
- As in other professional education programmes the teacher education curriculum has a knowledge base which is sensitive to the needs of field applications and comprises meaningful, conceptual blending of theoretical understanding available in several cognate disciplines. However, the knowledge base in teacher education does not comprise only an admixture of concepts and principles from other disciplines, but a distinct 'gestalt' emerging from the 'conceptual blending', making it sufficiently specified.
- Teacher education has become differentiated into stage specific programmes. This suggests that the

knowledge base is adequately specialized and diversified across stages, which should be utilized for developing effective processes of preparing entrant teachers for the functions which a teacher is expected to perform at each stage.

- It is a system that involves an interdependence of its Inputs, Processes and Outputs.

There are a number of sayings about the role of a teacher in the transformation of society. Keeping in mind the importance of teachers in the education system, the NEP-2020 has underlined the role of teachers along with the desired attributes of teachers for nation-building. In this policy, the teachers have been put at the centre of the most needed fundamental reforms in the education system. The policy has also emphasized re-establishing teachers, at all levels, as the most respected and essential members of our society, as they shape the future generation of the country. As a step forward, the NEP-2020 has also elaborated on the recruitment of good teachers in a transparent method, to give autonomy while also instilling a sense of responsibility and accountability in every teacher.

A multi-disciplinarian teacher becomes a successful teacher. NEP has mandated for holistic education which calls for the holistic outlook of a teacher for his/her subject without breaking the knowledge into discrete components such as Mathematics, Economics, and Physics etc. A teacher may have specialization in a particular subject or area, but he/she must be able to integrate different subjects and has a comprehensive outlook to inspire students to think beyond his / her subject. An ideal teacher must be responsive and adaptive to such changes and responsive to the changing needs of society with time. Bringing any innovative practice may be an important attribute of an ideal teacher. To value real-world learning is an essence for a good teacher. As described in NEP (2020), emphasis has been put on experiential or real-world learning. For this, it has been advised to reduce curriculum content to enhance experiential learning and critical thinking. Hands-on learning, arts-integrated and sports-integrated teaching may be more effective and adoption of these teaching methods by a teacher may lead to more enrolments in our education programmes.

The National Education Policy (2020) states that by 2030 the minimum educational qualification for teachers would be four-year duration integrated B.Ed degree. If this happens, only candidates with four year B.Ed degree and TET certificate will be eligible to apply for teacher recruitment in government schools.

Objectives of Teacher Education

The objectives of teacher education are stated as follows:

- Provide opportunities to observe and engage with children, communicate with and relate to children.
- Provide opportunities for self-learning, reflection, assimilation and articulation of new ideas; developing capacities for self-directed learning and the ability to think, be self-critical and to work in groups.
- Provide opportunities for understanding self and others (including one's beliefs, assumptions and emotions); developing the ability for self-analysis, self-evaluation, adaptability, flexibility, creativity and innovation.
- Provide opportunities to enhance understanding, knowledge and examine disciplinary knowledge

and social realities, relate subject matter with the social milieu and develop critical thinking.
- Provide opportunities to develop professional skills in pedagogy, observation, documentation, analysis, drama, craft, story-telling and reflective inquiry.
- To provide instruction in particular courses of study in B.Ed.
- To restructure the existing curriculum of teacher education programme completely.
- To build a national system of teacher education based on India's cultural ethics, its unity and diversity synchronizing with change and continuity.
- To facilitate the realization of the constitutional goals and emergence of the social order.
- To prepare professionally competent teachers to perform their roles effectively as per needs of the society.
- To upgrade the standard of teacher education
- To enhance the professional and social status of teachers and develop amongst them a sense of commitment.

Types of Teacher Education

The Education Commission (1964-66) after reviewing the status and service conditions of teachers have pointed out, "Of all the different factors which influence the quality of education and its contribution to national development, the quality, competence and character of teachers are undoubtedly the most significant. Nothing is more important than securing a sufficient supply of high quality recruits to the teaching profession, providing them with the best possible professional preparation and creating satisfactory conditions of work in which they can be fully effective". In view of the rapid expansion of educational facilities expected during the plan periods and especially in view of the urgent need to raise standards to the highest level and to keep them continually in proving these problems have now acquired unprecedented importance and urgency.

According to Mr. Oliver, "The development of teacher does not cease when he leaves the training college, he now begins to learn from a different kind of experience". To attain efficiency in every aspect of teaching, it is essential that a teacher should undergo a well-designed course of teacher education. Not only to this extent but teacher education should continue as long as teacher is in the profession.

Concept of life-long education has necessitated the continuation of teacher education. Because of the need of teacher education and its continuation teacher education has been divided into two types:

    A.   Pre-service Teacher Education

    B.   In-service Teacher Education

Meaning of Pre-Service Teacher Education

Pre-service teacher education means, the professional training undertaken by teachers before their joining in the service as teachers. People desiring to adopt teaching as their profession, are called upon to undergo and complete such pre-service training as they acquire necessary knowledge and skills that are necessary for improving their competence as teachers. These programmes are intended to support and enhance teacher's learning and to instil in them a greater degree of self-confidence. Their course of studies / curriculum includes appropriate content knowledge about essential qualities of a good teacher in relevant theory papers and provision of practice of effective domain related traits in school situations for transaction during sessions scheduled for the purpose. The programme is mainly aimed to make pupil teachers reflective, introspective and capable of analyzing his or her own life and the process of education at school so that after becoming a teacher, he becomes a successful agent to fulfil the goals of society. During the pre-service teacher education programme, it is important for teacher educators to learn the methodology of how to get in touch with the core qualities of a good teacher and how they can stimulate these qualities in student teachers. This will lead to a deeper involvement in the learning process of teacher educators as well as student teachers. There is an attempt to combine theory and practice in such a way that theory will be based on the accumulated results of practice, while at the same time practice should possess organizational and systematic characteristics deriving from generalization and principles. The theoretical and practical aspects of the programme contribute to the development of the ability of the teacher.

Pre-service teacher education develops the following aspects:

- It develops positive attitude and skills of pupil teachers, required for teaching profession.
- It helps to observe systematically and to analyze the relations and interactions taking place in classroom and at school in general.
- It helps to organize and direct the teaching process.
- It enables pupil teachers to critically analyze the teaching task.

On completion of the course of studies, the students or pupil teachers are required to appear at the examination and those who are found successful on the basis of their performance are given certificates or degree or diploma and they become eligible for entering into the teaching jobs according to their general and professional qualification.

The Education Commission (1964-66) laid stress on the professional training of teachers and made very useful suggestions for removing the isolation of teacher training and standard of training programmes. The NPE (1986) was the major document for giving utmost importance to the reorganization and reformation in teachers' training for pre-primary schools in the field of Teacher Education in general and pre-service training of teachers in particular. The NCTE has been given statutory status for setting and maintaining standards for pre-service training in Pre-primary, primary, secondary and higher secondary levels. It has also started to review the existing programmes of teacher education and developing suitable curriculum for pre-service teacher education at all levels. TheAcharya Ramamurti Review Committee (1990) recommended the need for an internship model as it is based on the primary value of actual field experience in a realistic situation on the development of teaching skills by practice over a period of time. NCFTE (2009) suggested guidelines for all aspects of teacher education with the focus on preparing humane teachers by integrating general education with professional development along with an intensive internship in schools.

The following are the types of teacher education programmes for various levels of education.

1. **Teacher Education for Early Childhood Schools / Pre Schools**: It caters to the needs of teachers for Kindergarten, nursery schools, and preparatory schools. Minimum qualification for admission to

this course is Higher Secondary (+2) with 50% of marks. This type of teacher training is called as Diploma in Preschool Education (DPSE), earlier known as Diploma in Early Childhood Education (D.E.C.Ed) and aims at preparing teachers for pre-school programmes. Teacher training institutes of this type are existing in different states. These are affiliated to association of Montessori international and recognised by NCTE.

2. **Teacher Education for Elementary Schools**: The Diploma in Elementary Education (D.EL.Ed) is a two year professional programme and aims to prepare teachers for the elementary stage of education i.e. classes I to VIII. The minimum qualification is higher secondary (+2) with 50% marks.

3. **Teacher Education for Upper Primary/Middle/Secondary/Senior Secondary Schools**: The Bachelor of Education Programme, generally known as B.Ed is a professional course that prepares teachers for upper primary or middle level school (classes VI-VIII), secondary level (Classes IX-X) and senior secondary (Classes XI, XII). It is of two years course after B.A/B.Sc or M.A/ M.Sc with 50% marks and Bachelor's in Engineering or Technology with specialization in Science and Mathematics with 55% marks.

4. **Teacher Education Institutes for Special Subjects**: These are special college for preparing teachers in certain subjects like physical education, home science, craft, language etc. The following training institutions prepare special subject teachers such as music, drawing, painting, fine arts, home science, etc.

- Viswa Bharathi University, Shantiniketan,
- Institute of Art education, Delhi.
- Government school of art, Lucknow
- Kalakshetra, Adayar, Madras

5. **Institute of Advanced Study in Education**: These provide M.A., M.Ed, and Ph.D. course in education.

6 **Training College for Special Education**: These prepare teachers for teaching handicaps, deaf and dumb child.

7 **Regional Institute of Education**: The Regional Institute of Education (RIE, formerly known as Regional College of Education), is a constituent unit of the National Council of Educational Research and Training (NCERT) New Delhi. The RIEs are set up in 1963 by Government of India in different parts covering various regions. The Regional Institutes were started with the objective of qualitative improvement of school education through innovative pre-service and in-service teacher education programmes and relevant research, development and extension activities. The Regional Institutes of Education have established themselves as institutes of repute in the area of school and teacher education. The institutes have endeavoured to shoulder the responsibilities and challenges generated by changes in the educational scenario of the country.

8 **Composite Colleges of Education**: Such colleges are to be meant for preparing teachers for several stages of education and have all teacher education courses i.e. D.P.S.Ed.El.Ed, B.Ed.,M.Ed., B.P Ed etc. in one campus.

Justice Verma Committee (JVC) Report on Improvement of Pre-service Teacher Education

- Government should increase investment in Eastern and North-eastern states to meet the increasing demand of teacher education.
- Institutionalising the transparent procedure of pre entry testing of the candidates of pre-service teacher education programmes.
- Teacher education must become a part of higher education with enhancing duration of D.Ed, B.Ed, M.Ed and four year integrated programme.
- Multi and inter-disciplinary approaches to be started in teacher education.
- Teacher education programmes should be redesigned according to National Curriculum Framework for Teacher Education NCFTE -2009.
- Teacher education institutions should have a dedicated school attached as a pedagogical laboratory for teachers and students.
- Establish a national body for continual reflection and analysis of entire teacher education programme.
- First professional degree /diploma programme should be offered only through face to face mode whereas other modes of education may be used for continuous professional development activities in teacher education.
- The institutional capacity should be increased for the preparation of teacher education along with starting of two year M.Ed programme.
- A broad-based qualification of teacher educators needs to be developed by NCTE.

- Faculty development programmes must be institutionalised through UGC-Academic Staff College.
- Research orientation needs immediate attention in teacher education and establishing inter University centre in Teacher Education for promoting research culture in this sector.

Meaning of In-Service Teacher Education

In-service Teacher Education refers to continuing education of teachers already working in schools for professional competence. It is, hence, a supplementary, additional training. The moment a teacher has completed his training in a college of education, it does not mean that he is now trained for all times to come. The professional growth of a teacher does not cease when he leaves the training institution. According to Lawrence (1992), "in service education is the education a teacher receives after he has entered the teaching profession". For a good teacher, every facet of his knowledge, skills, personality and interests is of potential value. Hence, every experience he undergoes during his career may be described as in-service education. In-service education may, therefore be taken to include everything that happens to a teacher from the day he takes up his first appointment to the day he retires which contributes, directly or indirectly, to the way in which he executes his professional duties. For administrative convenience, in-service education is a programme of systematized activities promoted or directed by the school system, or approved by the school system that contributes to the professional or occupational growth and competence of staff members during the time of their service to the school system. In general it can be defined as "structured activities designed exclusively or primarily to improve professional performance".

To equip a teacher with changing national goals, revision of school curricula, additional inputs in teaching-learning system and emergence of new concepts due to researches being conducted in the field of education, he requires in-service education. It develops a sense of security, a team spirit and allows for exchange of opinion, quality improvement and a sense of belongingness to the teaching profession.

Need and Importance of In-Service Teacher Education

In-service education as a programme of recent origin is the result of rapid changes in various fields of human activity and its need is felt in teaching profession because of rapid changes in content areas, pedagogical science, school curriculum, educational technology, socio-political scenario and job expectations of teachers etc. These developments demand from working teachers on acquisition of new knowledge and pedagogical skills to transact the curriculum effectively and to bring modifications in their perceptions about children and society. The need for in-service education of teachers was felt in 1949 when the University Education Commission stressed the need for it to keep teachers alive and fresh.

Following are the importance of in-service teacher education:

- It helps to equip the teachers with requisite additional knowledge, skills and competencies.
- It develops the habit of self-study with ultimate aim of keeping them abreast with the latest developments in their own and allied field.
- It suggests remedies for inadequacies of existing

method of teaching and teacher education.
- It gives an opportunity to practice new teaching techniques and to share experiences with other teachers.
- It gives an exposure to effective new techniques and developments in educational technology, such as computers, projectors etc,
- In-service education helps the teacher in becoming fully democratic. By in-service education programmes, the teacher can meet people of all types and he is also able to share his experience with others.

Justice Verma Committee (JVC) Report on Improvement of In-service Teacher Education

- An expert group to develop a policy framework for in-service teacher education is required in consultation with national and state level institutions.
- In-service teacher education institutions DIETs, SCERTs, BRCs, CRCs etc. need to be strengthened for elementary teacher education.
- Continuous professional development programmes for secondary school teachers in arrangement with CTEs, IASEs and University departments of Education.

In the world based on science and technology, it is education that determines the level of prosperity, welfare and security of the people. "Good education requires good teachers" so that it becomes essential that the most capable and appropriate teachers must be recruited into the teaching profession, provided with high quality pre-service programme of teacher education, and then offered opportunities to upgrade their knowledge and skills over the full length of their career through in-service education. It is, therefore, essential that teacher education must ensure that teachers are furnished with the necessary knowledge and skills to cope with the new demands of the society at every point of time.

The National Policy on Education (1986) linked in-service teacher education as a continuum with pre-service education. The Programme of Action (1992) stated that teachers have multiple roles to perform. In-service education must be mandatory for all faculty members. As teacher education is a continuous process, its pre-service and in-service education programmes are inseparable. The teachers must prepare themselves to respond to present day knowledge evolving society by furthering their professional competence.

Chapter-2

Issues and Challenges in Teacher Education

India is having one of the biggest and complicated teacher education systems in the world. The present teacher education remains isolated and incomplete. It is isolated from society and its' aspirations. The Kothari Commission (1964-66) points out that the teacher education suffers from three types of isolation. This isolation makes teacher education incomplete, valueless and worthless in our developing country. Over the last half a century and particularly in the recent decades teaching learning has been undergoing drastic changes. There has been a shift towards student centred classrooms with teacher's role more as facilitator of learning rather than an autocratic master. Now teacher education is facing a few issues and challenges.

Teacher Education: Issues and Challenges

Challenges play a key role for the development of every sphere. We have to face them and try to overcome with concrete solutions for upcoming generation. Martin Luther King Jr. said, "Our very survival depends on our ability to stay awake, to adjust to new ideas, to remain vigilant and to face the challenge of change". At present, our teacher education suffers from the following drawbacks:

- Inequality is a major issue in the field of teacher education. There is public-private dichotomy in teacher education. There is apathetic indifference in public sector institutions and rampant commercialization in private sector. The teacher education degrees conferred by the various universities and institutions are non-comparable. Inequality is also found in enrolment in teacher education programs. It varies from region to region. There are some areas in India where the enrolment in teacher education is near full, but the physical presence in the face-to-face mode is near nil. These are exclusively commercial centres than educational. These institutions should be immediately banned.

- There are problems in quality perception, quality scaling, and quality differentiation in teacher education. There is a significant difference between expected and actual quality. This is exemplified by the successive entrance tests for higher level, be it graduate, post-graduate or doctoral level. There is also problem in systematic parameters; input, process and output. The degeneration of quality of teacher education can be attributed more to the private sector.

- Inadequate technology infusion is a major issue at present. Teacher education programmes are largely traditional. Pace of modernization is very slow. We have not yet been in a position to infuse the technological innovations for transacting the education.

- Innovations in teacher education are very rare. Novel ideas do not incubate because of the adverse external conditions. There are wide gaps between the visionaries and actors. So, very often the innovations have short life and die down in the institutions, where these originate. Sometimes, the most innovative programmes fail in the formal system, because, these are beyond the view and purview of the apex bodies.

- Research in education is replicate and repetitive devoid of freshness, either of problem or of approach or methodology. There is more of quantitative research than qualitative. The studies are scattered and not linked properly. There is more of descriptive and evaluative research than suggestive.
- Teacher education programmes are largely traditional. Pace of modernization is very slow. We have not yet been in a position to infuse the technological innovations for transacting the education. There is more of knowledge deepening than knowledge construction. We have patents in Educational Technology.
- There is no well-established system for in-service training of teachers and teacher educators in most of the states. Whatever system of pre-service either at the national or state level exists could not show impact on the quality of teachers.
- Lack of effective monitoring is a double edged problem. First, the functioning of institutions is not being monitored periodically and also systematically. Hence, they are not able to get constructive feedback to improve the quality of teacher education programmes. Second, the credibility of monitors who are deputed to inspect the institutions is being questioned by society at large.

- It has been observed that ICTs are being underutilised by teacher educators while the teacher trainees are expected to make optimum use of innovative methods of teaching, including use of ICTs for delivery of lessons. Use of ICT is very dismal because of lack of interests among stakeholders: educational administrators, teachers and community at large.
- Manpower planning is improper in teacher education. There is remarkable increase in the number of teacher education institutions.
- There are mismatches between the teaching degrees and levels taught.
- Instead of appointing regular teachers, vacancy positions in different educational institutions of the states are filled with contractual teachers and guest faculties and management teachers with low salary.
- Education, research and development are the least priority as is evident through the investment by the state.
- Public at large is indifferent towards education.
- Content-pedagogy-technology integrated education is a big challenge.
- Absence of skill training and innovative courses in curriculum.
- Teacher Education on life skills, such as, lateral and critical thinking, innovativeness, problem solving etc. need to be strengthened.
- Teacher education lacks content on values of human life.
- It prepares teachers with limited classroom skills and narrow outlook.

- It fails to build up the right attitudes of teachers towards the teaching profession.
- It does not develop initiative and leadership qualities in our future teachers.
- Need of thorough preparation of teacher education at all levels, from pre-primary to higher education.
- Lack of Humane and Professional Teachers is another problem.

Quality control, leadership, culture, radical change etc. are many challenges in the field of teacher education. We can't avoid globalization because of rapid flow of technology, capital, and employment at international level for teachers.

Concept of Burnout

Burnout is a syndrome found among the people in every occupation. Matheny, Gfroerer, and Harris (2000), described 'burnout as a loss of idealism and enthusiasm for work'. Freudenberger (1974), a psychiatrist, is largely credited with first using the term burnout. Burnout is a work syndrome that stems out of the individual's perception of the inconsistency between the effort that one makes and the reward that one receives (Friedman, 1995). Burnout is observed mainly in people who interact directly with others, such as educators or doctors, and is manifested through emotional and physical exhaustion, as well as many psychological symptoms, such as edginess, anxiety, depression and low self-esteem (Farber, 1991). It should be emphasized that the burnout experienced by teachers is a process and not just a simple fact, so each individual tends to cope with it in his/her own special way (Farber, 1983). Burnout usually leads to decreased happiness and inability to perform adequately in everyday tasks (Burke and Greenglass, 1995).

According to Leiter and Maslach (1998) burnout is characterised by:

- Emotional exhaustion, which usually refers to a state of emotional drain and deprivation and often has physical manifestations, such as energy loss
- Depersonalization, which is described as cynicism, lack of idealism and negative or inappropriate attitudes towards other people; and
- Decreased individual achievement, which usually coincides with decreased professional efficiency, productivity or ability, low morale and inability to meet the work demands.

Teacher Burnout

Teaching is considered as the most important profession. Teacher provides knowledge and values to children. He prepares the child for life and makes him a good citizen. This profession has not been given proper recognition and status at present time. Presently teacher community faces many problems. Burnout is considered as one of the major problems of teachers at present time.

Education system has all the elements associated with stress; a bureaucratic structure, continuous evaluation process and increasingly intensive interpersonal interactions with students, parents, colleagues, principals and the community members. In addition, increased student misconduct, students apathy, overcrowded classrooms, inadequate salary, demanding or unsupportive parents, budgetary constraints, expanding administrative loads, lack of infrastructural support and an increasingly negative public opinion have caused an environment of stress. Teaching job is considered as one of the high-stress occupations, because teachers are in stress in teaching-learning environment. Burnout is a state of emotional, mental, physical and exhaustion caused by excessive and prolonged stress. It occurs when the teacher feels overwhelmed and unable to meet constant demands. As the stress continues, the teachers begin to lose the interest or motivation towards the job. Burnout reduces teachers' productivity and saps their energy, leaving their feeling increasingly helpless, hopeless, cynical and resentful. Eventually, they may feel like they have nothing more to give. The negative effects of burnout spill over into every areas of life, including home, workplace and social life. Burnout can also cause long-term changes to one's body that make vulnerable to illness like cold, mental tension, flu etc.

One of the major problems in the modern stressful lifestyle with special reference to the teacher is the occurrence of Burnout Syndrome among the teachers. Most of the teachers find it difficult to meet the challenges and demands of the society. Other professionals associated with the field of education too find it difficult to meet the challenges and demands of the society and adjust with their day to day functioning and subsequently develop burnout syndrome. It is evident from different studies in the area of burnout that there is a high relationship between job stress and burnout among teachers.

A good understanding of the different causes of burnout could facilitate the early recognition and treatment of burnout. Most of the researchers agree that burn out grows gradually over a period of time and can be considered a process.

Causes of Burnout

The causes of burnout are discussed below:

    i.   **Work related**
- Feeling that as if you have no control over your work

- Lack of recognition or rewards for good work
- Too much expectation from authority in job
- Doing monotonous or unchallenging work
- Working in a chaotic or high pressure environment

ii. **Lifestyle related**

- Doing too much of work, without getting time for relaxation and socialization
- Expectation of many things for many people
- Taking on too many responsibilities, without enough help from others
- Not getting enough sleep
- Lack of close and supportive relationships

iii. **Personality trait related**

- Perfectionist tendencies; nothing is ever good enough
- Pessimistic view of yourself and the world
- The need to be in control; reluctance to delegate to others
- High achieving, type A personality

Signs and Symptoms of Burnout

Burnout is a gradual process that occurs over an extended period of time. The signs and symptoms of burnout are subtle at first, but they get worse form as time goes on. The signs and symptoms are described as follows:

i. **Physical signs and symptoms**

- Feeling tired most of the time
- Lowered immunity, feeling sick a lot
- Frequent headaches, back pain, muscle aches
- Change in appetite or sleep habits

ii. **Emotional signs and symptoms**
- Sense of failure and self-doubt
- Feeling helpless, trapped, and defeated
- Detachment, feeling alone in the world
- Loss of motivation
- Increasingly cynical and negative outlook
- Decreased satisfaction and sense of accomplishment

iii. **Behavioural signs and symptoms**
- Withdrawing from responsibilities
- Isolating yourself from others
- Procrastinating, taking longer to get things done
- Use of food, drugs, or alcohol to cope
- Taking out own frustration on others
- Skipping work or coming in late and leaving early

Effects of Burnout

Burnout doesn't occur suddenly but occurs as a gradual deterioration. There are three stages that can occur in the burnout progression. The first stage is puzzlement, confusion and the appearance of frustration. The second stage is characterized by the tense, frustration and anger, the third stage is apathy, withdrawals and despair.

The present burnout stress syndrome affects the work output of the teachers both qualitatively and quantitatively. It causes deterioration in the quality of work of teachers.

Burnout occurs when teacher feels overwhelmed and unable to meet constant demands. As the stress continues, teacher begins to lose interest or motivation that leads him to behave indifferently in work place. Burnout reduces teacher's productivity and saps his energy, making him increasingly helpless, hopeless, cynical, and resentful. Eventually, he may feel he has nothing more to give to the society.

Steps to Prevent Teacher Burnout

Preventive measures can be taken at the organizational level or at the individual level to eliminate burnout. Teaching is a stressful job which sometimes leads to teacher's burnout. Interventions in the school system and other steps can prevent teacher burnout. These are:

i. Develop positive thinking within yourself which is the core of internal happiness
ii. Offer professional development activities
iii. Stress management workshops
iv. Relaxation training
v. Time management workshops
vi. Nutrition, exercise and coping skills training
vii. Improve working conditions
viii. Classroom environment
ix. Solution of salary issues
x. Accommodate cultural differences
xi. Religious events/ holidays

Top Ten Ways to deal with Teacher Burnout

Following top ten measures may help to combat teacher burnout. For this, the teacher is required to:

- Foster positivity
- Plan for his daily work and proceed accordingly
- Talk about teacher burnout
- Practice self-care

- Know when to take a break
- Plan for community
- Find out what actually went wrong
- Put things in perspective
- Try something new
- Ask for help when you need it

Strategies to overcome the Problems in Teacher Education

It was recommended by the Kothari commission (1964-66) that in order to prepare effective, efficient and successful teachers, teacher education must be brought into the main academic stream of the universities as well as school life and education department. Following suggestions may be taken into account for removing the isolation and bringing necessary improvement in teacher education programme:

- There is a need to restructure curriculum based on teacher's felt needs, viability and practicability. The re-structured curriculum should accelerate aesthetic and innovativeness in teachers.
- In order to make education responsive to the new needs of society, teacher education has to be reoriented in its aim and approach, curriculum and content.
- Periodical monitoring of the teacher education programmes being implemented is essential for improving and maintaining quality of teacher education.
- Teachers and teacher educators should be encouraged to design, develop, utilize and evaluate courseware so that they are able to own ICT as integral part of the teaching process. ICT can help overcome to a great extent the challenges of quantity and quality in teacher education.

- There should be adequate manpower planning for teacher education and school education.
- Educational curricula and modes of transaction ought to be practiced.
- There should be adequate focus on constructivists' approaches.
- Creative and innovative teaching-learning should be enhanced.
- All the teachers and learners should be techno savvy.
- A prospective plan for research and innovations should be framed with regional and national developmental priorities.
- The research problems must be compatible with the local problems.
- Programmes in teacher education and research related to education should be done in the universities and schools of education should be a part of the university.
- All teacher education institutions must organise extension work which should be included as an essential function of teacher education but for the benefit of others in the university system as well.
- The plan, the curricula and other training aspects of teacher education should be carried out with the help of effective alumni.

Chapter - 3

Teacher Effectiveness and Reflective Practice in Teaching

Teaching is an art. Teacher is an artist. To know the art of teaching, it requires considerable knowledge, a wide variety of interests and skills and a very positive attitude on the part of teacher. A teacher is to understand his subject as well as his pupils, he is to motivate, to instruct, to organise, to evaluate etc. It means that he is to play many roles and that too very efficiently. Academic qualification, subject matter knowledge, pedagogy and teaching skill are important factors in determining teachers' effectiveness and teaching efficiency. A knowledgeable teacher without motivation and dedication to teaching cannot provide quality education. The quality of teaching is not only governed by the knowledge, skill and competence of teachers but also their enthusiasm and commitment in teaching. When a teacher is motivated and loves the teaching profession, the students not only learn the content taught by the teacher, they may also be motivated towards learning (Czubaj, 1996). Teachers who are dedicated and committed to teaching might facilitate school based innovations or reformations that are meant to benefit students' learning and development. In fact, teachers' commitment and engagement has been identified as one of the most critical factors in the success of education (Nais, 1981).

Education System and Teacher

In ancient days, teachers were given equal status with God. They were held in high esteem. Teachers are the ideals to their pupils. An old Indian prayer says, "The teacher is God Brahma; he is God Vishnu; he is God Maheswara. He is the whole universe, obeisance to teacher". The ancient law-giver Manu has observed, "A teacher is the image of Brahma; a father is the image of Prajapati; a mother is the image of the Earth. By devotion for the mother the child obtains the world; by devotion to his father, the middle world; by devotion to his teacher the Brahmana world". According to Indian culture, a child receives his first physical birth from the parents and the second birth at the hands of the teacher. Rather, higher position is given to the teacher. Because he opens the pupils' eyes of knowledge and moulds his character, knowledge, skills, interests and attitudes. As it is said, God created man after his own image, the teacher fashions his student after his own image.

Teachers are the most important components of education system. It is no exaggeration to state that spacious building, costly equipment and sound syllabus will serve some useful purpose only when there are teachers who are fully aware to the nobility of the profession and its accompanying responsibilities and above all, the character and personality of the students. Present society needs professionally competent teachers. The teacher is the living idol, the fountainhead of knowledge and the potential guide to provide directive for the growth and development of students of today as the worthy citizens of tomorrow. Although in course of time the role and functions of teachers are changing, they are always regarded as the benefactors of mankind.

The National Knowledge Commission (2007) observes that, teachers constitute the foundation of the school education system. Teaching reflects a high degree of academic excellence and practical wisdom in one hand and a well-integrated value system on the other, both oriented towards altruistic service. Teaching involves unquestionable thirst for knowledge and its transmission to the future generation so that society may run on the path of progress and prosperity. Teachers are models to their clients – namely the students- who are highly impressionable.

The teacher performs multifaceted functions in classroom. She/he guides, understands, inspires the students. Teacher clarifies the doubts whenever the students face difficulties, creates learning environment and facilitate students' learning, shares ideas, experiences, he serves as a role model, touches and transforms the life of a student with care and compassion.

Teacher Effectiveness: The Concept

Teacher effectiveness refers to optimum level of perfection and productivity on the part of the teacher. Anand (1983) says, "Effectiveness is considered to be the finest trait of a person. As an attribute, it represents his personality in the best of his form". Combs (1961) defined the effective teachers as "a unique human being who has learned to use his self effectively and efficiently for carrying out his own on society's purposes".

Teacher effectiveness refers to the effect that the teacher's performance has on pupils. In other words, teacher effectiveness has a reference to the impressions that the teacher makes on his/her pupils as a result of teaching performance. It is, therefore, regarded as a product of teacher performance. It also depends on the learning outcomes of the learners or the learning experiences acquired by them as a result of the teacher's teaching performance.

Effective teachers are endowed with certain good characteristics which make them different from ineffective or poor teachers. Teacher education is an emerging area and a good number of researches have been made on characteristics of effective teachers. The findings of Anand (1971, 1979) Biddle and Ellera (1964), Kaul (1974), Paul (1950), Ryans (1960) and many others found that effective teachers are different from ineffective teachers on certain fundamental characteristics.

(i) Personal characteristics of teacher

Teacher effectiveness is concerned with personal characteristics of teachers. It is related with his qualification, intelligence, confidence, trustworthiness, analytical and conceptual thinking, drive for improvement, flexibility, accountability, love for children, passion for learning and so on.

(ii) Pedagogical content knowledge

Teacher should acquire pedagogical content knowledge. This refers to deep knowledge about the content and structure of a subject matter area. Teachers with more pedagogical content knowledge display a broad repertoire of teaching strategies for creating cognitive stimulating learning situations.

(iii) Self-efficacy of teacher

Self-efficacy influences students towards learning, even if they are not motivated towards learning. More efficacious teachers have more commitment. They believe in innovation, use more communicative based strategies and thus influence students' learning experiences and academic outcomes.

Ross (1994), reports that teachers with high self-efficacy are more likely to learn and use new approaches and strategies for teaching and provide special assistance to low achieving students. Teachers who have high sense of self-efficacy they are more creative in their work.

(iv) Commitment

Commitment is an important component of teacher effectiveness. It leads the teacher to effective achievement. Commitment is an attitude- a psychological frame of mind which motivates people to work towards certain goals. Teachers' commitment includes commitment to one's self, to one's students, to one's organisation and society as a whole. The impact of teachers on their students is subtle and long lasting. It is therefore, necessary that teachers should be committed, contented and devoted to their noble profession.

What makes a Great Teacher?

Today, world is progressing at an unprecedented pace where we need to equip our children with best education to match with giant leaps of human race. We as teachers have great responsibility for their success. Great teachers are amazing, enthusiastic and rare. If you wish to be a great teacher, please ask yourself the following: do you speak clearly, loud enough with proper speed and avoid unwanted pauses 'ums' or repeated words? Is your non-verbal communication appropriate? Are you understandable? Do you use soft and easy language? Do you emphasise important points and use logical sequence? Do you prepare teaching aids skillfully which are easy to understand? Is your style of presentation appropriate? If all answers of yours are 'Yes', you can be an excellent teacher.

A good teacher is one who creates good environment for teaching, able to effectively indulge his students in learning and help them understand the subject well. Not all students are quick in learning and some may have the problem of following too many instructions at one time, so a good teacher organizes his subject in an effective way, so that all the students are able to follow his method of teaching easily. The teaching method of a good teacher is simple and student directed which ensures the proper and complete command of student over the subject.

A good teacher masters his subject but a great teacher is an excellent communicator. He not only organises his course requirements but also asks intelligent questions. He provides platform for interaction to optimize the outcomes of the course for students in a worthwhile manner. There is a saying, 'A good teacher is a doctor who heals ignorance and an artist who inspires creativity'. Efficient teachers are able to listen attentively to their students, analyse their reflections and queries and also give effective feedback in a creative manner. The teacher to be great, following points may be taken into account.

- **Preparation**

If the teacher is not organised and prepared, he may have to compensate by spending more time with students outside of class. In preparing the lecture teacher should make it as a series of 10-15 minute mini-lectures and separate them by interactive activity.

- **Ask questions**

Questions are integral part of teaching which always stimulate students, engage them, strike their intellectual and thinking process. Good questions asked by a teacher are clear and precise. They are in various forms: an inquiry, a request, MCQ or a problem. Questions are productive, require thinking and lead to new questions. While evaluating always keep our grading policy consistent.

- **Make proper eye contact**

Teacher's eyes are most effective weapon to convince your students about your openness, honesty and confidence. Emerson has rightly said, "An eye can threaten like a loaded gun, or can insult like kicking; or in its altered mood, by beams of kindness, make the heart dance with joy".

- **Improve tone of voice**

One of the most valuable assets and powerful tool is voice through which you teach, instruct, control and educate. As a teacher, projection and modulation of your voice is very significant aspect of your communication. A good style is to be slightly louder and slightly slower in classroom teaching. You should know the importance of proper pronunciation, pause, pace, punctuation, pitch of your voice in any presentation and adjust it according to the environment.

- **Learn facial expression and body language**

Teacher should learn to use his whole body as a dynamic tool to reinforce his rapport with his students. Teacher will make hand movement to emphasise points but too much hand waving seems bad. Teacher should find a safe resting place for hands. His facial expressions enhance meaning to what he says. These are natural and do not repeat a gesture frequently. Teacher should look at the students in all directions and never fix eye on one student.

- **Emphasise important points**

When, a teacher says something that is important from the examination points of view, level of attention increases among the students. Teacher should take a pause in his lecture after making major points. A good teacher keeps balance among all types of students in his classroom and tries to bring forward slow learners in a modest way. When a teacher creates curiosity in his students, it leads to brainstorming and understanding which changes the tone of his classroom.

- **Print picture with words**

A great teacher makes complex concepts understandable to his students with his simplicity. This art is very important. When he uses metaphors or analogies to express a concept, it becomes more memorable and simple for the students. Explaining with practical examples makes difficult concepts understandable.

- **Be a good reader**

A teacher should be a keen reader of books and magazines. He should be well aware of current affairs: local, regional, national and international issues. He can surge the standards of education to any height.

- **Provide handouts**

Handouts of teacher should highlight important points, all information in a logical sequence and must be accurate and up-to-date. It should have active verbs, short sentences. The reader should understand the words and matter must be interesting.

- **Give assignments**

A teacher must give assignments, including grading criteria. Research shows that a series of short assignments throughout the semester is more helpful than a single long assignment. Besides always start with relatively easy problems followed by more challenging problems.

- **Keep focus**

A good teacher must try to learn and memorise names of his students with correct pronunciation and call them by name frequently. When the teacher focuses his attention upon the object, all his voluntary and involuntary action, drives him towards attaining that object. When he focuses his energies upon a thing, it generates a powerful force that can bring him what he wants. When he control himself, only then he can control others and by focusing on his thoughts, his strengths increases.

- **Be technology friendly**

Today we are living in digital age, where technology is everywhere. A teacher communicates ideas through various means. With the innovation in technology, students are now becoming not only literate of three R's i.e. reading, writing, and arithmetic but are also media literate i.e. production through text, graphics, music, voice and video. We all know about edutainment software which both entertain and educate. These have game like features. There are computer applications used to engage and enhance thinking which are classified as cognitive tools. These tools manage information and facilitate a teacher to think more creatively, critically and clearly. These include databases, tutorials, simulations, multimedia software and presentation and publishing tools. Integrating technology into teaching can change the way a teacher can monitor project, guide their efforts and provide feedback. His role changes from teller and tester into a new form. He becomes a coach, facilitator, co-learner and finally leader.

Teaching: The Concept

The profession of teaching is unique in several ways. Its very nature involves a complex and rich combinations of working relationships with not only the organization (schools and education system) but with a number of other stakeholders, the principal one among them are the learners. Teaching is a complex endeavour, involving classroom management, lesson preparation and organisation of teaching and learning activities, creating and maintaining a certain climate, evaluation and feedback.

Teaching is all about positive / negative attitude of teachers towards their job of imparting quality education. Teaching is that process in which the teachers prepare the learners for learning by using different methods, techniques and aids, and create suitable circumstances for learning for them, and assist them in learning. There is no meaning of teaching until the learners do not learn from this and desirable change does not occur in their behaviour.

Of all professions known in the world, only teaching is expected to create the human skills, potentials and capacities that can enable individuals to survive in today's knowledge society and develop the capacities for innovation, flexibility and commitment to change that are essential to economic prosperity of a nation (Hargreaves, 2003). Coolahan (2002) observes that, "teaching profession is a key mediating agency for society as it endeavours to cope with societal change and upheaval".

Teaching is a complex and demanding profession. To sustain their energy and enthusiasm for the work, teachers need to maintain personal commitment to the job (Day, 2000). Teaching, both as a profession and as mission, demands commitment by the teacher-as investment of his personal resources. As teaching is a continuous interaction between teachers and the taught, there is a daily need on the part of the teacher to fully engage in that work with not only their need, but also with their heart (Day,2004).

During the Vedic period, education was fully under the control of gurus (teachers). At that time, the gurus arranged education according to their own philosophy. In the beginning, when the written language had not been developed, the gurus transmitted their knowledge orally, and the pupils acquired those without any reasoning like passive listeners. The method of teaching then was called Sruti. The gurus during the Upanishad times made teaching a little wider. According to them, teaching is a process in which teachers and students both influence each other.

The western philosophers considered teaching as a one-way process, but after the development of question-answer and dialogue methods by Greek philosophers Socrates and his disciple Plato respectively, this process was given a two-way form, in which both teacher and students are equally active and influence each other.

Psychologists have taken teaching and learning as a joint concept. In their view, teaching has no meaning so long the act of learning does not take place. In the words of Hughes and Hughes,"Teaching means causing to learn. Nothing has been given until it has been learnt". Clark has defined, "Teaching is an activity which is designed and performed to produce change in student behaviour".

Some scholars call teaching as preparing students for learning. They reason that the function of a teacher is to prepare students for learning, they learn by themselves. However, the function of a teacher is not finished here, he has to assist the students in learning continuously. In the words of Thomas M. Risk, "Teaching may very well be defined as the direction or guidance of learning". William

H Burton has defined teaching in a little wider form. In his words, "Teaching is the stimulation, guidance, direction and encouragement of learning". Further Burton says, "Teaching is more than the efficient delivery of thoroughly prepared lectures".

Nature and Characteristics of Teaching

The nature of teaching is as follows:

- Teaching is a process, it has three components- teacher, learner and content or activity. The teacher may or may not be present personally.
- In its wider sense, the process of teaching continues at any place and at any time, but in its narrow sense, this is run at only definite places and at definite times.
- The process of teaching is purposeful, its aim is to acquaint the learners with newer facts and activities and bring about desirable change in their behaviour.
- In its wider sense, the scope of teaching is very wide, it cannot be bound in limits and in its narrow sense, its' scope is limited within the specified curriculum.
- In teaching, the teachers prepare the learners by the use of different methods, techniques, and aids and create learning circumstances for them, the learners take part in these to learn.

Teaching Effectiveness

Teaching effectiveness deals with the teaching process. Adaval (1978) suggests "Teaching effectiveness cannot be judged in a vacuum, it is to be related to the achievement of goals envisaged in terms of the aims of education embedded in the nation's philosophy of life. A teacher's success depends largely upon the capacity to reflect the national philosophy in his own life and action and to initiate the child into it".

Brophy (2001) advocated 12 principles of effective teaching. These are described below:

- **Supportive classroom climate**

    Students learn the best within cohesive and caring learning communities. The role of the teacher as a model and socialiser is emphasized.

- **Opportunity to learn**

    Students learn more when most of the available time is allocated to curriculum-related activities and the classroom management system emphasises maintaining students' engagement in those activities.

- **Curricular alignment**

    All components of the curriculum are aligned to create a cohesive programme for accomplishing instructional purposes and goals.

- **Establishing learning orientations**

    Teaching can prepare students for learning by providing an initial structure to clarify intended outcomes and desired learning strategies.

- **Coherent content**

    To facilitate meaningful learning and retention, content is explained clearly and developed with an emphasis on its structure and connections. When making presentations, providing explanations or giving demonstrations, effective teachers project enthusiasm for the content and organise and sequence it so as to maximise its clarity and learner friendliness.

- **Thoughtful discourse**

    Questions are planned to engage students in sustained discourse, structured around powerful ideas.

- **Practice and application activities**

    Students need sufficient opportunities to practice, apply and to receive improvement-oriented feedback.

- **Scaffolding students' task engagement**

    The teacher provides whatever assistance students need to enable them to engage in learning activities productively. Structuring and support can be lessened as the students' expertise develops.

- **Strategy teaching**

    The teacher models and instructs students in learning and self-regulation are sought in contexts like problem solving and general learning and student skills. For example, teacher thinks and tells loudly in use of strategy. Students are stimulated to monitor and reflect on their learning.

- **Co-operative learning**

    Students often benefit from working in pairs or small groups to build understanding or help one another in mastering skills.

- **Goal-oriented assessment**

    The teacher uses a variety of formal and informal assessment methods to monitor progress towards learning goals. Comprehensive assessment also examines student's reasoning and problem solving skills.

- **Achievement expectations**

    The teacher establishes and follows through on appropriate expectations for learning outcomes.

Role of Teacher in making Teaching Effective

Teacher effectiveness deals with characteristics of teacher whereas teaching effectiveness concerns the teaching process. Following role the teacher should play to make teaching effective. These are as stated below:

- **Be innovative**

    A teacher should always try something new: new methods, new techniques and new aids etc. It is necessary that a teacher does not become stagnant. A teacher may use a variety of teaching aids to avoid monotony of lectures. The teacher can only do this when he has knowledge of the application of devices.

- **Relationship building**

    Teacher student relationship can never be effective if it is just formal or confined to classroom teaching. A teacher should make sincere efforts to build healthy relationship through following ways:

    - Look in the eyes of students while teaching. It manifests confidence and preparedness of a teacher.
    - Always try to have a smile on face. A frown on the face always creates negative impression of teacher and unhealthy class-room environment. Remember as many names as a teacher can. It paves way for friendly and personal approach towards students.

- Admit mistake if made during delivering of a lecture.

- **Encourage interaction**

It has been accepted significantly that two way interactions is a better option in contrast to one way lecture. Students learn better this way when provided with an opportunity to mediate over various possibilities, thus, exploring their new horizons. Besides, discussions help them to be sensitive to the views, opinions and feelings of others, thus, providing them with an ample scope for learning behavioural aspects of life.

- **Scope for practical exercises**

The institutions providing higher education should have enough funds to facilitate practical exercises, workshops and field tasks to the students. Such practices can be effective when teachers are ready to devote extra time apart from their regular teaching hours. The assignments and project works given to the students have the touch of real life experiences.

- **Continue learning**

Learning is a life-long process. A teacher should read books concerning subject matter on personality development, motivation and other books concerning the interest of the teacher.

- **Guidance**

A teacher guides students both individually and through group work and making those successes. Again the guidance has to be academic as well as personal.

- **Collect feedback**

It becomes meaningful to collect feedback of teachers' performance on regular basis. This type of practice keeps them alert in all situations. Of course, care should be taken to see that such feedbacks are genuine and are free from any sort of bias.

- **Communication skills**
  - Communicate in simple language, the language in which students can easily understand the lecture. A highly sophisticated use of words may cause a feeling of inferiority complex among students which may lead to adverse psychological consequences.
  - Make use of appropriate gestures i.e. neither more nor less.
  - Make use of adequate audio-visual aids to make the lecture more simple and effective.
  - Lectures should be supported with live examples.
- **Discipline**

  It is rightly said that charity begins at home. A teacher expecting discipline must himself maintain discipline. A teacher should possess virtues such as regularity, punctuality, sincerity, etc. so that he can imbibe the same in his students.

- **Energetic**

  A teacher, whatever may be his physical appearance, should always be energetic and enthusiastic. A good teacher never gets tired of teaching activity. This is possible when a teacher considers his work as worship.

- **Teacher's commitment**

  The word 'commitment' derives from the verb 'commit' and it means 'pledge' or 'undertaking', 'being dedicated or devoted (to something)'- as the Oxford Advanced Learner's Dictionary defines it. Commitment implies a sense of fidelity and adherence to certain principles imposed by the individual upon himself to reach a goal. The sense of commitment makes the individual gather round a common value, aim and culture.

Teachers to describe themselves and each other frequently use the term 'commitment' (Nias, 1981). This commitment distinguishes those who are 'caring' 'dedicated' and who 'take the job seriously',-from those who put their own interest first'. Some teachers consider commitment as part of their professional identity. It defines them and their work and they 'get a lot of enjoyment from this'. (Elliott & Crosswell, 2001).

Teacher commitment has been identified as one of the most critical factors for the future success of education and schools (Huberman, 1993). Ebmeier & Nicklaus (1999) states that, "commitment is part of a teacher's affective or emotional reaction to his experience in a school setting".

Teacher's commitment is a key factor to student performance in school. Teachers with high level of commitment work harder, show stronger affiliation to their school and exhibit stronger desire to carry out the goals of teaching. Teacher's commitment is the psychological identification of the individual teacher with the learners. The goal of a committed teacher is to become involved in the development of students' personality well beyond his personal interest. Highly committed teachers are willing to do everything for the welfare of the learners under his supervision.

Classroom teachings by different teachers should be integrated rationally to attract and encourage the students and to help them excel in their study, they pursue. So, due care should be taken while preparing class routines for proper integration of lectures/demonstrations by different teachers/

instructors. Good teacher-integration needs each teacher to adjust the classroom lesson to complement the lessons and the students' progress. This classroom integration leads to the development of collaborative attitude and individual professional grooming in the teacher's concerned, and as a result they will be duly encouraged to think about new thoughts and practices of pedagogy. To keep up the most needed dynamism in our education-system, teacher should review it at regular intervals, so that, the way the teacher teach the learners, must co-ordinate and integrate the learning in the classroom with ever-changing real-life. Teachers are to undergo regular orientation/ refresher courses to update their skills and should use their minds to know and explore newer aspects of education.

The Organization for Economic Co-operation and Development (OECD, 1994) in its report quality in Teaching, states that a teacher should have:

- Knowledge of substantive areas and content
- Pedagogic skill that includes acquiring and using a range of teaching strategies
- The ability to be self-critical
- Empathy and commitment to the acknowledgement of the dignity of others and
- Managerial competence

With the opening up of various opportunities and prospects for career development consequent on rapid globalization, the longing for success and demand for skilled manpower have been the need of the hour. To bring success in student's learning, teacher's teaching must be more focused, real life oriented to make the learners educated in true sense of the term and trained in and aware of the latest trends in society and job market.

Reflective Practice in Teaching

The terms reflection and reflective practice have been very popular in education system at present. Many language educators still agree that some form of reflection is a desirable practice among teachers; however the agreement stops there because there is still almost no consensus as to what reflective practices and which reflective practices actually promote teacher development (Farrell, 2007).

John Dewey

John Dewey, the great educationist of America, in early 20th century suggested that one of the major aims of education is to help people acquire habits of reflection so that people instead of engaging them in routine thought and action, they can engage them in intelligent thought and action. Dewey developed revolutionary thoughts on reflective practice. Dewey opined reflective enquiry as, "active, persistent and careful consideration of any belief or supposed form of knowledge in the light of the grounds that support it and further conclusions to which it tends to constitute reflective thought". Dewey was concerned about routine thinking whereby actions are guided by impulse, tradition or authority.

According to Dewey, the cause of reflective thinking comes out of the feeling of doubt or conflict connected to teaching. He pointed out five main phases of reflective thought. These are as follows:

- *Suggestion*: A doubtful situation is understood to be problematic and some vague suggestions are considered as possible solutions.
- *Intellectualization*: The difficulty or perplexity of the problem that has been felt (directly experienced) is intellectualized into a problem to be solved.

- *Guiding idea*: One suggestion after another is used as a leading idea, or hypothesis; the initial suggestion can be used as a working hypothesis to initiate and guide observation and other operations in the collection of factual material.
- *Reasoning*: Reasoning links present and past ideas and helps elaborate the supposition that reflective inquiry has reached, or the mental elaboration of the idea or supposition as an idea.
- *Hypothesis Testing*: The refined idea is reached, and the testing of this refined hypothesis takes place; the testing can be by over action or in thought (imaginative action).

Zeichner and Liston (1996) have accepted Dewey's ideas and made a difference between routine action and reflective action and suggested that, for teachers "routine action is guided primarily by tradition, external authority and circumstance" whereas reflective action "entails the active, persistent and careful consideration of any belief or supposed form of knowledge".

Moreover, Dewey (1933) considered reflection as a form of freedom from routine behaviour: "Reflection emancipates us from merely impulsive and routine activity; it enables us to direct our activities with foresight and to plan according to ends–in-view or purposes of which we are aware, to act in deliberate and intentional fashion, to know what we are about when we act". Here he wanted to create interest in teachers to make informed decisions about their teaching, and these decisions be based on systematic and conscious reflections rather than fleeting thoughts regarding teaching. Dewey viewed that when teachers integrate these systematic reflections with their actual teaching experiences, then they could acquire more knowledge and this would lead to professional development of the teacher.

Donald Schon

Schon focused his research work on Dewey's theory of inquiry. The focus gave him a pragmatic framework was present in most of his later work. Schon was interested in organizational behaviour. His work centred on practitioner-generated intuitive practice. Schon (1983) in his book 'The Reflective Practitioner: How Professionals Think in Action' suggested that 'we are in need of inquiry into the epistemology of practice. What is the kind of knowing in which competent practitioners engage?

Schon & Chris Argyris (1974) together developed the notion of single-loop and double-loop learning. Single-loop learning is defined as planning, teaching and testing, and in double loop learning, thinking, practice and problems between the two are raised to an explicit level where they can be accessed.

Schon was interested in how professionals "know" through their practice because he was convinced that they know more than they articulate in language. This he called reflection-in-action. Reflection-in-action involves examining our beliefs and experiences and how they connect to our theories-in-use. However, in order to engage in reflection- in- action we must become aware of knowing-in-action, and this process moves beyond the usual established ideas as practitioners build up and draw on a collection of images, ideas and actions. According to Schon (1983), teachers use reflection-in-action to cope. Reflection-in-action involves a reflective conversation in which the practitioner is listening to the situations' back talk.

Reflection creates on-the-spot experimentation by the teacher. The practitioners engage in a process of problem setting rather than problem solving. Clarke (1995) explains, 'this conversation between the practitioner and the data which may then lead to new meanings, further reframing, and plans for further action'.

Dewey (1933) considered reflective practice as intentional, systematic inquiry that is disciplined and that will ultimately lead to change and professional growth for teachers (reflection-on-action). Schon added to this idea of a practitioner being able to reflect on his or her intuitive knowledge while engaged in the action of teaching (reflection-in-action). Both types of reflection, in and on action, can encourage teachers to reflect for action. In view of both Dewey & Schon, reflective teaching is evidence based; teachers collect data that means they collect evidence about their work, and then reflect on that evidence to make informed decisions about their practice.

The work of both Dewey and Schon suggests that teachers look at what is actual and occurring (theories-in use) in their practice and compare this to their beliefs (espoused theories) about learning and teaching. This productive tension (personal communication of Freeman,) between espoused theories and theories-in–use provides teachers with the opportunity to systematically look at their practice so that they can deepen their understanding of what they do and thus come to new insights about their students, their teaching, and themselves. Dewey (1933) recommended development comes from a "reconstruction of experience". Teachers by reflecting on experiences can reconstruct their own approaches to teaching.

Dewey (1933) in his work on reflective inquiry

opined that teachers to be engaged in reflective practice need to have at least three attributes:

- Open-mindedness
- Responsibility
- Wholeheartedness

Open-mindedness is a desire to listen to more than one side of an issue and to give attention to alternative views. Responsibility refers to careful consideration of the consequences to which an action leads or what is the impact of reflection on the learners. Wholeheartedness is concerned with the aspect that teachers can overcome fears and uncertainties to critically evaluate their practice in order to make meaningful change. On the whole, reflective practice can help the teacher to create more learning opportunities for students.

Teacher as a Reflective Practitioner

Reflective practitioner is meant to such person who sum up and find fault with his working system concerning his occupation, examine its merits and demerits and attempts to improve it. Because a teacher has to do this work in a clearer manner, then people look at him in the form of a reflective practitioner.

During the Vedic period, teacher completely controlled the education system. Teachers were responsible for the determination of its form, aims, curriculum and methods of teaching and so on. History tells us that during the Vedic period, the teachers first thought was what they have to teach, why they have to teach, and then how they have to teach the subject. During teaching, teachers solved the problems of their students. The lecture method, the illustration method and analogy were mainly used. History tells that the teachers used to develop their work. In this context, it is better to mention Acharya Vishnu Sharma. When Acharya Vishnu Sharma was given the responsibility of teaching morality to the dull princes, he invented the story-telling method to impart moral education to them. During the Buddhist period, a sound educational system existed in India, starting from primary education to university education. The aims of education for different levels were specified, the curricula were created, the teaching methods were decided, the rules of admission in universities were identified, the methods of examinations were specified, different degrees were determined for different curricula and all this was the contribution of reflective teachers.

It is essential that the teacher must be trained in a way to enable him to adapt his teaching skill to the basic requirements of any education system. These four principles of learning and teaching procedure point towards the differential needs of the students, their maturational level, and the burden of learning materials and lastly the skill and art of teaching. All these aims can be attained if the teachers and the administrators have better idea of individual differences and their implications in teaching. Each individual is unique, so it is the responsibility of the teacher to provide appropriate teaching techniques and learning materials in a justway. National Curriculum Framework for Teacher Education (NCFTE, 2009) promises to translate the vision into reality and prepare humanistic and reflective teachers they have the potential to develop more professional teachers and improve the quality of education.

Schon has expressed the role of a teacher in the form of a reflective practitioner in the following ways:

(i) The teacher should accept the responsibility that he has to reflect on and has to improve all aspects of education in the democratic polity.

(ii) He should effect a change in his attitude, and that is, he should analyze everything in place of accepting everything as it is, he should verify its merits and demerits and should make attempts for continuous improvement in them.

(iii) Teacher should make exhaustive plan for teaching before starting his teaching. In this plan, he should determine the teaching objectives along with the analysis of the content and should provide them in objective form. He should diagnose the physical and mental capacity of the students and their previous knowledge (behaviour) also, and should select teaching methods, strategies and teaching aids accordingly. He should also guess the forthcoming problems at the time of teaching and should determine their solutions.

(iv) While teaching he should proceed forward as per his plan, but he should not enslave himself to the plan, he should change it as per the need and according to his insight and reflection.

(v) Teacher should keep the students motivated from beginning to end during teaching and should keep them active.

(vi) He should keep diagnose and remedy the difficulties of the students. He should not flee from the problems, he should solve them immediately. Teacher should perform this task with the cooperation of students, he should guide them and should provide them individual assistance.

(vii) What he teaches, he should give feedback to it.

(viii) He should evaluate his teaching, and if he has not succeeded in it fully, then he should diagnose its causes. A reflective teacher should analyze the content, teaching objectives, previous knowledge of students, use of teaching methods, strategies and teaching aids, his behaviour and activities of students. He should look for their merits and demerits and should take rest after optimum success. At this level, he should also give suggestions for the improvement in the curriculum, teaching objectives and teaching methods.

(ix) The schools also hold other co-curricular activities along with class teaching. The reflective teachers should plan for their organization and should improve upon their working system and should benefit others with their experiences.

(x) Generally the problem of indiscipline is faced at the time of morning assembly, class teaching and organization of other programmes. A reflective teacher should at first diagnose the causes of indiscipline and then should remedy them. Which activities have helped him under which circumstances; he should benefit himself and his co-workers continuously.

(xi) A reflective teacher does never rests; he is always sensitive to the problems of the educational field and keeps thinking about their remedies. This is the difference between a common teacher and a reflective teacher. He should do this work continuously.

Presently, the teachers in democratic countries are not only expected to develop their teaching methods continuously, but also need to participate in the whole educational process. All teachers cannot do this work, but only reflective teachers are required for this. From this view, Schon has developed such teaching steps according to which very reflective teachers can participate in the improvement of the whole educational process. These steps are planning, teaching activity, monitoring and feedback.

Chapter-4

Quality Management in Teacher Education

Quality of teacher education is one of the factors affecting the overall education of the country. Last decade has manifested an unprecedented growth in teacher education leading to quality degradation in this sector including unplanned mushroomed institutional growth, under supplied institutions for teacher educators, lowering criteria for teacher educators and uncontrolled indulgence of local market forces. Kothari Commission (1964-66) univocally held that the quality, competence and character of teachers to be the most significant factors, influencing the quality of education and its contribution to national development. Quality of school education is undoubtedly the direct consequence and the outcome of the quality of teachers and the teacher education system. Therefore quality improvement and excellence of teacher education programme is now considered a sine qua non for quality education. At present there is persistent strong demand for the search for quality and excellence in teacher education programmes which can infuse in future teachers a set of desired competencies, values and sense of commitment and willingness to perform.

Concept of Quality

Quality refers to basic and essential character, the distinguishing element or characteristics of a product, service, organisation or entity. It is defined as "the degree to which an object or entity (e.g., process, product, or service) satisfies a specified set of attributes or requirements". The quality of something can be determined by comparing a set of inherent characteristics with a set of requirements. Quality lies in the perception of the consumer. Quality has been the goal since the existence of human civilization. It has been the driving force for all human endeavours. Quality is the inspiration for transcendence from the mundane to the higher realms of life.

Definition of Quality

Quality has several definitions. These are described below:

Crosby (1979) defines quality as, "conformance to requirement".

Juran & Gryna (1980) define quality as, "fitness for use".

Deming (1986) defines quality as, "a predictable degree of uniformity and dependability at low cost and suited to the market".

Deming (1986) does not define quality directly but in one of his popular fourteen points for management says: Improve constantly and forever the system of production and service. Quality must be built in at the design stage. It may be too late, once plans are on their way. There must be continual improvement in test methods and ever better understanding of the customer's needs and of the way he uses and misuses a product. The quality desire starts with the intent, which is fixed by management. The intent must be translated into plans, specifications, and tests in an attempt to deliver to the customer the quality intended, all of which are management's responsibility.

The concept of quality is based on the above definitions reveal two important dimensions: customer's satisfaction and continuous improvement.

Characteristics of Quality

(i)   Quality is a matter of perception, not logic

It is the perception that resides outside the product, service or organisation. Peter Drucker (1990) says the results of an organization are always outside the organization. Inside, there are only costs. The result of a business is a satisfied customer, the result of a hospital is a healed patient and the result of an educational institution is a student who has something of value which he/she can use ten years later. Thus, quality is perceived by the consumer.

(ii)   Quality is relative and not absolute

It is a matter of degree. Theoretically, there are no maximum or minimum limits. Quality improvement, like pursuit of excellence, is a journey without a destination. There is nothing that cannot be little better in some way or the other.

(iii)   Quality is subjective

The criteria for judging quality can be substantially different from people to people, based on experience, values and culture.

(iv)   Quality is a contextual idea

Indicators of quality are institution specific. A high rate of job placement of graduates is a legitimate indicator of quality for vocational- technical-professional education programmes, but would not hold for humanities and liberal arts education. Each institution has a mission, a clear understanding of what it is, why it exists and what its primary obligation is? All functions and activities are informed by this mission. Assessment of performance and quality are valid only in terms of mission and goals.

(v)   Quality can be measured inferentially

Like intelligence, motivation, attitude and other educational outcomes indicators of quality are established that serve as a basis of measurement.

(vi)   Quality is attainable

Quality is not something that is bestowed by others, it is attained and maintained as a result of ceaseless striving (Spare, 1999).

(vii)   Quality is applicable to the system and its parts

Quality is applied to each component of a system i.e. input-process-output.

Quality Indicators for Teacher Education

- Curriculum Design and Planning
- Curriculum Transaction and Evaluation
- Research, Development and Extension
- Infrastructure and Learning Resources
- Student Support and Progression
- Organisation and Management

Quality Enhancement in Teacher Education

Now- a-days the entire teacher education system in India is in the process of change and reforms to meet the quality. The NCTE Regulations, 2014 which has brought reformation and innovations in teacher education will be successful only if the quality of teacher education gets improved. Hence, sound programme for professional preparation of teachers at all levels of teacher education is essential for imparting quality education for which well recognised programme and activities must be introduced.

Quality of education is a multi-dimensional concept, with varying conceptualizations. It includes, within its ambit, the quality of inputs in the form of students, faculty, support staff and the infrastructure; the quality of processes in the form of learning and teaching activity: and the quality of outputs in the form of the enlightened students who move out of the system (Sahney, Karunes and Banwet, 2001). With more attention being paid to the quality of higher education, quality has also increasingly been seen as something that can and should be managed and approved (Seymour, 1992). Quality management in higher education had already been introduced during the 1980s, and in the beginning of the 1990s the idea of applying the popular industrial quality models such as Total Quality Management (TQM), aiming at customers' satisfaction to the higher education area was also quite widespread. TQM can be considered as the first quality management model in higher education that cause a lot of discussions about potential relevance for the sector, as well as its educational and social implications (Stensaker, 2007).

For enhancement of total quality in teacher education, the educational institutions and universities should follow certain standard parameters in admission procedure to take the quality intake of students, quality faculty, appropriate teaching pedagogy, quality infrastructure, quality control and proper leadership and management etc. There are following important dimensions of quality enhancement in teacher education. The quality in teacher education can be enhanced by implementing these important quality dimensions such as:

- Quality in students' intake
- Quality in faculty members

- Quality in academic infrastructure
- Quality in teaching methodology and technology
- Quality in uniform examination system
- Quality in evaluation procedure

Due to the existing main challenges in teacher education, it is very difficult to maintain the total quality in teacher education at present in India. First, we must solve these main problems in teacher education then after, the quality in teacher education can be maintained.

The Secondary Education Commission (1952-53) has rightly observed the need of teacher for improving the quality and standard of education. After reviewing the status and service conditions of teachers, the Kothari Commission (1964-66) has pointed out, "Of all the different factors which influence the quality of education and its contribution to national development, the quality, competence and character of teachers are undoubtedly the most significant". The Ministry of Education Document "Challenge of Education: A Policy Perspective" (1985) has mentioned, "Teacher performance is the most crucial input in the field of education. Whatever policies may be laid down in the ultimate analysis these have to be interpreted and implemented by teachers as much through their personal example as through teaching learning process". National Policy on Education (1986) has also stated, "The status of the teacher reflects the socio-cultural ethos of a society; it is said that no people can rise above the level of its teachers. The Government and the community should endeavour to create conditions which will help motivate and inspire teachers on constructive and creative lines. Teachers should have the freedom to innovate to devise appropriate methods of communication and activities relevant to the needs and capabilities of the concerns of the community".

Total Quality Management (TQM): The Concept

Total Quality Management was originally developed by W. Edwards Deming, an internationally renowned quality expert, known as the father of TQM. Other persons who are associated with this philosophy are Juran, (1988, 1989), Crosby (1979, 1984), Ishikawa, (1983, 1985). The Approach of Total Quality Management in Education (TQME) is an adoption from the concept of W. Edwards Deming's, 'Total Quality Management (TQM)'. After World War-II, Deming conceptualised it for improving the production quality of goods and services. Deming indicated, TQM can be used in any type of organisation regardless of size or orientation (e.g., public, private, profit, non-profit, service, manufacturing, etc.) to create an efficient, effective environment for both employees and customers.

Total Quality Management (TQM) is a well-known approach by organizations that strive to make quality assurance as their business culture. There are also various definitions by different writers. Berry (1996) defines TQM as an approach to improve the effectiveness and flexibility of business as a whole. It is essentially a way of organizing and involving the whole organization; every department, every activity, every single person at every level. In the context of education, Harris (in Kwan, 1996) defines three common approaches to TQM, namely, customer focus, staff focus, and service agreement stance.

The theory of TQM rests on two tenets (Weaver, 1992). The first and most important is that customers are vital to the operation of the organization. Without customers there is no business definitely, and without business there is no organization. Consequently, it should be the primary aim of any group to keep customers satisfied by providing them with quality product (Deming, 1986). The second tenet is that management needs to listen to non-traditional sources of information in order to institute quality. This is based on the belief that employees want to do quality work, which will be possible if managers listen to them and create a workplace based on their ideas (Deming, 1986).

Total Quality refers to not only the product but also to the way the product is made as well as presented to the customer. Total quality also asks for customer orientation, process orientation, people management and leadership. It can work only when stakeholders understand the importance of guaranteeing quality and improving continuously unless the institutions and the stakeholders have a keen desire and a constancy of purpose. For achieving total quality, three things are essential (i) meeting customers' requirements, (ii) continuous improvement through management process and (iii) involvement of all employees.

Quality management adopts a number of management principles that can be used to guide the organizations towards improved performance. Providing quality education to large numbers at affordable costs is the primary concern of developing countries. The three aspects to be managed are academic, administrative and financial as well as the human and physical resources. In other words management of input-process-product is of utmost concern of the system of teacher education.

TQM in Education

TQM has become increasingly popular in education. TQM has also spread into mainstream of educational organisations. In support of the TQM initiatives in education,

Crawford and Shulter (1999) applied Crosby (1984) model to suggest a practical strategy for using TQM principles in education. Their strategy focused on the quality of the teaching system used rather than on students' examination results. They argue that examinations are a diagnostic tool for assuring the quality of the teaching system. To satisfy the educational needs of students, continuous improvement efforts need to be directed to curriculum and delivery services.

Implementation of Total Quality Management

Deming (1986) has suggested certain steps for implementation of TQM in any organisation. These are as follows:

- Lay down policies and objective of TQM. Determine what the customer is supposed to receive and what they are receiving.
- Chalk out the methods to achieve TQM objectives.
- Educate and train workers and managers to understand and meet the requirements of TQM.
- Observe results of operation and find out the causes of non-conformance and place the report before the top management.
- Present undesired effects in quality improvement. Establish personal relationships with employees so that they can voice their concerns and ideas.
- Suggest measures for improvement of methods and design in future.

Mukhopadhya (2005) has proposed a workable strategic plan in seven steps: (1) belief, vision, mission, goals (2) learner's need assessment and client education (3) institutional assessment and SWOT analysis, (4)

Quality policy and intervention plan (5) cost of quality (6) planning for implementation (7) Evaluation and feedback.

TQM in Teacher Education

Considerable effort has gone into translating ideas generated by TQM to Teacher Education. For TQM, the role of teachers and students are very much important.

- **Role of students**

TQM recognises students (student teachers) as both customers and employees of the educational system. Administrators need to involve students in their own education by training them to question the learning process, and once the students have questioned it, administrators need to involve students in their own education by training them to question the learning process, and once the students have questioned it, administrators need to seriously consider student proposals for change.

- **Role of teachers**

TQM calls changes in teachers' relationships with both students and administrators; teacher's need to view education through students' eyes, and they need to work with administrators as a team. This teamwork is largely the responsibility of administrators, who need to delegate some of their responsibility and power to teachers.

- **Testing and evaluation**

Instead of using standardised tests and grades to measure students' progress, institutes that embrace TQM often try to assess student progress regularly throughout the year. By doing so, they avoid bringing problems to student's attention at the end of the year, when it is too late to do anything about them.

Suggestions for Improving the Total Quality of Teacher Education Program in India

The findings of the various studies have many implications on maintaining the total quality in teacher education institutions. It has implications on quality development of teacher education, teachers' job satisfaction and linkage with community, focus on leadership quality of the principal, experience of the teachers on TQM. The following suggestions are put forth:

- Teacher education plays a vital role in human capital formation. Economic development of a country is also correlated with the development of higher education (World Bank, 1998). In any educational programme, the teacher is the most important element. Adequate number of quality teachers can implement the educational process through which the desired development of the student is achieved. The quality of the teacher, to a large extent, depends on the quality of teacher education received by him/her (NCTE, 1998).

    (i) All teacher education institutions should ensure that quality management is implemented at all levels. These institutions should be subjected to periodical assessment and accreditation from the national assessment bodies like NAAC and ISO.

    (ii) Internal and external periodical assessment cells should be formed to monitor and promote quality in teacher education programmes as per the guidelines of national agencies like National Council for Teacher Education (NCTE), NAAC etc.

- (iii) Establishment of teacher education institutions should be according to the demand and supply policy. Quality of teacher education should be ensured when there is quantitative expansion.
- Various studies show that most of the teachers in government aided institutions and self-financing institutions, though they maintained quality in teaching, did not have job satisfaction. As a result, they did not attempt to contribute more to improving the linkage with community. The following strategies should be worked out to enhance the job satisfaction of the teachers and their linkages with community:
  - (i) The management and the head of the institution should have frequent interaction with the teachers to understand their needs.
  - (ii) More opportunities for professional development must be provided.
  - (iii) Transparent administration would certainly enhance quality improvement.
  - (iv) Teachers are to be given quality assignments to go with the community to conduct extension service activities such as awareness camps, campaigns, parents meet and social gatherings. Community participation in institutional activities will strengthen the teachers' linkage with community.
- It is indicated by various studies that the principal as leader is stronger in all types of institution such as government, government aided and self-financing institutions. The leader of the institution needs to

possess important qualities such as leadership, manager, administrator and researcher.

- Around 90% of pre-service teacher education institutions are in the non-Government Sector and most of the states of the eastern and North-Eastern Region of the country are facing acute shortage of institutional capacity of teacher preparation in relation to the demand. It is recommended that the government should increase the institutional capacity of teacher preparation, especially in the deficit states.

- Government may explore the possibility of instituting a transparent procedure of pre-entry testing of candidates to the possibility of instituting a transparent procedure of pre-entry testing of candidates to the pre-service teacher education programmes, keeping in view the variation in local conditions.

- Teacher education should be a part of the higher education system. The duration of programme of teacher education needs to be enhanced.

- The teacher education institutions which are located in multi and interdisciplinary environment need to redesign the norms and standards of various teacher education course specified by the NCTE. This will also have implications for employment and career progression of prospective teachers.

- As per the recommendations of the Education Commission (1964-66), every pre-service teacher education institution may have a demonstration school (teaching practice school) attached to it as a laboratory where student teachers get opportunities to experiment with new ideas and develop their capacities and skills to become reflective teachers.

- The institutional capacity should be increased for preparation of teacher educators. There is a need to make the Masters of Education programme of two year duration with the provision to branch out for specialization in curriculum and pedagogic studies, foundation studies, management, policy and finance, and other areas of emerging concerns in education.

- There is an urgent need to develop comprehensive programmes for continuing professional development of secondary school teachers. Towards this, existing institutions arrangements have to be significantly enhanced, along with strengthening of CTEs and IASEs. Besides, some post-graduate colleges and Department of Universities may also function as training centres, especially for secondary school teachers.

- It would be better for M.Ed. students to learn more about the practice of education by teaching a few years before taking the Master's Degree in Education at all stages as recommended by different commissions' earlier (Radhakrishnan Commission,1948-49 and Mudaliar commission ,1952-53).

- For professional preparation of Elementary Teacher educators, many programmes in the line of RIEs of NCERT, M.Ed. (Elementary) should begin to equip prospective teacher educators with the required capacities, sensibilities and skills.

- More and more studies should be encouraged and

conducted on the efficacies and effectiveness or different programmes both in pre-service and in-service levels (D.Ed., D.El.Ed., B.El.Ed.,B.P.Ed.,M. Ed. (Elementary, Secondary, Special) so as to bring out the required modifications in the current programmes.

- Teacher education programme should be organised on the basis of evidence obtainable from researching such areas as follows: (i) Teacher behaviour Developing conceptual framework and a theory of institution (ii) Innovative practices of teaching such as microteaching, simulation and interaction analysis procedures.

- For professional growth of teacher educators there should be seminars, summer institutes and research symposia at more frequent intervals.

- Competency Based Teacher Education Programme- Competency means the right way of conveying units of knowledge, applications and skills to the students. Competency based teacher education programme should make teachers discharge their duties efficiently for achieving success in providing quality education. It should also enhance the teaching skill of teachers. Morphy (1992) has emphasized the competency based Teacher Education programme. NCTE has identified ten competencies such as:

- contextual competencies
- conceptual competencies
- curricular and content competencies
- transactional competencies
- competencies in other educational activities

- Competencies related to the preparation of teaching learning materials
- Evaluation competencies
- Competencies related to parental contact and co-operation and competencies related to community contact and cooperation

The most important and urgent reform needed in education is to transform it, to endeavour to relate it to life, needs and aspirations of the people, and thereby make it a powerful instrument of social change necessary for the realization of national goals. The reforms in teacher education are necessary to achieve national goals. For this purpose, education should be developed to increase productivity, achieve social and national integration, strengthen democracy, accelerate the process of modernisation and cultivate social, moral and spiritual values. The national goals cannot be achieved without educational development. Teacher education has a significant role to play in maintaining the quality of education. Quality management is not an overnight process and it is not the product of a single hand.

Chapter- 5

Information and Communication Technology Integration in Teacher Education

In the present age, globally educational systems are under great pressure to adopt innovative methodologies and to integrate new Information and Communication Technologies (ICTs) in the teaching-learning process to prepare students with the knowledge and skills they need in the 21st century. Teaching profession is evolving from an emphasis on teacher-centred, lecture-based instructions to student centred interactive learning environments. Today a variety of ICTs can facilitate not only delivery of instruction but also learning process itself. There is a range of ICTs options, from videoconferencing through multimedia delivery to websites which can be used to meet the challenges that teachers face today. Undoubtedly, a teacher being pivot in the process of teaching-learning, knowledge of ICTs and skills to use in teaching-learning has gained immense importance for today's teacher. A teacher is expected to know successful integration of ICTs into his or her subject area to make teaching and learning meaningful.

Information Technology: The Concept

Information technology is a technology in which

both telecommunication and computer techniques work together to provide information. It is that technology by which information is processed, displayed, communicated and retrieved at a faster rate without error. It is a scientific system which accelerates the process of exchange of information between information sender (server) and information-user. Information technology refers to "tools and application support" by means of which information is recorded, edited, stored, analysed and disseminated with accuracy in the minimum possible time.

Fundamentals of Effective Communication

The word communication is derived from the Latin word 'communis' which means to share. The desire to share one's thoughts, ideas, feelings and emotions is inherently deep-rooted in the human psyche and man has devised ways and means of sharing and transmitting these. Communication is a process of transmitting and receiving verbal and non-verbal messages. Communication is considered effective when it achieves the desired reaction or responses from the receiver. Simply stated communication is a two way process of exchanging ideas.

Communication plays a very central role in our lives and it is the vehicle through which basic human activities are carried out. It is the life blood of any organization and it is indispensable to the success and well-being of people. The main objectives of communication are to give and receive information, to provide advice and counsel, to impart education and training and to use orders and instruction. The varieties of technological tools have made communication faster, smoother, and more efficient. The internet, e-mail, fax, messages, voice mail, teleconferencing and wireless devices have transferred the way people communicate.

In today's rapidly evolving environment, effective communication helps us to adapt to the new scenario. The revolution in the field of information and communication technology has led to a virtual paper-free system but this still does not undermine the value of the operator who will ensure effective communication. No matter how much technology will develop in the future, high standards must be set to ensure that communication is not only appropriately worded and logically structured, but it should also be consistently and attractively presented.

Communication technologies used in e-learning are generally categorised as Asynchronous and Synchronous. Asynchronous activities use technologies such as blogs, wikis, and discussion boards. The idea here is that participants may engage in the exchange of ideas of information without the dependency of other participants' involvement at the same time. Electronic mail (e-mail) is also asynchronous, as the mail can be sent or received without having both the participants' involvement at the same time.

Synchronous activities involve the exchange of ideas and information with one or more participants during the same period of time. A face to face discussion is an example of synchronous communication. Synchronous activities occur with all the participants joining in at once, and with an online chat session or a virtual classroom or meeting can often use a mix of communication technologies. In many models, the writing community and the communication channels relate with the e-learning and the m-learning communities. Both the communities provide a general overview of the basic learning models and the activities required for the participants to join the learning sessions across the virtual classroom or even across standard classrooms enabled by technology. Many activities, essential for the learners in these environments require frequent chat sessions in the form of virtual classrooms and/or blog meetings.

Knowledge Revolution through ICTs and Teacher

Traditionally, the teacher used to be the source of knowledge for the students. The main source of knowledge was limited to the text book. Now the pace of technological revolution and emergence of a knowledge society can change the traditional role of the teacher and the students. In many cases, the teachers do not possess adequate knowledge to supplement the requirements of the student. At present, in a number of cases the student is more informed than the teacher. Furthermore, there is likely to be confusion in the teacher's mind about his or her role in relation to the use of different technologies i.e. teacher finds himself in a situation where he/she is no longer the principal source for delivery of information. In the new phase of the knowledge revolution, the source of knowledge has shifted from one source to different sources. In other words, we can say that there is a decentralisation of the knowledge source. This has an overall impact on the development of learning abilities among the children. Teachers as members of learning communities are always learning from each other, exchanging ideas or solving problems together. But the demands of teaching have often prevented regular or sustained sharing. At this juncture, technology can provide some solutions to structural problems that serve as obstacles to sustained collaboration among teachers.

The world is changing very fast. Using modern invents of science and technology, the world is getting closer to us day by day. Access to information has become easier. The teachers have to keep them informed with the vast changing world. Over and above these, modern information and communication technologies are being introduced in the curriculum time to time. This also demands teachers' competencies. Mere introduction of modern technologies and pedagogical principles will not yield good fruits, unless and until the teachers are fully acquainted with their theory and practice. The teachers have the responsibility of changing the content of education to make it meaningful for the young generation.

Internet has become an integral part of our life. We need to accept and adopt it to make our teachers and teacher educators updated in the modern technological society as it has great relevance for 21st century pedagogy. The international commissions and national level committees in India in the past 30 years have stressed on a paradigm shift in the area of education, teaching and instruction. As a result, learning stands recognised as a life-long process, supported by a system called multi-channelling with the use of ICT which offers the possibility for active, interactive and parallel interaction.

The UNESCO World Education Report on 'Teachers and Teaching in Changing World' describes the radical implication that information and communication technologies have for conventional teaching and learning. It predicts the transformation of teaching-learning process and the way teachers and learners gain access to knowledge and information. The report states,

- Students and teachers must have sufficient access to digital technologies and the internet in their classrooms, school and teacher education institutions.
- High quality, meaningful and culturally respon-

sive digital content must be available for teachers and learners.
- Teachers must have the knowledge and skills to use the digital tools and resources to help students to achieve high academic standards.

Table-1-ICT involves a change in the Role of Teacher and Student

Changes in teacher's role	Learning facilitator, collaborator, coach, mentor, knowledge navigator and co-learner
	Teacher gives students more options and responsibilities for their own teaching
Changes in student's role	Active participant in the learning process
	Producing and sharing knowledge, participating at times as expert
	Learning collaboratively with others

Researchers' and academics' conceptualization of pedagogy has changed with recent developments in ICT and models of learning (Walkins and Mortimore, 1999). Many writers have suggested the need to design a new integrated pedagogy (Cornu, 1995) and the changing pedagogical roles of teachers, setting joint tasks, promoting student self-management, supporting meta-cognition, fostering multiple perspectives, and scaffolding learning (McLoughlin and Oliver, 1999).

Challenges

(i) ICT has brought about many challenges and opportunities for education. The challenge in teacher education has been to create a new generation of teachers capable of employing a variety of technology tools into all phases of academic, administrative, research, and extension functions.

(ii) The most important obstacle to the effective use of technology in instruction and in professional development is inadequate training. Teachers have not received enough pre-service training in technology.

(iii) Integration of ICTs in education system may face various challenges with respect to policy, planning, infrastructure, learning content and language, capacity building and financing, ICT-enhanced education also requires clearly stated objectives, mobilization of resources and political commitment of the concerned bodies.

(iv) Teacher education institutions are faced with the challenges of preparing a new generation of teachers to effectively use the new learning tools in their teaching practices. For many, teacher education programme is a daunting task that requires the acquisition of new resources, experience, expertise and careful planning. In approaching this task it is helpful to understand:

- The impact of technology on global society and its implication for education.
- The extensive knowledge that has been generated about how people learn and what this means for creating more effective and changing student centred learning environment.
- The stages of teacher development and levels of adoption of ICT by teachers.
- The critical importance of context, culture,

- leadership and vision, life-long learning and the changes in planning for the integration of technology into teacher education.
- The ICT competencies required by teachers related to content pedagogy, technical issues, social issues, collaborative and networking.
- The importance of developing standards to guide implementation of ICT in teacher education.
- The essential condition for successful integration of ICT into teacher education.
- Important strategies to consider in planning for infusion of ICT in teacher education and managing the change.

Online Education

Online education is the type of education that is also called e-learning; where, the methodology of learning is unusual as compared to the traditional classroom type of learning. The synonyms of e-learning are Online Learning, Multimedia Based Learning, Technology Enhanced Learning (TEL), Computer Based Training (CBT), Internet Based Training (IBT), Web Based Training (WBT), and online virtual education. Content delivery in case of online education is with the help of Internet, intranet, extranet, audio or video tape, satellite TV, and CD-ROM and it includes media in the form of text, image, animation, streaming video and audio. It allows us to learn at our own way i.e. on our own time with a flexible, interactive and engaging online experience. For education, the internet is making it possible for more individuals than ever to access knowledge and to learn in new and different ways. The internet is enabling us to address educational challenges, bringing learning to students instead of bringing students to learning. It is allowing for the creation of learning communities that defy the constraints of time and distance as it provides access to knowledge that was once difficult to obtain.

The main attribute of online education is the flexibility of accessing information and resources. It refers to the access for the use of information and resources at any time, any place or pace according to one's convenience. Moreover, the information and communication technology provides the individual an opportunity to capture, store, and distribute information in the form of text, pictures and illustrations which includes multimedia-based simulations of simple and complex processes which are cheaply accessible.

Integration of ICTs in Teacher Education

To meet the educational needs of the present society the teachers are required to be ICT competent. The ICT competencies are organised into four groups; (i) Pedagogy is focused on teacher's instructional practices and knowledge of the curriculum and it requires that they develop applications within their disciplines that make effective use of ICTs to support and extend teaching and learning. (ii) Collaboration and networking acknowledges the communicative potential of ICTs to extend learning beyond the classroom walls and the implications for teacher's development of new knowledge and skills. (iii) Technology brings with it new rights and responsibilities, including equitable access to technology resources, care for individual health and respect for individual property included within the social issues aspect of ICT competence (iv)Technical issues are the aspects of the life-long learning theme through which teachers update skills-hardware and software, as new generation of technology.

Teacher education institutions and programmes have a critical role to provide the necessary leadership and adopting pre-service and in-service teacher education to deal with the current demands of the society. They need to model the new pedagogies and tools for learning with the aim of enhancing the teaching-learning process. Moreover, teacher education institutions and programmes must also give guidance in determining how the technologies can best be used in the context of culture, needs and economic conditions of the country.

The International Society for Technology Education has released its educational technology standards for teachers. These standards include 21st century skills. Some of these skills are:

- finding and managing resources
- Publishing on the web
- Connecting with colleagues, students, parents and local / global communities

Teachers must be proficient in the above skills in order to develop good practices for their students and help students include these skills for learning. Teacher and teacher educators also need computer literacy and technical skills to be able to utilise ICT in educational settings. Teachers also need knowledge about how to use the tools available in pedagogically meaningful ways.

Technology has the potential to transform the professional environment for educators. Through the application of network technologies to research and collaborative planning, teachers can break loose from the isolating environments that the teaching profession had imposed on them in the past. Technology impacts not only on the teaching and learning process but also on the ways and opportunities through which educators learn.

Technological developments influence two aspects of education. One is the way the Teacher Training College train up prospective teachers (pre-service) and the other is how the Training Colleges design continuing education for their teachers to learn on the job either at the physical workplace or at virtual learning (in-service).

Following steps can be taken to integrate ICT in teacher education:

- **Easy access to computer and internet**

Teachers must be provided free and easy access to computers and internet. Teachers may be given pre-paid internet cards to be used in cybercafé in the neighbourhood when institutional access to the internet is inadequate.

- **Access to technical and curriculum support**

Technology infusion in various subject areas is a complex innovation that requires a considerable change in and possibly a shift in the personal beliefs of a teacher and how teaching and learning takes place. If a teacher has not seen technology infusion modelled in pre-service, he/she would have a greater need for technical and curriculum support. This support can be provided by teacher mentors or coaches who have experienced in technology integration.

UNESCO planning guide for ICT in teacher-education cites three key principles for effective ICT development in Teacher Education that were put forward by the society for Information Technology and Teacher education. The application of these three principles will be a mile stone towards effectively integrating ICT in Teacher Education and staff development programmes.

- That technology should be infused into the entire teacher education programme, implying that ICT should not be restricted to a single course but needs to permeate in all courses in the programmes.
- That technology should be introduced in context. Accordingly, ICT application like word processing, databases, spreadsheet and telecommunications should not be taught as separate topics rather encountered as the need arises in all courses of teacher education programmes.
- That teacher trainees should experience innovative technology supported learning environment in teacher education programmes. This requires that students should see their teachers engaging in technology to present their subjects utilizing power point or simulations in lectures and demonstrations. Students should also have the opportunity to use such applications in practical classes, seminars and assignments.

In planning for infusion of ICTs into teacher preparation programmes, the factors that are important to a programme's success must be considered. A holistic framework proposed by the UNESCO (2002) takes into account the factors, e.g. cultural, educational, technology resources that are important in planning the integration of technology into pre-service curriculum.

Following factors should be taken into consideration for inclusion of ICTs into curriculum of teacher education:

(i) The use of technology in culturally appropriate ways and the development of respect for multiple cultures and contexts, which need to be taught and modelled by teachers.

(ii) Leadership and vision are essential for the successful planning and implementation of technology into teacher education.

(iii) Life long learning acknowledges that learning does not stop after school. Planning and Management of change is the final theme, born of today's context and accelerated by technology itself. It signifies the importance of careful planning and effective management of the change process.

Role of ICT in Professional Development of Teacher

There are various approaches to professional development of teachers in the context of use of ICTs in education. For professional development, ICT needs to be incorporated into teaching and learning which is an ongoing process and should not stop at one training. Teachers need to update their knowledge and skills as school curriculum and technologies change. There are two fundamental aims of teacher training; (i) teacher education in ICTs (ii) teacher education through ICTs.

The most obvious technique for professional development of teachers is to provide courses in basic ICTs knowledge and skills. It is necessary for teachers to become skilled in operating the new technologies and in exploiting them effectively as educational tools. Teachers must master the use of information: skills of research, critical analysis, linking diverse types and sources of information, reformulating retrieved data, if they are to teach their pupils to develop these same skills. More emphasis need to be placed on training in pedagogy, as opposed to the current trend in many education systems where the major focus is on specialized knowledge in specific curricular subjects. Teachers must be adequately equipped with more didactic competencies to assume their new role as experts in the learning process.

ICTs can support effective professional development of teachers. Using ICTs as tools for training of teachers is as important as introducing the basics of ICTs to the prospective teachers. As sources of information and expertise, as well as tools for distance communication, ICTs can offer many new possibilities for teacher education. Teachers may go through the regular use of these technologies. Use of new media, new rules of communication, even a new language has to be learned. ICTs can promote international collaboration and networking in education and professional development. In fact, there has been increasing evidence that ICTs may be able to provide more flexible and effective ways for life-long professional development of teachers.

To remain updated of the knowledge base regularly is inevitable to teacher's advancement in career and overall development. Information comes from multiple media, but filtering it down to what is relevant and authentic is very important. To read from books, magazines, and journals a lot about the concerned sector is essential when teacher is looking for a career entry or advancement, along with authentic content assessed from the World Wide Web.

Teacher Education institutions should perpetually endeavour to use the latest technologies in order to support the process of education. We need a system that can sustain the increasing demands and the challenges of the present world to stay updated with the ever changing world. Techno-pedagogy which refers to weaving the techniques of teaching into learning environment can do wonder in providing multi- sensory learning that is possible through e-learning. For the professional development of teacher educators, there is a dire need of use of electronic modes as it provides remarkable speed in accessing various resources and skills.

In the process of professional development, e-resources are useful in the following ways:

- Promoting high level decision making and reasoning abilities
- Obtaining errorless and updated knowledge of concepts
- Processing information more efficiently and effectively
- Getting new information about various training programmes, seminars, conferences and workshops for development of professional abilities and insights towards new methodology and advancement in teaching-learning process.
- Technology can be effectively used in orientation programmes, refresher courses, seminars, workshop, conference, e-learning, e-content, video recording and playback.

Advantages of ICT Tools for Teacher

- Through ICT, images can easily be used in teaching and improving the retentive memory of students.
- Through ICT, teachers can easily explain complex instruction and ensure students' comprehension.
- Through ICT, teachers are able to create interactive classes and make the lessons more enjoyable, which could improve student attendance and concentration.

Now the whole world has shrunk to a small

village. The development of ICT changes the epic centre of knowledge. Teacher education plays a vital role in developing quality education which is the present requirement in the modern information and communication era. There ought to be technology culture in the educational institutions. Every teacher ought to be Techno-savvy. ICT Aided Constructivists approach should be practised by every teacher for promoting innovation, creation and construction.

Chapter- 6

Innovative Pedagogy and Teacher Education

At present, there is an unprecedented level of support for doing things differently and widespread recognition that new approaches and new methods are essential to address the educational needs of today's society. There is a lot of promising energy behind innovation in public education today. Teaching-learning process is tuned with innovation. New ways of doing things often bring about an improved result. The community expects teachers to be sufficiently acknowledgeable in the subjects they teach and proficient in different pedagogy. To satisfy diverse needs of different categories of students effectively, teacher's role is not only to disseminate knowledge but also to create and generate new knowledge among students by using innovative pedagogies.

What is Innovation?

The present world is ever changing. Now students want to be innovative and to make learning environment more exciting, challenging and rewarding. The term innovation does not simply mean a moment of invention: it is a cycle that includes several stages and the work of many stakeholders. The term innovation has been defined and understood in a number of ways. Innovation in the field of education refers to an idea or practice new to a specific educational context that meets unsatisfied needs. It is the introduction or promotion of new ideas and methods that are devised in education and /or school practices.

Innovation is concerned with the following features:
- It is concerned with a new or novel element which deviates from existing structures
- Its' objective is relevant to the needs of the community and to national development
- It is renewable from time to time based on appropriate feedback
- Innovation should permit flexibility during the experimental stage
- Innovation needs to be both cost and time effective

Innovation is based on a broad set of strategic, marketing, operational and technical skills. Creativity plays important role as the prime source for innovation. It is seen as a process of generating ideas, expressions and forms, which can amplify knowledge and lead to new ways of using the knowledge. Enhancing creativity and innovation at all levels of education and training has been considered as one of the objectives of Indian education system.

Oxford English Dictionary (1970) says innovation is the introduction of novelties, something newly introduced. The idea or conception also may find a place in such a broader meaning of the term innovation, as compared to invention. The Dictionary of Education (1977) has also defined innovation as promotion of new ideas or practices.

Change is another term used to describe innovation. The Oxford English Dictionary gives 'a change made' as one of the meanings of innovation. Innovation refers to the planned or deliberate type of change. In other words, an innovation is something better than what it replaces (Per Dalin, 1978). This view is shared by Munro (1977) when he states that innovation is a deliberate attempt to improve educational practice. Innovation is a deliberate effort directed towards the significant improvement of the system (Havelock). The word 'deliberate effort' includes both conceptualising and implementing. Since our concern here is teacher education, innovation in teacher education can be defined as a 'deliberate effort directed towards the significant improvement of teacher education'.

Teacher Education and Pedagogy

Teacher education has to be conceived as an integral part of educational and social system and must primarily respond to the requirements of the school system. It can no longer remain conventional and static but should transform itself to a progressive, dynamic and responsive system.

Quality process in teacher education programme is concerned with the proper method of transacting the curriculum, practical based training with constructive feedback system and democratic teacher-student interaction system. Keeping in mind the thrust areas highlighted by the NCF (2005) and the NCFTE (2009) in terms of the development of content knowledge as well as the pedagogical competencies a basic structural change is required which can provide necessary scaffoldings for quality teacher education programme.The teachers have to keep abreast of the latest developments not only in their field of specialization but also in areas of educational developments and social and cultural issues through continuous in-service orientation.

Teachers in the 21st century must be prepared for the classroom in ways beyond what is presented in textbooks.

In an ever-increasing diverse society, the acquisition of content knowledge and limited field experience by pre-service teachers fall short of preparing them for teacher effectiveness in the diverse classroom. They must be equipped with knowledge and skills that are not articulated in textbooks. The present teacher education programme is inadequate to meet the challenges of diverse Indian socio-cultural contexts and the paradigm shift envisaged in the NCF(2005). The pedagogic reform from this perspective need to invest on building the teachers' capacity to act as autonomous reflective groups of professionals who are sensitive to their social mandate and to the professional ethics and to the needs of heterogeneous groups of learners.

Teacher is the only person who imparts knowledge to the students to attain desirable changes among his students. To achieve desired goals teacher will have to take many decisions for the smooth and efficient functioning of teaching learning process. In teaching learning situation he takes the decision, use different methods / strategies. Teaching strategies refer to methods used to help students learn the desired course contents and be able to develop achievable goals in the future. Imparting knowledge is the most fundamental part of a teacher's job.

Teaching means interaction between teacher and students. No two teachers are the same. The way the teacher teaches is unique to him. In the process of teaching the teacher plays the role of independent variable that is responsible for the functioning of the dependent variable i.e. students. He does the planning, organizing, leading and controlling of teaching so that desirable outcomes of his teaching may be properly obtained. He is free to perform various activities for providing learning experiences to the pupils.

Teaching is a skill that can be learned and teachers need to ensure adherence to fair play while teaching. Teacher's professionalism contains the essential characteristics such as competence, performance and conduct which directly impact the effectiveness of teaching. Teacher educators must be able to demonstrate not only general and specific knowledge and skills of their technical special; they must also demonstrate ability to translate the knowledge and skills into pedagogy.

Every region has its typical cultural identity, and there is a need to utilize the same as a basis for developing meaningful relevant pedagogies. Since there is no one universal way in which a child is placed, pedagogy must be culture specific. Cultural specificity should get embedded in the pedagogical practices which should be evolved for tribal, rural, urban communities and other ethnic groups.

Innovative ideas are germinated in the field of education. Some innovative methods of teaching could be multimedia, integrated multi-sensory interactive application etc. Any innovation in education sector, be it in student assessment, curriculum design, use of technology, content organization, or approaches to learning, aims at promotion or advancement of learning.

Pedagogical Innovation in Education

Traditional teaching is concerned with the teacher as the controller of the learning environment. Power and responsibility are held by the teachers and they play the role of instructor and decision maker (in regard to curriculum content and specific outcomes). The delivery of lesson is considered to be the most important and students master knowledge through drill and practice (rote learning). As traditional methods or strategies of teaching have some limitations, so teacher educators are compelled to take a shift from traditional to new innovative strategies (Teacher centred to learner centred) in order to make the teaching learning process more effective and to make the content more understandable to students keeping in view of present situations. Following factors are responsible for the shift and use of new pedagogies in the field of education:

- Explosion of knowledge
- Development of new technologies
- To provide practical knowledge to students
- Utmost utilization of students' abilities
- Emphasis on child centred education
- To create learner centred environment

In education, teachers facilitate student's learning through the use of appropriate pedagogy. The different ways to teach are often referred to as the teacher's pedagogy. A good teacher helps students to understand the material and to understand what it means. This can be achieved by finding innovative and creative ways to make complicated ideas understandable to the students. Teacher's work is to show students the techniques needed to find the answer for themselves and they can become self-sufficient in the field. The innovative pedagogies for teaching-learning processes are discussed below:

i. **Collaboration**

Collaboration is 'to work with another or others on a joint project'. It involves two or more teachers' planning, teaching and assessing the same students in the interest of creating a learning community and maintaining a commitment to collaboration with students and each other. Collaboration develops new ideas or change old ones depending upon supportive and frequent conversations with respected peers. It pushes the participants to engage in conversations through a lens that is multi-cultural and multi-dimensional, it pulls at the boundaries. Working collaboratively helps create energy for the teachers and that energy provides motivation to keep striving to improve teaching and complete projects. Co-teaching can provide support to try new methods/strategies in the co-teachers' own individual classrooms. Co-teaching can provide a vehicle for change. For some co-teachers, personal change, such as increased confidence about teaching, is a result of simply having someone else understand and appreciate their teaching experiences; for others, change is brought about by planning curriculum together, reflecting on what topics are taught, and the justification for those topics in conversations that never occurred previously.

ii. **Team teaching**

Team teaching/co-teaching is defined as the collaboration between teachers in teaching. In a co-taught classroom, two teachers work together to develop a differentiated curriculum that meets the needs of a diverse population of students. In a co-taught classroom, teachers share the planning, presentation, evaluation, and classroom management in an effort to enhance the learning environment for all students. Team teaching is an approach in which two or more teachers join together, plan together, teach together and evaluate together. In inclusive schools the regular education teacher and the special education teacher also work together in providing service to children with special need in the classroom. In inclusive education, meeting the special educational needs of children is the joint responsibility of the regular teacher, the special teacher and other professionals. For team teaching one has to plan jointly with others for teaching and evaluating a particular topic or subject depending upon one's expertise/experience.

iii. Peer supported learning

Peer supported learning is based on the idea that more heads are better than one. Using peers as a resource can be useful in many different situations. It is possible to learn from others in many different situations including: tutorials/seminar; web based discussion forums; e-mail groups; in-class discussions/debates; working as a group on an assignment. Peer tutoring involves one-to-one instruction from a student to another.

iv. Cooperative learning

Cooperative Learning is a strategy used by group/number of students to achieve a common goal with mutual collaboration and support in an inclusive classroom where many children with and without disabilities have been enrolled. Children can be taught with the help of cooperative learning in which they have common goals. The teacher would operate only as planner, facilitator, evaluator and monitor.

v. Problem solving

The problem solving method has several advantages over expository methods. It assumes that students are active participants in the construction of new knowledge rather than passive receivers of knowledge. The problem solving strategies give students opportunities to think rationally. The higher levels of learning e.g., reasoning, critical reflection, imagination, which involve transfer and application of knowledge and understanding to new situations, can be achieved through problem solving. Learning through problem solving is more meaningful, permanent and transferable compared to learning through traditional expository methods. The process of problem solving includes the major steps of scientific method such as; (i) recognising the problem (ii) interpreting, defining and delimiting the problem (iii) formulating hypotheses (iv) collecting relevant data/ conducting experiments (v) organising and evaluating the data (v) arriving at conclusions (vii) verifying conclusions and generalizations.

Problem solving method presupposes that students can take on some of the responsibility for their own learning and can take personal action to solve problems, resolve conflicts, discuss alternatives, and focus on thinking as a vital element of the curriculum. It provides students with opportunities to use their newly acquired knowledge in meaningful, real life activities and assists them in working at higher levels of thinking. For this students take the help of technologies. It is student centred teaching strategy which requires students to become active participants in the learning process. With problem based learning, students engage themselves in real experiences of life. It is social and collaborative learning in which the students learn the important skills for life. Students are presented with problems which require them to find either a scientific or technological solution.

vi.   Problem posing

Problem posing is the core of the survey method. It is a systematic approach to empowering learners to control their own learning. To problematise a term, a text, an opinion, or personal perspective, it is essential to construct them as challenges that encourage learners to attempt to transform their circumstances or views. Problematisation is based on a dialogue or process that takes the common knowledge about a situation and transforms that knowledge into a problem. This allows the learners to adopt new points of view, to reflect and to move towards action. One way to problematise a statement is to get the learner to ask some simple questions about the statements. This approach helps learners question and challenge their beliefs and achieve critical consciousness.

vii.   **Critical pedagogy**

Critical pedagogy is based on the assumption that students are not just young people for whom teachers should devise solutions. They are critical observers of their own condition and needs, and should be participants in discussion and problem solving relating to their education and future opportunities. They should be made aware that their perceptions and experiences are important; and should be encouraged to think independently and to have courage to dissent. Critical pedagogy provides an opportunity to reflect critically on issues in terms of their political, social, economic and moral aspects. It entails the acceptance of multiple views on social issues and a commitment to democratic forms of interaction. Thus, critical pedagogy facilitates collective decision making through open discussion and by encouraging and recognising multiple views (NCF, 2005).

viii.   **Culturally situated pedagogy**

Culturally situated pedagogy/Responsive Pedagogy highlights the centrality of culture in students' understandings of the world. It addresses the need for teachers to acknowledge students' diversity and incorporate their backgrounds and experiences into the learning experiences and classroom environment. In "culturally relevant pedagogy" (Ladson-Billings, 2001), "culturally responsive teaching" (Gay, 2000), and "culturally-situated pedagogy" teachers develop the knowledge and skills to teach children from diverse racial, ethnic, language, and social class backgrounds (Weinstein, Curran,& Tomlinson Clarke, 2003). Culturally relevant pedagogy aims to ensure that educators acknowledge and honour the diverse viewpoints of their student population and refrained them from promoting homogeneous perspectives. Dingus (2003) further emphasized the importance of this perspective: "No student should have to sacrifice cultural heritage, ethnic identity, and social networks in order to obtain an education."

ix. Concept mapping

Concept mapping as a teaching strategy was first developed and used by J. D Novak of Cornell University in early 1980s. Concept mapping is a technique of graphically representing concepts and their hierarchical interrelationships in a meaningful network. Its origin was derived from Ausubel's learning theory which places central emphasis on the students' prior knowledge in subsequent meaningful learning. Concept mapping can be used both as an instructional tool and as an evaluation tool. As an instructional tool it helps to organize and represent knowledge in a subject, facilitates information processing, deep thinking and making thinking process explicit, visualise the cognitive structures of knowledge, links and determines the relationships between textual and visual information, enhances mastery and retention of facts, and facilitates meaningful learning.

Generally, the concept mapping is a state of knowledge representation and consists of extracting concepts and their relationships from a text or other content, plotting these concepts on paper or a computer screen, and finally naming the relationships.

x. **Constructivist theory of teaching and learning**

Constructivism is 'an approach to learning that holds that people actively construct or make their own knowledge and that reality is determined by the experiences of the learner' (Elliott et al., 2000).Constructivist teaching is based on constructivist learning theory. This theoretical framework holds that learning is always based upon knowledge that a student already knows; this prior knowledge is called a schema, because all learning is filtered through pre-existing schemata. Constructivists suggest that learning is more effective when a student is actively engaged in the learning process rather than attempting to receive knowledge passively. A wide variety of methods claim to be based on constructivist learning theory. Most of these methods rely on some form of guided discovery where the teacher avoids most direct instruction and attempts to lead the students through questions and activities to discover, discuss, appreciate and verbalize the new knowledge. The primary responsibility of the teacher is to create a collaborative problem-solving environment where students become active participants in their own learning.From this perspective, a teacher acts as a facilitator of learning rather than an instructor.

Scaffolding is a key feature of effective teaching, where the adult continually adjusts the level of his or her help in response to the learner's level of performance. In the classroom, scaffolding can include modelling a skill, providing hints or cues, and adapting material or activity (Copple & Bredekamp, 2009).

xi. **Blended learning**

Blended learning is a teaching and learning approach that combines face-to-face classroom methods with computer mediated activities to deliver instruction. This pedagogical approach means a mixture of face-to-face and online activities and the integration of synchronous and asynchronous learning tools, thus providing an optimal possibility for the arrangement of effective learning processes.

It can be applied to any program which holds on to the values of traditional learning and incorporates digital media with that. A blended learning mode provides ultimate flexibility in many aspects. It can be applied to any program which holds on to the values of traditional learning and incorporates digital media with that. It is a lot more effective and likeable than anything that has been ever before. Students, academicians, policy makers etc. appreciate the needed freedom/flexibility. Only a well-crafted blended solution can provide a seamless transition or vice versa. Though there are many teaching methods and techniques, available resources indicate that blended learning mode is the "best of all worlds". It is the best because it helps all learning requirements and styles through a variety of mediums and techniques. It is one of the most adopted learning tools. Recently many learning platforms globally have adopted blended learning.

The important features of Blended Learning are as follows:
- Increased student engagement in learning
- Enhanced teacher and student interaction
- Responsibility for learning
- Time management and flexibility
- Improved student learning outcomes
- Enhanced institutional reputation.
- More flexible teaching and learning environment

- More amenable for self and continuous learning
- Better opportunities for experiential learning

xii. Computer assisted instruction

Computer Assisted Instruction (CAI) refers to the application of computer software to address student needs. It involves online interaction between a learner and a computerized delivery system. CAI programmes use tutorials, drills, and question and answer session to present topic or to test students' performance.

ICT is used in teaching in the following ways:

- Developing understanding and application of the concepts
- Developing expression power
- Developing reasoning and thinking power
- Development of judgment and decision-making ability
- Improving comprehension, speed and vocabulary
- Developing self-concept and value clarification
- Developing proper study habits
- Developing tolerance and ambiguity, risk taking capacity, scientific temper etc.

xiii. e-learning and multimedia technology

e-learning encompasses learning at all levels; both formal and non-formal. e-learning is essentially the network-enabled transfer of skills and knowledge. It refers to using electronic applications and processes to learn. Web-based learning is a subset of e-learning and refers to learning using an internet browser (such as Netscape or Internet Explorer). e-learning application and processes include web-based learning, computer based learning, virtual classrooms and digital collaboration. Content is delivered via the internet, intranet/extranet, audio or video tape, satellite TV, and CD-ROM. e-learning was first called 'Internet-Based training" then "Web-Based Training". Today, e-learning has more use among students. There is also an increased use of virtual classrooms (online presentations delivered live) as an online learning platform and classroom for a diverse set of education providers.

e-learning is naturally suited to distance learning and flexible learning but can also be used in conjunction with face to face teaching, in which the term blended learning is commonly used. Bernard Luskin, the pioneer of e-learning argues that the 'e' must be understood to have broad meaning. If e-learning is to be effective, Luskin says that the 'e' should be interpreted to mean exciting, energetic, enthusiastic, emotional, extended, excellent, and educational.

e-learning is commonly referred to the intentional use of networked information and communications technology in teaching and learning. It comprises a lot more than on-line learning, virtual learning, distributed learning, net worked or web-based learning. As the letter "e" in e-learning stands for the word "electronic", e-learning would incorporate all educational activities that are carried out by individuals or groups working on-line or off-line, or synchronously or asynchronously via networked or standalone computers and other electronics devices.

The modalities of e-learning are individualised self-paced e-learning off-line, Individualised self-paced e-learning online, group-based e-learning synchronously, group-based e-learning asynchronously.

Advantages of e-learning

It helps the teachers to:
- master a skill quickly
- study easily
- make learning enjoyable
- make learning experience intellectual
- reduces social differences
- share resources across networks
- use face book, twitter, etc
- allow flexibility with time and place

Implementation of new means of technology changes the classroom environment. There are many multimedia technologies that are available for developers to create these innovative and interactive multimedia applications such as Adobe Photoshop and premier, Sound Forge and 3D Studio Max etc. The teacher uses multimedia to modify the contents of the material. It helps the teacher to present the content in a more meaningful way using different media elements. These media elements can be converted into digital form, modifies and customized for the final presentation. By incorporating digital media elements into the project, the students are able to learn better since they use multiple sensory modalities, which would make them more motivated to pay more attention to the information presented and retain the information better. In addition, PCs, compact computers that allow the teacher to write notes directly on the screen with a special pen, replace the archaic projector. Technology allows teachers to make notes on charts and spreadsheets and send them directly to their students' PC.

Traditional Pedagogy vs. Pedagogy in Information Society

Introduction of ICTs have brought paradigm shift in the area of teaching and learning. The following table shows a comparative study of Traditional Pedagogy vs. Pedagogy in Information Society.

Table-2

Aspect	Traditional Pedagogy	Emerging Pedagogy for the Information Society
Active Learning	Activities prescribed by teacher	Activities determined by learners
	Whole class instruction	Small group
	Slight variation activities	Many different activities
	Pace determined by the programme	Pace determined by learners
Collaborative	Individual	Working in teams
	Homogeneous group	Heterogeneous group
	Every one for him/herself	Supporting each other
Creative	Reproductive Learning	Productive learning
	Apply known solutions to problems	Find new solutions to problems
Integrative	No link between theory and practice	Integrating theory and practice
	Separate Subjects	Integration between subjects
	Discipline based	Thematic
	Individual Teachers	Teams of teachers
Evaluative	Traditional pedagogy	Emerging pedagogy for the information society

Adapted from a comparative study of ICT and Traditional Pedagogy of Voogt (2003) and Tinio (2002).

The process of students' learning assumes centrality in the whole process of education. Thus, it is not sufficient just to present the learning material before the students or to put them into the internet. Pedagogy, as it is understood here, mainly focuses on the activities of the learners and the teachings primarily from the point of view of support. This is known as student centred pedagogy. In this context, the construction of learning environments is evolving as one central task of the teachers. This task is not as simple as it appears to be. It requires teacher to get rid of his traditional role as 'a sage in the stage' and to collaborate with the other stake holders of education. There is no universal or readymade approach to do this. S/he must find his/her ways to support students for optimum learning. The teachers need to seek not only support but also ideas from parents and other members of community in bringing out pedagogical innovations.

Chapter-7

Teacher Education and Inclusive Practice

Inclusive education has been internationally recognised as a philosophy for attaining equity, justice and quality education for all children, especially those who have been traditionally excluded from mainstream education for reasons of disability, ethnicity, gender or other characteristics. Education for all with quality and equity has a high priority in our country. In this way, teachers are of central importance and should develop specific skills and vision to contribute to this goal. The goal is to eliminate all barriers in order to achieve learning (Lipski, 1998). Inclusion promotes quality and equity education for all, without any type of barrier or exclusion, including those who may be potentially marginalized due to disability, gender, emotional behaviour problems, family background, ethnicity, giftedness, migrants, poverty, hearing or visual impairment, language delay etc. A majority of the developing countries has made significant improvements in mandating inclusion of all children through policies or legislation, but implementation of such policies or legislation at classroom level has not been achieved and remains a distant reality. There are many reasons for progress or no progress in this regard. One area that has been most neglected in this regard is the training of teachers.

Inclusive Education: The Concept

Inclusive education is a human right approach. Now-a-days it has been widely acclaimed nationally as a philosophy for attaining equity, justice and quality education for all children, especially those who have been traditionally excluded from mainstream education due to disability, ethnicity, gender or other characteristics. The policy at national and international level envisages for inclusive education for children and their right to quality education to the extent possible to their individual needs. The National Curriculum Frame Work (2005) advocates a policy of inclusion to be implemented in all schools throughout education systems. It is an entry point to improve the quality of school education.

Inclusive education "is a process of strengthening the capacity of the education system to reach out to all learners". It involves restructuring the culture, policies and practices in schools so that they can respond to the diversity of students in their locality. Inclusive education means that all children, regardless of their ability level, are included in a mainstream classroom, or in the most appropriate or Least Restrictive Environment (LRE), that students of all ability levels are taught as equals, and that teachers must adjust their curriculum and teaching methodologies so that all students are benefited. This also avoids wasting of resources and "shattered hopes", which often occurs in classroom that are "one size fits all".

Inclusive education is brought about by having all children of society to become students of the same school. Inclusive education means the act of ensuring that all children despite their differences, receive the opportunity of being part of the same classroom as other children of their age, and in the process get the opportunity of being exposed to the curriculum to their optimal potential. Inclusive education is very important as it fulfils constitutional responsibility (RTE, Sarva Shiksha Abhiyan, compulsory primary education etc.), helps in achieving universalization of education. It develops nation, break barriers of poverty. The main goal of inclusive education is to improve the quality of education and helps in achieving social equity. It also helps in the growth of individual life and development.

Inclusive education according to UNESCO means that "the school can provide a good education to all pupils irrespective of their varying abilities. All children will be treated with respect and ensured equal opportunities to learn together. Inclusive education is an on-going process. Teachers must work actively and deliberately to reach its goals".

The Draft Action Plan for Inclusive Education prepared by the MHRD (2003) defines, "Inclusive education means all learners, young people with or without disabilities being able to learn together in ordinary pre-school provisions, schools and community educational settings with appropriate network of support services (MHRD, 2003)".

The Draft Action Plan for Inclusive Education of Children and youth with Disabilities (MHRD, 2005) defines inclusive education as "An approach that seeks to address the learning needs of all children, youth and adults with a specific focus on those who are vulnerable to marginalization and exclusion. It aims at all stakeholders in the system (learners, parents, community, teachers, administrators, policy makers) to be comfortable with diversity and see it as a challenge rather than a problem".

Kothari Commission (1964-66) emphasised that the education of children with disability should be "an inseparable part of general education system". The commission is also specially emphasized the importance of integrated education in meeting its target.

Underlying the process of inclusion is the assumption that the general classroom teacher has certain knowledge and understanding about the needs of different learners, teaching techniques and curriculum strategies. Florian and Rouse (2009) state, "The task of initial teacher education is to prepare people to enter a profession which accepts individual and collective responsibility for improving the learning and participation of all children".

The fundamental principle of inclusive school is that all children should learn together wherever possible regardless of any difficulties or differences they may have. UNESCO, in 2005, has defined that it is a process of addressing and responding to the diverse needs of all learners by increasing participation in learning and reducing exclusion within and from education. In the context of education, the restructuring of school on inclusive lines is a reflection of the social model in action (Mittler, 2000). The fundamental principle of inclusive school is that all children should learn together wherever possible regardless of any difficulties or differences they may have.

The International Commission on Development of Education (1972) felt, "Foreseeing the advent of democracy to the world of education is not an illusion. It may not be a perfect democracy, but when has this ever existed? Yet it will at least be a real, concrete, practical democracy, not inspired and built by bureaucrats or technocrats, or granted by some ruling caste. It will be living, creative and involving". Article

30 (1) of the Indian constitution states that, "All minorities, whether based on religion or language, shall have the right to establish and administer educational institutions of their choice". Article 30 (2) states that, "The state shall not in granting aid to educational institutions, discriminate against any educational institution on the ground that it is under the management of minority, whether based on religion or language". The government will not foist any language of its own choice on any minority. The minority status of a group will be determined based on its population. The reservation of the particular group is not considered as a violation of the constitution. No educational institution will be entitled to refuse admission to any child on the basis of religion, caste, creed or language.

Need of Inclusive Education for the Society

The 21st century is regarded as an era of inclusion and knowledge. One of the most important goals of educational institution is to impart quality education among all regardless of any discrimination on the grounds of age, caste, creed, socio-economic background, gender, disability, ethnicity, religion or any other belief in order to envisage the path of building a completely just and inclusive society. Government of India has also undertaken a number of initiatives by framing various acts and legislations, launching schemes, and implementing programmes to ensure quality, equity and accessibility in education for students with disabilities.

Inclusive society is the need of the hour that can be made possible only when there is total inclusion in education. Now inclusive education is the most feasible plan of getting across of education to each child. Inclusive school must recognise and respond to the diverse needs of their students, accommodating both different styles and rates of learning and ensuring quality education to all through appropriate curricula, organizational arrangements, teaching strategies, resource use and partnership with their communities (Lipsky & Gartner, 1999). The basic purpose of inclusive approach is to improve the quality of life through facilitating interactions between the children with and without special needs that would contribute to both bonding and building a complete society.

Inclusive education is not an end itself but a means to an end which signifies the importance of it in the present day society. A cohesive society can be formed without any discrimination of caste, creed, colour, sex, gender, social background and above all disability among children. Inclusive education can bring a new social order by integrating all children forming a uniform society. Inclusion is a system of education that provides inclusive education programs where children with diverse characteristics will be able to learn together.

Inclusive education is essential for economic and social development of country and building of a truly democratic society, and in the promotion of national integration. Inclusive education can be considered as a powerful instrument of social and economic progress.

Education acts as the lever for enhancement of society especially for socially and economically weaker sections. The Kothari Commission (1964-66) observed, "On grounds of social justice as well as for the furtherance of democracy it is essential to make special efforts to equalize educational opportunities between different groups". Commission added that, "one of the important social objectives of education is to equalize opportunities, enabling the backward or underprivileged classes and individual to use education as a lever for the improvement of their condition. Every society that values social justice and is anxious to improve the lot of the common man and cultivate all available talent must ensure progressive equality of opportunity to all sections of the population. This is the only guarantee for the building up of an egalitarian human society in which the exploitation of the weak will be minimised". Prem Kripal observed, "education as an equalizing factor, the quest for the quality of life which is the essence of modern education offers new hope and opportunity to poor and materially deprived societies." There have been many efforts taken by international and national organisation for promoting inclusive education which have been explained in the following paragraph.

The SC, ST and OBC population, women, children, minorities and other excluded groups require special attention for their mainstreaming in national life. To achieve inclusiveness or equity in all these dimensions require multiple interventions by the central and state governments, private sector, NGOs, civil society and each one of us. Its success will depend not only on new policies and government programmes, but on a collective and conscious effort of all sections of society.

Inclusion in National and International Context: Some Research Studies

In India inclusive education is a human right which refers to embracing all without excluding any one whosoever. It addresses learning and other needs of everyone. It lays much emphasis to include those who are vulnerable to marginalization and exclusion. It implies that all learners with or without disabilities are able to learn together in an inclusive and enabling environment. Inclusive education as a notion seeks to develop a just and humane society, a value that resonates with the constitution. It is also concerned with the creation of quality education system, which, if coupled with access, makes the core of what Akoojee and Nikomo (2007) regard as a successfully transformed higher education. The adoption of an inclusive education and training system is a significant reflection of both social and human right model in action.

According to Loreman and Deppeler (2001), "Inclusion means full inclusion of children with diverse abilities (that is both giftedness and disability) in all aspects of schooling that other children are able to access and enjoy. It involves 'regular' schools and classroom genuinely adapting and changing to meet the needs of all children as well as celebrating and valuing differences". In an ideal system of inclusive education, the general education itself should make the education of children with special needs as its integral part. The implied meaning of this is that general educators should be equipped with knowledge and skills to address the learning and other needs of children with special needs with minimum or no assistance from special educators. This demands the requirement of incorporating all those components in the pre-service as well as in-service training curriculum which are needed to prepare a teacher suitable for inclusive education. It is commonly thought that education of a child with special needs in general school is inclusion but it cannot be treated as total inclusion. Total or full inclusion refers to when general school system including teachers take most of the responsibilities for education of children with special needs.

Extending access to education is a part of worldwide agenda. The Education for All (EFA) initiative from the

United Nations is an essential element of the Millennium Development Goals in part because education is seen as being crucial to human development, and because so many children do not have access to children (UNESCO, 2005). Across the world, there are many reasons why children do not attend school, including high levels of mobility, social conflict, child labour and exploitation, poverty, gender and disability. Many children are at risk of not attending school, or of receiving a substandard education. In such countries, the concern is not only about access to schooling, but it is also about ensuring meaningful participation in a system in which achievement and success is available to all (Black-Hawkins, Florian & Rouse, 2007). But, why is there such a long tail of under achievement in many countries?/ why do educational systems have institutional barriers to participation and achievement? And why do so many teachers think that the problems that some students have in learning should not be their responsibility because they have not been trained to deal with these matters? Throughout the world, there is an increased awareness of differences in access to and outcomes of education. This has to be understood in the power of education to reduce poverty, to improve the lives of individuals and groups, and to transform societies (Grrub & Lazerson, 2004). Developing 'schools for all' is important because schooling is linked to human, economic and social development goals. The development of successful inclusive schools, 'schools for all' in which the learning and participation of all children is valued, is an essential task for all countries. It is hardly surprising therefore that tackling under-achievement and increasing inclusion are a part of worldwide agenda. The process of mainstream education reform began in many countries in the mid 1980s when concerns about economic competitiveness and the efficiency of school systems led to the introduction of marketplace principles in education (Ball, 2006). Children who are considered difficult to teach and those who find learning difficult are at increased risk for exclusion when schools operate in a competitive educational marketplace (McLaughlin & Rouse, 2000, Gillborn & Youdell, 2000). According to Kaufman et al. (2005), successful teaching of children who are different, requires that they are grouped homogeneously so that special pedagogical approaches can be deployed by teachers who have been trained to use them. It could be argued that when special education is conceptualised in this manner, it is a barrier to the development of inclusion because it absolves the rest of the education system from taking responsibility for all children's learning.

The research literature suggests that the implementation of inclusion policies have been uneven (Evans & Lunt, 2002). There are many success stories to be told about inclusion (e.g., Ainscow, 1997; Black-Hawkins, Florian & Rouse, 2007), there have also been failures and difficulties. It has also been suggested that one of the greatest barriers to the development of inclusion is because most teachers do not have the necessary knowledge, skills and attitudes to carry out this work (Forlin 2001). Therefore, although inclusion is seen as important in most countries, experience tells us that it is difficult to achieve for children with additional support needs for a number of reasons including:

- Uncertainty about professional roles and the status of teachers especially those who have responsibilities for additional support needs
- A lack of agreement about the nature and usefulness of specialist knowledge

- Territorial disputes between professionals associated with certain 'special' practices
- Inadequate preparation of teachers and a lack of on-going professional development opportunities

Inclusive education is an important aspect which is a partnership between disabled adults and the parents of disabled children regardless of their physical, emotional, intellectual, linguistic and other conditions. The underlying premise of inclusion is that all children can learn and belong to the mainstream of school and community life. Inclusive is about the child's right to education and to participate with others in all spheres of school activities and school has to accept him with all his limitation and liabilities.

"The government and the community should endeavour to create conditions which will help motivate and inspire teachers on constructive and creative lines. Teachers should have the freedom to innovate, to devise appropriate methods of communication and activities relevant to the needs and capabilities and the concerns of the community" (NPE, 1986).

The prime goal that has guided the policy on higher education includes expansion, expansion with inclusiveness (equal access to all), quality and relevant education. The inclusive education was brought at centre stage in the 11th Plan (2006-2012). The focus on inclusive education has continued in the 12th plan as well (2012-2017). Inclusive education with equal access to those who desire and deserve is based on the understanding that the state should develop a policy in a manner such that, it provides equal opportunity to all to realize their capabilities and potential individually and collectively, so that they can participate in economic development and also benefit out of it.

What does inclusive policy involve? Inclusive policy involves strategies that increase access to higher education to those groups who lack access, both in absolute and relative terms (compared with the others). Among other things, the identification of such groups with their group specific constraints is critical for developing policy of inclusive education. The exclusion from access to higher education occurs for number of reasons and reflects in the disparities not only between poor and non-poor, but also on caste, ethnic, religious and gender lines.

Teacher Education for Inclusive Education

Criticisms of the ways in which teachers are prepared to deal with diversity and learning difficulties are two-fold. As noted previously, one view holds that there is a specific body of knowledge and a set of skills for working with 'special' children and that initial teacher education courses do not adequately cover these matters. The second claims that because education is not only about 'special' pupils, teacher education should focus on improving teaching and learning and should help beginning teachers to reduce the barriers to learning and participation of all pupils. Both these views are right to an extent, but each response is insufficient. A new way of thinking about the problem of teaching which does not deny human differences, but attempts to respond to them within what is ordinarily available in schools, rather than by making some children as different, is needed (Florian, 2007). This requires all teachers to accept responsibility for all the pupils they teach with confidence that they know how to access appropriate support when necessary. The position of teacher training in relation to its contribution to the development of inclusive thinking and practice on the part of student teachers is of fundamental importance.

Teacher issues are high on policy agendas in many countries and increasing attention is being given to teacher education for inclusion in particular. Peters and Reid (2009) propose an advocacy model for teacher education based on principles of inclusive education and disability studies. They point out, however, that moving from the prevalent technical-rational discourses based on (special) education towards a socio-political takes time because they are 'so enmeshed in our national psyche, legislation, school procedures and daily classroom practices'. They highlight the need for societal reform, disability/diversity reform and school reform to be addressed together, bring about a shift away from the medical or deficit model of special education. Slee (2010) says, 'just as normalization was rejected by many disabled people as a form of assimilation that invited them to deny difference, inclusive education is compromised by holding the extent regular school as the model for reform'. Garcia Huidobro (2005) points out that equity must be at the centre of general policy decisions and not limited to peripheral policies oriented to correct the effects of general policies that are not tune with logic of justice or prevention. In some countries the involvement of a large number of decision- making bodies fragments policy and practice including debates around teacher education programmes (Brownell et al., 2005; Sindelar & Rosenberg, 2000). This indicates the need for clear vision and purpose and parallel changes in policy and practice to remedy discrepancies in legislation (Lesar, 2007).

Need of Quality Teacher Education for Inclusive Education: Some Reviews

Savolainen (2009) notes that teacher's competence plays an essential role in quality education. Studies of Sanders & Horn,1998; Bailleul et al.,2008, suggest that the quality of the teacher contributes more to learner achievement than any other factor, including class size, class composition or background. The need for 'high quality' teachers equipped to meet the needs of all learners become evident to provide not only equal opportunities for all, but also education for an inclusive society. Reynolds (2001) says that it is the knowledge, beliefs and values of the teacher that are brought to bear in creating an effective learning environment for pupil, making the teacher a critical influence in education for inclusion and the development of the inclusive school. Romi and Leyser (2006) reported that favourably disposed teachers toward the inclusion of students with disabilities in regular education classrooms employ more effective instructional strategies than those who hold negative attitudes. Literature indicates that teachers' actions and performance in classrooms are greatly influenced by their knowledge of the learning characteristics of their students and these have profound impact on learning processes (Philpott, Furey, & Penney, 2010; Pinar & Sucuoglou, 2011). Regular teachers are increasingly required to be sensitive to the curricular needs, styles and rates of learning and levels of motivation of students with special needs. They are expected to design, implement and evaluate the educational programme based on the students' assessed needs and create active and appropriate learning situations through integrative, flexible and interdisciplinary instructional strategies (Kochhar & West, 1996). They would also be required to participate in Individual Education Programme (IEP) meetings and work in partnership with special education teachers, para professionals, parents, and other service providers (Ashman & Elkins, 2009). Therefore, it is evident that the learning and achievement of the learner are highly dependent upon the quality and competence of teachers. Competent teachers can only be possible when there is quality in pre-service and in-service teacher education.

Barriers in the way of Inclusion

UNESCO (2003) has pointed out three barriers in the way of inclusive education.

Social barriers

Social barriers include negative thinking of society about disabled and handicapped children; discrimination, belief that special education is a good alternative; resistance to accept change, etc.

Educational barriers

Educational problems include lacking characteristics of acceptability, availability, accessibility, adaptability and attention in teachers and organizations towards children. Teachers, administrators etc. are less sensitive towards diversities; prefers rigid, inflexible curriculum, views inclusive education as a technique for lowering of quality of education and regards it as additional burden. Besides shortage of trained teachers are also great problem.

Economic barriers

Economic barriers like expanding grant-in-aid in a wasteful manner. The money provided under SSA to teachers for purchasing material or aid useful for children is not spent accurately as they regard this grant as wastage of money, etc.

Problems in Inclusive Education with Special reference to Teacher Preparation

Rigidity in general education system, lack of community and family involvement, inadequate teacher development programme and lack of strong advocacy are some of the major problems in the way of inclusive education.

Inclusion requires a large vision and specific competencies for all teachers. Now the teachers need to know that diversity is present in the classroom, and that they should attend to learners with a range of diverse needs. In this frame, it is imperative to prepare teachers for inclusion in all curricular plans for pre-service teachers, also for teachers in services, with the professional aptitudes.

Some problems related to inclusive education with special reference to teacher preparation are mentioned below:

- Lack of Teacher preparation institution
- Lack of competent teacher educator
- Lack of infrastructure and resources
- Lack of proper curriculum with special reference to inclusive education during teacher preparation
- Lack of proper strategies to improve practical skill and competency development on the part of student teachers
- Lack of time for preparing teachers for inclusion in general classes
- Lack of continuous workshop, seminar, projects, internship for special children education
- Lack of adequate pedagogy and strategy to educate children with special need

Role of Teacher in Developing Inclusion

Teachers are crucial in determining what happens in classrooms and there are those who would argue that the development of more inclusive classrooms require teachers to cater for different student learning needs through the modification or differentiation of the curriculum (Forlin, 2004). For some this approach has been interpreted as requiring individualisation. At its most extreme, this view can be seen in the call for one-to-one teaching of students with learning difficulties. Questions about the sustainability of such provision are rarely adequately answered. Further, there are those who argue (e.g. Kaufman et al,. 2005) that there are specialist teaching approaches for children with different kinds of disabilities and that specialist training is required. An unintended consequences of these views is that most mainstream teachers do not believe that they have the skills and knowledge to do this kind of work and that there is an army of 'experts' out there to deal with these students on a one to one basis or in small more manageable groups. Nevertheless teachers do have concerns about inclusion and many surveys have found that teachers' attitudes towards inclusion are not particularly positive (Ellins & Porter, 2005). Further, they express concerns about their lack of preparation for inclusion and for teaching all learners (Forlin, 2001).But in settings where teachers are encouraged to try out a range of teaching strategies, they report that they knew more than they thought and, for the most part, children learn in similar ways. Although some children might need extra support, teachers do not distinguish between 'types' of special need when planning this support, (Florian & Rouse, 2001). Many teachers reported that they did not think that they could teach such children, but their confidence and repertoire of teaching strategies developed over time. Rouse (2007) suggested that developing effective inclusive practice is about not only extending teachers' knowledge, but it is also about encouraging them to do things differently and getting them to reconsider their attitudes and beliefs. In other words, it should about 'knowing', 'doing, and 'believing'. But what might this look like in practice? For many years, teacher development courses focused extending knowledge and skills. Courses would often concentrate on the characteristics of different kinds of learners, how they should be identified and the current policy context. In addition, they would cover the specialist teaching strategies that should be used. In other words these courses focused on:

Knowing about
- Teaching strategies
- Disability and special needs
- How children learn
- What children need to learn
- Classroom organisation and management
- Where to get help when necessary
- Identifying and assessing difficulties
- Assessing and monitoring children's learning
- The legislative and policy context

It is important to point out that such content knowledge is important, but the evidence suggests that it is insufficient to improve practice in schools because many teachers did not act upon this knowledge when they returned to the classroom. It was clear that there was a big gap between what teachers knew because of being on a course and what they did in their classrooms. In an attempt to bridge this gap, initiatives have been designed to link individual and institutional development. In other words 'doing' has become essential element of professional learning and institutional development. In many cases this involves action research type initiatives built around school or classroom based development projects and new ways of:

Doing
- Turning knowledge into action
- Moving beyond reflective practice
- Using evidence to improve practice
- Learning how to work with colleagues as well as children
- Becoming an 'activist' professional

Believing
- That all children are worth educating
- That all children can learn
- That they have the capacity to make a difference to children's lives
- That such work is their responsibility and not only a task for specialists

Inclusive Education Programmes

Inclusive education programmes are as follows:
- It is a process whereby the personal and educational needs of the disabled and marginalised groups of students are looked into more empathically than ever before.
- It is a new approach in education to include all those in the general mainstream system of education who previously have been excluded from it for one reason or the other.
- Inclusive education is a system where emphasis is not on training the deficit but on adapting to environment to accommodate the disability perceiving it as a natural difference.
- It is an enthusiastic optimistic endeavour through

education for restructuring an equalitarian society where everyone may have space.
- Inclusion is a process by which a school expands its resources to meet the learning needs, physical and emotional needs of all children.

Responsibility of Teacher in Promoting Inclusive Education

Teachers have the responsibility in promoting inclusive education. To teach in inclusive settings, cooperation and understanding among regular, special and resource teachers are an essential condition. The teacher for teaching in inclusive classrooms must be aware of 3R's i.e., Rights, Roles and Responsibilities. The teacher is expected to welcome all children, without any discrimination by making necessary accommodations and arrangements for their education in the same school and classes along with the non-disabled peers. The teacher should help the child to grow his or her potentiality to the maximum and making students to understand and accept human differences, provide opportunities for overall development of child's physical, cognitive, emotional and social skills. A teacher is to follow zero rejection policy according to which everyone should be welcomed to the class and foster positive attitudes among students: also help to preparation of curriculum which includes effective learning for all students. A teacher has to maintain contacts and linkages with other professionals working for the welfare of disabled students and appreciate the need for modification of the school or classroom organisation for the curriculum of teaching techniques plus appreciate special services available to children with special needs. A teacher should also help parents, voluntary organizations and educational planners in understanding the problems of exceptional children, possesses knowledge of various technologies, understand the value of parents and contributions which parents can make to their children's development. The basic responsibility of a teacher is to identify the children who need special attention and also those children suffering from any kind of disability and refer them to their parents, schools so that necessary steps can be taken at right time.

Strategies for Teaching in Inclusive Setting

Following strategies may be adopted by the teacher for teaching in inclusive setting:

- **Pedagogy in inclusive classroom**

School must provide a chance at placement of students with disabilities in a "normal" classroom environment before putting them into a special needs classroom. As such methods of instruction that benefit these students, along with their non-disabled classmates must be implemented in order to serve the needs of all involved. Methods of teaching are commonly used in full inclusion classrooms to support the load of diversified students now entering the classrooms. There are some important methods which can be adopted in inclusive classroom.

- **Collaborative method**

Collaborative learning is a situation in which two or more learner learn or attempt to learn something together, in which learners engage in a common task where each learner depends on and is accountable to each other. These include both face-to- face conversations and computer discussions (on line forums, chat rooms, etc.). In inclusive classrooms teachers use this method to teach students one-on-one when needed. In this method, teacher supports one another by rotating roles and sharing instructions and ideas. This collaborative approach allows all students to remain in the general education classroom.

- **Multi-sensory instruction**

In this method of teaching teachers take sample lesson assignments and design presentations for auditory, visual, tactile, kinaesthetic and special needs students. Where possible, teachers can create lessons that include experimental components and practical applications. Class participants can take lesson packets and share additional suggestions and critique. Pairs of small groups of teacher participants can work together to practice methods of inclusion instruction.

- **Co - teaching**

A co- teaching method consists of combination of a special education teacher, general education teacher, and/or a related service provider. In co-teaching, both professionals coordinate and deliver substantive instruction. They plan and use high involvement strategies to engage all students in the instruction. Co-teachers provide instruction for a diverse group of students, including those identified with disabilities and others who are not so identified. Professionals should consider the defining characteristics of co-teaching and their own professional strengths as they initiate co-teaching relationships.

- **Cooperative learning method**

There are several benefits of cooperative learning structures for students with disabilities. Students with disabilities are more engaged in classroom activities where cooperative learning structures are in place compared to more traditional classroom interventions. Specifically, in inclusive classes cooperative learning is used, students articulate their thoughts more freely, receive confirming and constructive feedback, engage in questioning techniques, receive additional practice on skills and have increased opportunities to respond. Further, when students are thinking aloud while discussing, teachers are better able to assess student and group needs and intervene if needed.

- **Team teaching**

Team teaching is an approach in which two or more teachers join together, plan together, teach together and evaluate together. In inclusive schools the regular education teacher and the special education teacher also work together in providing service to children with special need in the classroom. In inclusive education, meeting the special educational needs of children is the joint responsibility of the regular teacher, the special teacher and other professionals. For team teaching you have to plan jointly with others for teaching and evaluating a particular topic or subject depending upon your expertise/ experience.

- **Peer tutoring**

Peer tutoring involves one- to-one instruction from a student to another in the tutoring role and the tutee who receives instruction. Peer tutoring meets the individual needs of the child with disabilities by providing remedial or supportive instruction.

- **Language experience approach**

The Language Experience Approach (LEA) integrates the development of reading skills with the development of listening, speaking and writing skills. What the child is thinking and talking about would make the material for developing the lesson. LEA deals with the following thinking process (a) what a child thinks about, he can talk about (b) What a child says, he can write (or someone can write for him) and (c) what a child writes (or others write for him), he can read.

- **Task analysis**

In task analysis, the task to be learnt by the child is broken up into small teachable components. The components are sequenced and each component is transacted to the child. The next component to be taught is taken up only after the child masters the initial ones. Children with special need cover a large range of disabilities. For each child the basal level and the profile have to be assessed and accordingly considering his pace of learning, the task is to be broken down. Various activities of daily living as need academic activities can be taught through this method.

- **Modifying materials and activities**

Teaching social studies can involve many different instructional practices. Within the classroom setting teachers can employ discussions and demonstrations. Other intriguing techniques involve simulation activities, role-playing or dramatic improvisation.

Inclusive education is an innovative step towards quality of education and helps in developing each child fully and helps in universalisation of education. Therefore, inclusive education should be utilised effectively in schools and other institutions. As the teacher is the pivot of the entire education system and is the main catalyst agent for introducing desirable changes in the teaching learning process, all attempts need be made to improve the teacher education programme so that it can gift us the quality and competent teachers capable of meeting the diverse needs of each and every student irrespective of their abilities and disabilities in an inclusive classroom. They are to be motivated to become dynamic, enthusiastic, positive, innovative, and creative. Teacher education programme should be structured and modified based on the findings of the researches in the field of education. Content, pedagogy, and technology are to be integrated. Furthermore, at the time of planning for teacher education programme, policies, legislations, needs of the society and students, futuristic perspective, employ ability, technological advancement and infrastructural issues should be given due attention. Teacher education plays an important role in making this goal of inclusive education achievable. For this purpose teachers, administrators, organisations, etc. should be trained and have broad mind in order to accept diversity and fulfil their responsibility. Adequate steps should be taken by different organizations for promoting inclusive education. For a school to be inclusive, the attitudes of everyone in the school, including administrators, teachers, and other students, are positive towards students with disabilities.

Chapter-8

Professional Development of Teacher

A profession may be defined as an occupation which requires specialized knowledge or advanced learning. A professional is one who can acquire funds of knowledge, range of skills and their application in the service of humanity. Hence professional means belonging to a profession; showing the skill of a trained person; doing specialised work for payment. Thus a teacher is considered as professional because he is trained to teach and has acquired skills. Thus to meet the need of fast generation learner, the globalized world demands the type of teacher who must have administrative knowledge as well as teaching skills and knowledge. Professional development is the foremost need which helps teachers to develop new insights into their practices.

Teaching profession comprises of teacher's competencies, obligations, devotions towards teaching and leadership in the field of education. It has been pointed out that teachers can act as trail blazers in the lives of learners and in the process of education for development (Dave, 2003). As teaching profession is considered as the respectable profession world over, teachers have the responsibility to shape the future of children in terms of educating them in a best possible way. They are considered to be the most important resources for all levels of education to nourish and develop the system.

Teacher and Teaching Profession

Teachers must view teaching as profession, this would require professional attitude on their part (Singhal, 2003). Teaching profession needs change in attitudes and value systems of the teachers. Apart from teaching, their multiple roles include that they have to act as the agents of change and modernization, cultural reconstruction and social development to earn recognition as professional from society by acquiring new competencies and commitments. The task of sensitising teachers about their commitment to the learner, society, profession, institute and values is a great challenge before teacher education (Walia, 2003). Steps should be taken for their professional growth and development on a continuous basis to enable them to keep abreast with the changes and developments in their respective fields. Besides, the teachers are expected to develop necessary skills for professional development.

The NEP (2020) puts forward many policy changes when it comes to teachers and teacher education. To become a teacher, a 4-year Bachelor of Education will be the minimum requirement needed by 2030. The teacher recruitment process will also be strengthened and made transparent. The National Council for Teacher Education will frame a National Curriculum Framework for Teacher Education by 2021 and a National Professional Standards for Teachers by 2022. The policy aims to: Ensure that all students at all levels of school education are taught by passionate, motivated, highly qualified, professionally trained, and well equipped teachers.

We have enormous opportunity for ensuring

teacher's quality well into the 21st century if we recruit promising people into teaching and give them the highest quality preparation and training.

Professional Development: The Concept

Professional development refers to various activities that enhance professional career growth. Such activities include individual development, continuing education and in service education as well as curriculum writing, peer collaboration, study groups and peer coaching or mentoring. Fullan (1991) states that, the sum total of formal and informal learning experiences throughout one's career from pre-service teacher education to retirement. Teachers' professional competence and commitment determine the quality of education. Delors Commission (1996) has rightly emphasised that "there is need to update and improve teacher's knowledge. In-service education is as good as the pre-service education, even better for quality improvement".

Professional development is the driving force which helps to bring much change in the area of teaching and learning. As in any other profession, it is vital that teachers keep up-to-date with the most current topics, thinking and research in their field. This in turn supports them in their life-long learning. It is a worldwide experience that professional development is the key determining factor for improved student performance. Effective professional experiences are designed to help teachers for better understanding of teaching and learning. "To be effective, professional development must provide teachers with a way to directly apply what they learn to their teaching" (Resnic, 2005).

Professional development plays an essential role in

successful education reform and serves as a bridge between where prospective and experienced teachers are now and where they will need to meet the future challenges of guiding students in achieving higher standards of learning and development.

It is well recognised that the quality of education depends invariably on teachers. Which in turn depends on teacher education programmes which prepare them. Twelve Five year plan has also highlighted in strengthening teacher education in India. Now the MHRD Department of Higher Education, New Delhi has launched a scheme of Pandit Madan Mohan Malavya National Mission for Teachers and Teaching. The mission is envisaged to address comprehensively all issues related to teacher, teaching, teacher preparation and their professional development. The mission would pursue long term goal of building a strong professional cadre of teachers by setting performance standards and creating top class institutional facilities for innovative teaching and professional development.

Professional Crisis

Teacher education is currently facing a professional crisis. The profession has not been able to organise itself into a dynamic forward-looking professional organisation. The Indian Association of Teacher Educators, which had a glorious past, is under a cloud. The professionals are reluctant to mobilise round the Association. Attempts at vitalising the profession have not been planned and sustained. The administrators and other social scientists are looking with suspicion at the entire programme of teacher preparation. The Education Policy of 1968 talked about revamping teacher education. The National Policy on Education of 1986 has mentioned overhauling teacher education, but the programme of action is silent about the academic uplift of teacher education. There is an undertone to the effect that the existing teacher education institutions need to be replaced by new institutions.

Why is Professional Development of Teacher Necessary?

For a teacher it is very important to be well educated as well as dedicated. If one of the two traits is missing the teacher becomes only a professional. With the rising standards of education, it has become essential for the teachers to concentrate on their education. From play group to college level the teachers are educated and trained in a specific way to be able to teach their group.

Teachers are lifelong learners. In fact, ongoing education is a requirement for teachers at all levels of education. Professional development is necessary for the following reasons:

- To keep abreast of the developments in the teaching profession
- To maintain membership in key professional organizations relevant to his subject or area of speciality
- To maintain ethical behaviour in his relations with fellow teachers and educational associates
- To exercise professional discretion in his relations with parents and others
- To keep abreast of subject matter by study of books, periodicals, newspapers and other sources concerning development in his field
- To utilize films, filmstrips, T.V and radio as a means of keeping abreast of new and advanced knowledge in his field

Aims of Professional Development Programme for Teachers

The broad aims of professional development programs for teachers are to:

- Explore, reflect on and develop one's own practice
- Deepen one's knowledge and update oneself about one's academic discipline or other areas of school curriculum
- Research and reflect on learners and their education
- Understand and update one on educational and social issues
- Prepare for other roles professionally linked to education / teaching, such as teacher education, curriculum development or counselling
- Breakout of intellectual isolation and share experiences and insights with others in the field, both teachers and academics working in the area of specific disciplines as well as intellectuals

Professional Ethics for Teacher

Teaching being an important profession, there is urgent need to develop professional ethics, responsibility and obligation among teachers. Teachers like other professionals, have the similar responsibility, not only to their students but also to the society in which they are treated as the conscious and learned members.

Ethics is defined as a moral philosophy or code of moral conducts practiced by a person or group of persons. Basically it is a science of discrimination between the right and wrong. It governs a person's behaviour and dealing with values relating to human conduct with respect to the rightness or wrongness of certain action and to the goodness and badness of the motives of such action (Sinha, 2009). On the other hand professional ethics is a field of applied ethics whose purpose is to define, clarify and criticize professional work and its typical values. It encompasses the personal, organizational and corporate standards of behaviour expected of the professionals. Professions are characterized sociologically by means of their member. Their service ideal can be understood with reference to value that define the goals of their work, e.g., a teacher's primary goal is all round development of personality of all students and a doctor's primary goal is to promote health. Professional ethics can also be understood from the point of view of its service ideal and its related values. Thus professional ethics are the set of broad principles, derived from a spectrum of values, which are arrived at after deep philosophical reflection on the nature and role of the profession (Saxena & Dargan, 2014).

Accordingly, professional ethics of the teachers can be deduced as a set of moral conduct and values of the teachers towards their own students, schools, colleagues, community and professions. Jayamma and Sumangala (2012), define it as "a set of dignified principles put into practice by them. They are the valuable tactics that are exhibited and enforced by teachers in relation to the students, colleagues, community and to oneself, to produce a profound effect on strategy of education". Conduct and character development should be integral part of teaching profession, which can be cultivated through both pre-service and in-service training programme. In this regard IGNOU (2009), states that the profession of teaching reflects a high degree of academic excellence, repertoire of teaching skills and practical wisdom on one hand and a well-integrated value system on the other, both being oriented towards altruistic service. Thus professional ethics of a teacher is the core of professionalization and forms the base for professional development.

Professional Ethics in the light of Professional Development of Teacher

Professional development is a range of learning activities through which professionals improves and broadens their knowledge, skills and attitudes and develops their personal qualities necessary for the execution of professional duties (UNICEF, 2014). On the basis of this definition, it can be deduced that professional development includes mastery over content knowledge, pedagogical skills, professional competencies, organizational competencies and professional ethics. Hence development of professional ethics is an essential component of professional development of teachers, which can directly or indirectly strengthen its other components. Once morality and values are shaped strongly in the teachers, content knowledge, professional and pedagogical skills will follow it automatically.

On the other hand, a teacher is known by his professionalism, with unparallel commitment and higher standard of values. He is an embodiment of morality and symbol of sacredness. "Professionalism of the teacher has two aspects e.g., knowledge and ethics. So far as knowledge aspect of professionalism is concerned, a professional man is required to have mastery over his subject matter and exercise control over the development and maintenance of organized body of knowledge. As regards the ethical aspect of professionalism, a professional person is expected primarily to meet the best interest of the clients whom he serves by dispensing his acquired knowledge and skills with devotion, commitment and with missionary zeal" (Das, 2000).

Keeping in view the sacredness of the teaching profession a significant number of teachers have excelled in the profession by exhibiting their godly conduct towards their students, colleagues and community. In spite of it the teaching community has been defamed in the contemporary society owing to some teachers having no professionalism within them. There has been a wide spread violation of professional ethics by those teachers when they receive bribe from the students, use the students for their personal purposes, exploit them physically and mentally, discriminate them in the name of caste, creed, class, race, religion and gender.

In this connection National Education Association (1975) states, "the educators recognize the magnitude of the responsibility inherent in the teaching process. The desire for the respect and confidence of one's colleagues, of students, of parents and of the members of the community provides the incentives to attain and maintain the highest possible degree of ethical conduct". In order to protect the rights of students, to sustain the moral standard of teaching profession and to make the human relationship sacred, worthy, fruitful and productive in the school, there is an urgent need of inculcating a well-defined code of professional ethics within them. Hence professional ethics, if inculcated, can help the teachers in the following ways:

- To inspire the teachers to reflect and uphold the honour and dignity of the teaching profession
- To develop a positive attitude and interest towards teaching profession
- To develop a strong sense of commitment and dedication towards the profession
- To guide ethical decisions and actions in the teaching profession

- To identify the ethical responsibility and commitments in the teaching profession
- To promote public trust and confidence in the teaching profession
- To make the teachers accountable to their students and community
- To honour the right of the children in the schools and to protect the students from wide spread exploitation
- To develop their pedagogical beliefs and competencies
- To develop professional and organizational skills and create a sustainable academic atmosphere in the school
- To develop interpersonal relationship among the students and colleagues

Recommendation of Committees on Professional Development of Teachers

Kothari Commission (1964-66) suggested that for the professional preparation of teachers of higher education orientation is necessary especially of junior teachers. The commission recommended that orientation course should be organised for the new staff in every university.

Mehrotra Committee (1987) suggested for 3 to 4 weeks duration orientation programme for the newly appointed teachers. The emphasis should be laid on the methodologies of teaching in the concerned subject.

Ramamurti Committee (1990) recommended that there should be one year training after recruitment of the teachers for their professional development. All the commissions and committees always felt the need of professional development of teachers of higher education. Programme of Action (1992) proposed:

- To organise specially organised orientation programme for all new lecturers
- To organize refresher courses for all the teachers' at least once in five years
- To organize orientation programme for the teachers
- To encourage teachers to participate in workshop, seminars, conference and symposia etc.

Need for Continuous Professional Development (CPD)

The teacher has to develop professionalism as part of his continuous professional development. Continuous Professional Development (CPD) is a planned, continuous and lifelong process whereby teachers try to develop their personal and professional qualities, and improve their knowledge, skills, and practice, leading to their empowerment, the improvement of their agency and the development of their organizations and their pupils. It is "the process by which teachers review, renew and extend their commitment as change agents and by which they acquire and develop critically the knowledge, skills, planning and practice through each phase of their teaching lives" (Day, 1999).

CPD is needed to remain professionally alive. In the present globalised world wherein knowledge is the currency, professionals need to keep progressing in their field of work. Some of the reasons CPD is needed for those in the profession of teaching at various levels have been enumerated below:

- To attain quality in teaching and to uphold high standards

- To ensure meaningful student support
- To gain career security
- To fulfil the onus of preparing a cadre of young professionals of posterity-scientists artists, teachers, lawyers, engineers, doctors, etc.
- To be equipped to face the increasing competition from other fields
- To attain higher levels of accountability and risk taking
- To create learning ambiance and a competent workforce
- To build bridges with the community by assuring the public that individual professionals are well equipped for their work
- To continue to conduct research and innovate
- To satiate one's thirst for excellence

Suggestions for Promoting Professional Development of Teachers

Since teachers are expected to perform multiple roles in the present time, their continuous professional development becomes inevitable. The following suggestions deserve attention for professional development of teachers.

- **Participation in seminar, conference and workshop**

Teacher must keep abreast of current developments. He should find a forum to exchange ideas and share suggestions with the peers. This interaction will enable to enhance his knowledge. Teacher should regularly participate in conferences, seminars and workshops to expose his academic knowledge.

- **Academic development**

Teachers should make efforts and manage time for their academic development, increasing and updating their subject-matter knowledge. They must enrol themselves for Ph.D. programmes and do coursework, revision of notes, adding new materials, referring to latest books and journals. They should develop the habit of regular reading of professional journals and periodicals. Teachers should maintain a good personal library at home and make a regular use of internet to provide adequate knowledge and information to students.

- **In-service programmes**

Knowledge explosion in every discipline is the main source of development. The teacher has to continuously update his/her knowledge in his/her field of expertise. In service training programme is more valuable for the teachers. In service training programme is an organized need based continuing programme. For college and university teachers, orientation, refresher like courses are offered by HRDC of universities. These courses provide opportunities to the teachers to keep themselves abreast of latest advances in their fields. College Development Councils of universities should plan a variety of need based in service programmes for teachers. The higher the quality of teacher training programs, the more effective teachers will be (Berry, Daughtrey, Wieder, 2010, Farooq, Shahzadi, 2006).

- **Life-long learner**

Teacher must continue his learning throughout his life. Teachers need to be aware of new ideas, to refine decision making skills and to become more effective in integrating theory to practice. A teacher has to be ensured that whatever a student learns, he must learn for himself.

Colleges and universities are offering teacher education programme need to give priority to purchase latest books and subscribe to research journals in order to help the teacher in updating his knowledge. Library should be equipped with internet and other modern facilities.

- **Conducting research activity**

Teachers should undertake research activity on pertinent issues of the society. Research activities will involve them in exploring ideas and creating new knowledge. This will upgrade their competence. Moreover, with growing experience and knowledge, the teacher develops insight into educational process. He should spread widely his thoughts through articles/research papers for development of society.

- **Exposure to innovations**

In order to bring excellence in imparting knowledge, teachers should get exposed to innovations. The innovations in various teaching institutions can be compiled and disseminated among teachers. There is a need to develop linkage with other teacher education institutions all over the world for meaningful interaction and sharing for development.

- **Use of ICT**

The role of the teacher has been multiplied as instructor, constructor, creator, facilitator of learning situations. The teacher training programmes cannot be success if the teaching pedagogy is not properly matched with the emerging learning environment. Information technology has created opportunities for better education. The teacher should be aware of ICT programmes. But, our teachers are still uncomfortable with the use of latest tools of technology; such as e-learning, use of computers, e-mail,

OHPs, etc. They should be trained to use the technological innovations that are readily available. Effective use of information and communication technologies in teacher education institutions can ensure qualitative teaching and bring a change in the pedagogy and a shift in the teaching-learning paradigm.

- **Self-study**

Self-study is another effort to develop professional skills of teachers. Every teacher must carry out self-study for one's own professional needs, interest and teaching responsibilities. Self-learning helps to upgrade the competencies and skills of teachers. A competent teacher must be familiar with the day to day improvement of modern knowledge and technology. Self-learning is to be pursued by teachers through books, journals, audio-visual aids and sources of electronic medias. A successful and dynamic teacher is always a self-directed and self-motivated learner throughout his career.

Reflection and Professional Development

Dewey was among the first to promote reflection as a means of professional development in teaching. He believed that critical reflection is the most important quality a teacher may have and that it has much more impact on the quality of schools and instruction than the teaching techniques one uses. Dewey (1933) added that when teachers speculate reason, and contemplate using open-mindedness, wholeheartedness and responsibility, they will act with foresight and planning rather than basing their actions on tradition, authority or impulse.

Valverde (1982) viewed reflection as examining one's situation, behaviour, practices, effectiveness and accomplishments by asking: what am I doing and why? The self-evaluation that follows involves active, persistent and careful consideration, speculation and contemplation of the practitioner's beliefs and knowledge and leads to professional development, growth and greater understanding of self and the profession. Valverde went on to say that to be truly considered a reflection, this self- examination must be constructive, deliberate, and undertaken periodically.

In the context of education, reflection involves teachers thoughtfully adapting, applying and evaluating their knowledge of pedagogy and content, in order to improve student learning in a particular context (LaBoskey, 1994). Reflection can have many faces and offers varied benefits. Reflective practices offer support, assist in gaining of knowledge, give opportunity for the growth and challenges, open more perspective and solution possibilities and help to bridge the gap between theory and practice. Ginsburg (1988) wrote that in order to reflect in a manner that promotes professional growth and development, educators must use problem solving skills to modify and enhance their understanding of professional practice. Problem solving skills are necessary when trying to make sense of difficult situations, identify areas in need of improvement, clarify goals for improvement and develop an action plan to accomplish them. Smylie and Conyers (1991) added that teachers use and strengthen their problem solving skills as they focus less on the transfer of knowledge and more on analytical and reflective learning.

Reflection fosters professional growth and development, critical thinking, self-assessment, and self-directed learning. It promotes the development of new knowledge, leads to broader understanding, and creates greater self-awareness. It facilitates sorting through and selecting from many ideas, helps confront and challenge one's current conceptions of teaching and learning and assists in identifying how these affect classroom decision making. Therefore, reflection is an invaluable tool in facilitating life-long learning and professional growth. In addition to the aforementioned effects of reflection on professional growth and development, reflection also aids the educator in becoming a moral steward. By reflecting on daily practice, the educator is more likely to understand and practice the standards of professional conduct.

In the present learning age, professional development is very essential for all teachers. It improves the quality and excellence of teacher in all walks of life. Continuous professional development is essential to increase teachers' competency, knowledge, skills, attitude and confidence by which they can improve the quality of education. Government, universities, colleges of teacher education and other organizations need to take initiatives for professional development of teachers which will enable them to create best educated individuals to cope effectively with fast emerging challenges of the century.

Chapter-9

Life Skills Education for Teacher

With the change of society, teachers are required to modify their roles in view of changing demands of school curriculum, students' needs and emerging concerns of society. Preparing humane and professionally trained teacher is the need of the hour. Along with content and pedagogy, there is need to integrate life skills in teacher education. Teachers are to be trained in life skills such as self-awareness, empathy, problem solving, decision making, effective communication, interpersonal relation, creative thinking, critical thinking, coping with emotions and coping with stress (UNICEF, 2006). Teacher education institutions have a vital role to enrich the professional competency of teacher by providing them life skills education through various programmes. Training of life skills education will surely enable the teachers to play their multifarious roles in school, home and society most effectively and to achieve professional success. These skills will also enable them to develop their own identity in the society.

Life Skills Education: The Concept

The important landmark in the area of life skills education came in the year 1993. World Health Organization (WHO) clearly defined Life Skills as the "abilities for adaptive and positive behavior that enables individual to deal effectively with the demands and challenges of everyday life". Life skills are the abilities for positive behaviour that help individual in making correct choices in life. Life skills enable people to translate knowledge (what one knows) and attitudes/values (what one believes and feels) into action (what to do and how to do it). "Life skills education is an important vehicle to equip young people to negotiate and mediate challenges and risks in their lives, and to enable productive participation in society" (UNICEF).

The concept of life skill has made a very recent entry into the field of education. Life skills education is an interactive methodology, which focuses on knowledge, attitudes, skills and is specially designed to enhance efforts to develop positively and bring goodness in behaviours and manners. At present, life skills education seems very essential for all individuals because everyone in the society in some way or other is confronting conflict, competition and stress in every walk of life. It is more observed in young children, who are future of the nation. They indulge themselves in many anti-social activities and spoil their valuable time and energy. In order to save the young generation from various problems and its possible consequences and to direct the young minds into constructive channels, it is very important that teachers should be trained in life skills education.

Life skills can be classified under three main categories

Thinking skills	Social skills	Negotiation skills
Self-awareness, problem solving, decision making, critical thinking, creative thinking	Interpersonal relationship, effective communication, empathy	Managing feeling/emotion, Coping with stress

Need and Importance of Life Skills Education

Life skills education promotes mental well-being among teacher and makes them able to face the realities of life. Life skills education equips teachers to behave in a socially desirable way. It empowers teachers and enables them to take more responsibility in their lives. If life skills education programmes are effectively implemented in schools, it will able to change outlook of the students about others and themselves, resulting in improvement of their self-esteem and self-confidence. Life skills education helps teachers in developing their emotional and psycho-social competencies and interpersonal skills which results in an attitude for solving problems, taking right decisions, thinking critically and creatively, communicating effectively, creating good relationships, empathize with others, and managing their lives in a healthy and perfect manner. In fact, teachers need life skills for their healthy and positive ways of living at one or other step. Teachers can learn and enhance life skills throughout the life. Practicing the use of life skills in simple day to day situations makes it easy for utilizing them in complex life situations too.

It is of high importance for every individual to acquire adequate skills beyond academic or technical knowledge. Life skills mean those essential skills developed through a higher order thinking, that enable a person to perform effectively in his or her life, and thus become a socially acceptable and successful person.

Life Skills Education: A Research Review

The topic has been a significant area of interest to the researchers, theorists, and practitioners, and there have been numerous research carried out to emphasize the importance and effectiveness of life skills education in the development of students' social, emotional and cognitive development and dealing with their psycho-social problems and issues.

Garland (1999) investigated the perceived effectiveness of a life skills education program for youth. Results revealed the improvement in most of the skills by youth, parents and class teachers. It was reported by the class teachers that the children showed better performance in 12 out of the 15 skill areas.

Gulati (2006) posted an article named Empowering Teachers and Children through Life Skills Training. It was a report of a life skills training for teachers which was organized by UNICEF India in 2006 in collaboration with the Education Department of the Gujarat government in three districts of Gujarat namely, Patan, Chhota Udepur and Valsad covering about 147 schools. A total of 20 teachers were trained. It was a four day interactive training program which covered ten life skills suggested by WHO. Results revealed that student teacher relationships have become stronger and students have become more participative, creative and interactive.

The Hindu (August, 2012) published an article in a newspaper on the topic Life Skill training for teachers to help students. This article explained the efforts of Gandhigram Trust, Madurai, India in the area of life skills. The trust arranged a seminar on life skills education for school teachers at Gandhigram. Trust secretary K. Shivakumar addressed the seminar and said that life skills education is very important for teachers who prepare the young minds. Trust has developed a module on life skill education (based on the skills suggested by UNICEF) for eighth, ninth and tenth class students to enhance their skills and help them handle things efficiently.

Life Skills for the Teacher

Life skills are the personal, interpersonal and cognitive psychosocial skills that enable teachers to interact appropriately manage their own emotional states and make decisions and choices for an active, safe and productive life. Life skills develop right attitudes to think smartly, act smartly and to live consciously. Life skill education is very necessary for teacher to lead an ideal life. The main goal of the life skills approach is to enhance teacher's ability to take responsibility for making healthier choices, restricting negative pressures and avoid risk behavior.

Now, life skills education is considered as one of the most effective approaches for preparing teachers for their professional development. In view of this, teachers are required to develop the following life skills. There are about 10 core skills which have been identified by World Health Organizaion to be developed by the teacher. These are described as below:

- **Self-awareness**

It includes recognition of oneself, of one's values and beliefs, of one's strength and weakness, desires and dislikes. Developing self-awareness gives importance on ourselves when we are stressed or feel under pressure. Teachers need high self-awareness in order to recognize and manage their own behaviour. If a teacher develops awareness about his worth, he becomes more self-confident. Self-awareness skill enables teacher to understand himself and establish his personal identity. It also helps to establish a positive image and sound career perspective.

In case of lack of self-awareness, there are quite several ways to build it up. Introspection and feedback from others are just two ways for this. Teacher may begin self-introspection with a single thought related to some period in the past. Then he allows his mind to gradually work backward, recalling specific incidents. People, places and events associated with that particular period. This type of reflection about the past gives insight about him or he may ask one of his close relatives/friends for feedback. This will enable him to have another's opinion about his strength and weaknesses and to get assurance whether/not what he is doing is right, to verify himself.

Feedback, be it positive or negative, is important. It gives another's opinion on how he behaves. It is a way of learning more about himself and the effect of his behavior has on others. In the absence of feedback, no change can be worked out.

- **Empathy**

Empathy is the ability to understand other's needs, accept others, to put oneself in the other person's position. It refers to the feeling of emotional understanding and unity with another, such that an emotion felt by one person is experienced to some degree by another who is empathetic to them. This skill will assist teacher to reduce animosity with himself and increase respect for different people of the society and also help in understanding the view point of others. It involves the ability to mimic externally the feelings of another person. To build good and successful relationship with other person, a teacher must understand others and their nature. This understanding will help him respond appropriately to others moods, temperaments, motivations, desires and act wisely in their interactions and dealings. When one attains proficiency in empathetic listening, he stands to benefit in several ways. Through it, one can build good study relationships. As there is good understanding between teacher and other persons, he can engage in collaborative learning and cooperative management of study tasks. A teacher's ability to empathize will lead him to a stage wherein harmony, collaboration and synergy are possible.

- **Problem solving**

Problem solving is a life skill. Problems are situations that are not easy to surmount. Problems, be they big or small, have to be faced and overcome. It is a deliberate and sincere act involving the use of some new methods, higher thinking and systematic planned steps for the realization of set goals. It develops analytical mind, strong work ethics, tolerance etc. that enable the teacher to put his heart and soul into the work.

Problem solving is a process and so it involves a number of steps:

Step-1 - Find and frame the problem
Step-2 - Develop a good problem solving strategy
Step-3 - Evaluate the solution
Step-4 - Rethink and redefine problem and solution over time

- **Decision making**

Decision making can be defined as the ability of a person to be able to decide what he/she wants in life.

Decision making is one of the life skills that we have to utilize before solving problems and handling issues. This skill enables the teacher to gather information about issues and to decide for him/herself what is right for him/her as he/she will be able to evaluate the future consequences of his/her own actions. It helps the teacher to deal constructively with all critical decisions of his professional life.

The model of decision making uses various steps. These are as follows:

(i) Problem finding: This step involves locating the problem and analytically studying in detail.

(ii) Problem Stating: This step looks into all the dimensions of the problem and coming out with its definition.

(iii) Option Finding: Decision maker has to generate as many alternatives as possible through which the problem in question could be solved.

(iv) Decision making: It is at this stage, the decision maker critically studies each option and arrives on the most appropriate option.

Decision making as the above steps reveal, involves choosing a course of action from among the several well defined and frequently competing alternatives after due deliberations.

- **Effective communication**

Communication skills are essential ingredients in the complex craft of teaching. Good communication skills are a prerequisite for teaching profession. Effective communication is all about conveying one's messages to others clearly and unambiguously. This skill includes written, verbal, body language and presentation skills. Nothing can make as much of a dramatic effect on teachers' personal and school life as speaking well. The impression he makes on others mostly depends on the way he speaks the pitch, expressiveness and clarity of his voice. From the tone of his voice and his manner of saying things, his listeners can deduce a lot about his feelings and personality. They will be able to tell him whether he is confident or frightened, excited or depressed and friendly or aggressive.

A teacher, who is able to communicate well with students, can inspire them for fruitful learning. It is only through communication skills, teacher can introduce creative and effective solutions to the problems of the students.

It is necessary to learn and practice a few habits; teacher will be able to make his communication much better. If he is able to cultivate the habit of thinking before he speaks, believe the message he conveys, keep him talk at the audience perception level, avoid annoying mannerisms and gestures, repeat major points and use generalization sparingly and avoid expressions that hurt, his communication would rise above the mediocre.

- **Inter-personal relation**

Inter-personal skills help individual relate to others. These skills are give and take in any relationships. It helps person relate to people of his surroundings. This may mean being able to make and maintain friendly relationship which can be of great value to one's mental and social well-being. It may also mean having good relations with family members who are important sources of social support. Understanding human nature is one of the first steps in developing good relationships. For this, one must concentrate on others, pay close attention to them, listen to them properly and look for clues in their body language. Body language is a language of signals. When one interacts with others, he generally expresses his feelings through his gestures, facial expressions and body postures. One's success in life depends to a great extent, on his ability to understand his friends and act wisely. To be successful in life, one ought to pick up inter-personal skills.

Inter-personal skills are interactive skills. A successful teacher develops an affinity with, an understanding of and a harmonious inter-relationship with his/her pupils. It inspires the teacher to keep positive relation with the students, teaching and non-teaching staffs, administrators, parents etc. that helps him to give and receive social and personal support.

- **Creative thinking**

Creative thinking encourages the teacher to create, discover or produce a new idea or object including the re-arrangement or reshaping, of what is already known. It involves the ability to think about something in novel and unusual ways and come up with unique solutions to problems. Creative thinking skills belong to such skills as brain-storming, lateral thinking, divergent thinking etc. There are several ways in which creativity can be developed. You can come up with creative ideas, play off each other's idea and say practically whatever comes to mind that seems relevant to a particular issue. Identifying creative people and finding out what helped them to be creative, fostering flexible and playful thinking and getting internally motivated are some other techniques for fostering creativity.

The teacher is required to be mastered in the following factors of creative thinking such as ideational fluency, originality, flexibility, divergent thinking, self-confidence and persistence, ability to see and build relationship.

- **Critical thinking**

Critical thinking is an ability to analyze information and experiences in an objective manner. Critical thinking can contribute to recognize and assess the factors that influence attitude and behavior. Critical thinking represents a challenging thought process, taking to new avenues of knowledge, understanding to a set of higher cognitive abilities and skills for the proper interpretation, analysis, evaluation and inferences. This skill is of great value to teacher in making his teaching effective.

It is necessary for a teacher to develop this skill. There are several ways to develop this skill. One of these is to focus on 'how' and 'why' in addition to what happened when you read reports on events and incidents. The habit of comparing various answers to a question and finding the best one is yet another way to develop critical thinking. It is also developed through asking questions to himself and to create new ideas.

- **Coping with emotion**

    Emotion plays a significant role in individual's life. Emotions are powerful feelings that are directed at something or someone. Emotions can be positive or negative. Anger, fear, anxiety, worry etc. are examples of negative emotion while hope, optimism, love etc. are examples of positive ones. Emotions, be they positive or negative, would keep on crossing the mind. We cannot stop them. Emotional management, however, doesn't mean total suppression. Coping with emotion refers to recognizing emotions of oneself and others, aware of how emotions influence behaviour, able to respond emotions appropriately.

    There are different ways to cope with our emotions. Controlling emotions is easier said than done. This doesn't mean that we should allow our emotions to go unchecked. Once we can identify our inner feelings and sources from which they arise, we are in a better position to bring our discretion and rationalization to bear upon them. Teacher should be aware of common emotions like anger, fear, sadness, disgust, love, joy or happiness and should make positive decisions for different emotions.

- **Coping with stress**

This skill involves recognizing the sources of stress, its impacts on the life of individual, and the ways that help to control the levels of stress. Stress generally refers to the reaction that people show when they encounter excessive pressure. Stress is a highly emotional experience. Everyday a teacher confronts with several situations that produce stress. Depending upon our attitude and our level of tolerance, the pressure we experience may keep varying. Stress is a combination of physical, mental, emotional feelings that results from pressure, worry and anxiety. It is nothing but the body's response to any unpleasant situation.

When the stress is excessive, it is harmful; a slight amount of stress is a great source of assistance. Stress is the main cause of many illnesses. If a teacher learns to manage the stress, he must avoid preoccupation with removing negative thoughts and focus only on his strengths and victories. Similarly, he must avoid the habit of worrying and projecting the worst that can happen. Similarly, by getting organized, avoiding procrastination, developing a good sense of humour, striking a balance between study and leisure, teacher can keep stress at bay to a great extent. Teacher should develop the values like tolerance, courage and perseverance to cope effectively with stress.

Importance of Life Skills Education for Teacher

The main component of education system is the teacher. For success of education, it is essential to produce capable professionally developed teachers who can understand problems and needs of students and respond accordingly. Life skills education will enable teachers to translate knowledge, attitude and values for handling real life situations of the children helping them decide what to do, when to do and how to do it with ease. This was also an approach towards integrated self-empowerment.

The importance of life skills education for the teacher is as follows:

- Life skills enable the teacher to establish positive vibes with his students and make him feel the delightful chemistry being generated between him and students.
- Practice of life skill helps teacher to develop qualities like punctuality, honesty and integrity and the like.
- Life skills education is essential to promote healthy interaction and positive behaviour among students and other staff of the institutions.
- Teachers need life skills to adjust and cope with stressful situation that they experience in school and society etc.
- Life skills education gives importance on the teachers to enhance quality of education through innovation, creative thinking, effective communication and equip children to become more analytical in approach.
- It enables the teachers to understand that education means more than just giving students the knowledge of textbooks.
- It promotes positive attitudes towards cultural, ethnic and religious diversity and gender equality etc.

- Life skills education is necessary to explore feelings and emotions in order to create a greater self-awareness and to develop the skills to manage that better.
- Life skills education is very important for the teacher as it contributes to the promotion of personal and social development, the prevention of health and social problems and the protection of human rights.

Now teachers should not only be trained in pedagogy but also in life skills through teacher education programme. Once the teachers acquire these life skills, they can apply that in their personal life as well as implement in teaching. This will enable the teachers to think independently, to upgrade themselves to respond according to students' needs. National Curriculum Framework, 2005 also puts forth need of imparting life skills to teachers. NCF, 2005 has following expectations about preparation of teachers.

- Teacher must be co-operative, feel belongingness, respect other groups and respect democratic values.
- Teacher must realize the need to upgrade continuous knowledge gaining.
- Teacher must have ability to communicate clearly and think logically to understand the world around him and to fulfill social responsibility towards national development.
- Teacher should be emotionally developed, happy and cheerful.
- Teacher should guide their students to think.

To fulfill these expectations teachers must be provided professional knowledge, skills and education of life skills too. The major lacuna in existing teacher education is that life skills were never taught to would be teachers.

Integrating Life Skills in Teacher Education

Life skills education needs to be integrated in teacher education curriculum. Preaching and practicing of life skills need to be developed as part of a support of healthy behaviour and mental well-being of the teacher. Moreover, they are more vulnerable to behaviour related problems. The teaching of life skills should be associated with the teaching of health information and development of attitudes and values. To accumulate particular life skills involves active support of the teachers, friends and a positive and supportive classroom climate. Moreover, the methods and strategies are based on a social learning process which further includes learning and explanation about any skill, observing how others behave and what consequences arise from that particular behaviour, practicing of the skill in a planned and friendly learning situation and feedback about individual and group performance of skills. This provides a deep insight into the various approaches which can be used for development of life skills. Further, life skills learning may be both active learning and experiential learning. Active learning engages the teacher trainees in a dynamic and evolving process of learning by using approaches like group discussion, brainstorming, quiz contest, debates and case studies. Experimental learning is the actual practice of what is being taught which involves games and role play.

Following steps may be adopted to promote life skills among teachers:

- Life skills education needs to be emphasized in both pre-service and in-service education of teachers.
- Special educational programmes on life skills should be organized for would be teachers and life

skills education needs to be incorporated in their curriculum.
- Teachers should be given orientation in life skills education (both in theory and practice). Practical work should include role play, simulation and games, group discussions, group interactions, brain storming, sharing experiences and self-demonstrations etc.
- Life skills education should be imparted in a supportive environment.

Effects of Life Skills Education on Teacher

Training of life skills education has a number of impacts on teacher. These are as follows:
- Knowledge of life skills enables the teacher to create a student friendly classroom environment that paves the way to make his teaching both effective and reflective.
- Teachers become more affectionate and caring to students.
- Students become more participative, creative and interactive. It helps to develop healthy interpersonal relationships instead of creating rivalry with one another.
- Life skills education helps the teacher to establish meaningful interactions not only among teachers but also with administrators, parents and other community members.
- Students learn many things from teachers such as how to be courageous, how to solve problems, how to understand others and to be independent thinkers. The performance of students becomes more satisfactory.

- Once the teacher is trained in life skills, he/she will definitely use the knowledge of it in helping his/her students to develop properly. This will lead a teacher as professionally talented teacher.

Teaching Techniques for Life Skills Education

Following teaching techniques should be adopted for teaching of life skills to teacher trainees:

i. **Brain Storming**

Brainstorming implies gathering of various ideas regarding a particular topic or problem related life. It enhances the capability of the teacher trainees to think freely and express quickly. It is highly essential to analyze the merits and demerits of any idea in the light of discovering a plausible solution of a particular problem. After brainstorming they should be encouraged to reflect their ideas which ultimately bring them nearer to the appropriate conclusion.

ii. **Role play**

Role play provides an opportunity to the teacher trainees to have a useful experience of applying life skills in an organized real-life situation. Several trainees can participate to play certain roles through an imaginary situation. Skill of assertiveness, inter-personal relationship, and effective communication ability of the trainees can be developed through role playing.

iii. **Quiz contest**

It is a very interesting activity both within and outside the classroom, which inspires the teacher trainees to acquire knowledge vividly regarding a topic or a selected theme. They acquire thorough and accurate knowledge which enhances their power to think critically and communicate courageously with the values of perseverance and concentration.

iv. **Storytelling**

Storytelling can help teacher trainees think about local problems and develop critical thinking skills, creative skills to write stories, or interact to tell stories. Storytelling lends itself to draw analogies or make comparisons, help discover healthy solutions. It also enhances attention, concentration, listening skills and develops patience and endurance.

v. **Debates**

Debate provides opportunity to address a particular issue in depth and creatively. Teacher trainees can debate, for instance, whether smoking should ban in public places in a community. It allows trainees to defend a position that may mean a lot to them. It offers a chance to practice higher thinking skills.

vi. **Group discussion**

Through the process of group discussion, trainees can get an opportunity to express their views freely and fluently. The critical feeling can also be activated, and they would learn not to hesitate or show inhibition while trying to express. Topics relating to various important aspects can be discussed which will increase the sphere of their knowledge and will built confidence among them to face those challenges in life.

vii. **Case studies**

Case studies are like powerful catalysts for thought and discussion. Trainees can learn better through case studies as an effective way of accumulating in-depth data about a case, mainly from their complexities and ambiguities. Thus, case studies are significant medium of learning by identifying a particular problem and its parameters, and will try to find out the possible solutions to overcome that problem. These approaches develop the skill of empathy, problem solving, communication and decision making ability among them.

From the above discussion, it is concluded that present society needs professionally competent teachers well equipped with life skills. Life skills education enables the teachers to exercise their decisions with responsibility and accountability, cultivate democratic values, develop positive attitude and enrich their personality. Training in life skills not only empowers the teachers, but also saves them from obsolescence, reutilization and burn out. Life skills education of teacher has tremendous influence on students' personality development. Hence, it should be a part of teacher education. Sincere and continuous efforts must be made for the inculcation of life skills among teachers through various programmes. No doubt, training in life skills education will enrich and enlighten the teachers and make them most effective and successful in their profession.

Chapter-10

Creativity and Teacher

There are some teachers in teaching profession who are different from others. They are different not in terms of their educational qualifications or length of service but in terms of some characteristics or quality of teaching. They are the teachers who see the worth of students and do not encourage rote learning of their students. These teachers bring newness into whatever they undertake with children. They are different and they boldly explore new and creative ways of teaching and learning (Acharyulu, 1995).

What is Creativity?

Creativity is a cognitive activity that engages a range of mental abilities and processes such as remembering, imagining, planning, anticipating, judging, organising, storing, deciding, determining, perceiving, comprehending, learning, recognizing and interpreting. However, the important and essential features of creativity are problem redefinition and ideation. Redefining the problem provides an opportunity to look at a problem from different perspectives which is not available immediately. Ideation involves the generation of alternatives triggered via the use of imagination, associative thinking and other generative processes such as conceptual combination, analogical transfer and so on. Both problem redefinition and ideation result in novel and unique ideas to emerge. Creative outcomes are characterised by (a) originality, uniqueness and novelty, (b) appropriateness, relevance, effectiveness, utility (c) ethics.

"Creative thinking applies to a thought process that constructs original answers, solutions, or ideas. Usually creativity is associated with responses that are novel to the society as well as to the individual. Problem solving entails the correct answer. For creativity there is no correct response. It is new or original and unique" (Travers, 1982).

Creativity is generally associated with divergent production which is a problem-solving activity involving originality, flexibility, fluency and sensitivity to new problems, ability to abstract, synthesize, organize a wide variety of ideas into a coherent, meaningful whole not seen before etc. For instance, if a child is asked to write the use of a knife in as many cases as possible, he exercises his divergent mental operations and gives several novel uses of the knife, different from the ordinary or traditional functioning of the equipment. This unconventional or unusual style of thinking or mental operation is, according to Guilford, the typical form of creativity.

Creativity is regarded as "the ability for divergent thinking or open ended thought" (Page & Thomas, 1979). The factors of creativity are generally described as "associative and ideational fluency, originality, adaptive, and ability to make logical evaluation" (Good, 1950). Creativity is a novel problem-solving behaviour and is expressed through original discoveries, new innovations, and unconventional approaches to problems in systematic and organized ways. There are different kinds of creativity and are identified in various forms like music, dance, painting, art, sculpture, literature, science, mathematics, industry, technology, and so on.

Creativity is not the prerogative of a selected few. It is distributed among all people in a continuum. It is universally found in all persons in varied degrees and shades. The most salient feature of creativity is originality. It is revealed through uncommon clever responses to new situations. It is usually displayed in the form of original capacity to organize ideas in novel juxtapositions. It is the capacity to grasp vast complex and intricate conceptual structures. It is viewed not in conformity, but in novelty.

Creativity stands for "the capacity to accept challenge", "the readiness to change oneself", "the capacity to change one's environment". According to many psychologists, creativity should form an integral part of intelligence. There have been a lot of controversies about the relationship between intelligence and creativity (Getzels & Jackson, 1962, Torrance, 1962). In general, there seems to be almost no relationship between measures of figural creativity and measures of intelligence, and only low positive relationship between verbal measures of creativity and intelligence.

It was the belief that at birth there are individual differences in characteristics associated with creativity, e.g., responsiveness to environment, curiosity, etc. But a study by Pezzullo, Thorsen & Madaus (1972) showed no evidence of hereditary variation in either verbal or figural forms of creative thinking. According to Torrance (1977), the "heritability index for the figural and verbal measures of the Torrance Tests of Creative Thinking approached Zero and were statistically insignificant".

Torrance (1971) summarised the results of 16 different studies conducted in various localities in order to ascertain the relation of creativity with socio-economic and radical factors. It was revealed that in some studies, there were no racial or socio-economic differences and in a few others, black children excelled whites on certain tasks and whites excelled blacks on others. The same was true where socio economic differences were studied. Overall, there was no racial or socio-economic bias to the distribution of creativity.

All creative tests do not measure every creative ability equally. Tests of divergent thinking alone do not constitute complete tests of creativity. They, of course, represent an important factor of creative thinking ability. There are a number of personality traits which are also involved in the making of a creative person. According to Torrance, we miss about 70 per cent of our more creative youth when we depend on IQ tests alone.

Nature of Creativity

(i) It is a power within the individual.
(ii) It is the ability to produce uncommon and unusual responses to a problem.
(iii) It is related with divergent thinking abilities.
(iv) Novelty is an important characteristic of creativity.
(v) It is concerned with some original, uncommon, unconventional and unusual mode of behaviour, creation or product.
(vi) It exists in degree and kind.

Who is a Creative Teacher?

A creative teacher may be described as an individual who introduces changes and novelties in day-to-day teaching and learning activities thus making education meaningful, enjoyable, useful and explorative experience to children. A creative teacher is seen as an information- processor, a problem finder, a problem poser and problem solver. Teaching is seen by the creative teacher as an exercise of imagination to generate fluent and novel ways of organising ideas, content and materials for solving problems. Every teacher can be a teacher of creativity. Fontana (1981) wrote, "just as all teachers are teachers of language whatever their actual subject so all teachers are teachers of creativity".

A teacher should be creative in teaching. He should adopt such teaching pedagogy which would make even difficult subject also very easy. He should develop new methods depending upon the calibre of students to transmit knowledge with minimum difficulty. The pedagogy should be such so that it enables a student to develop conceptual clarity, analytical and quantitative skills.

Characteristics of Creative Teacher

For a long time educators everywhere believed that one of the important determinants of successful teaching concerns with the characteristics of teachers. This resulted in considerable research on teacher characteristics as related to instruction and achievement of pupils.

- **Cognitive Characteristics**

Cognitive characteristics refer to the traits, abilities and styles of information processing used by creative teachers. Originality relatively high intelligence, good imagination and verbal fluency are often the traits associated with creative teachers. The abilities of the creative teachers include flexibility, skill in decision making, coping with novelty, visualisation, ability to break away from the fixed set of ideas and rigid thinking, sensitivity to problems and finding order in chaos. The commonly mentioned processing styles include using wide categories and images, preferences for non-verbal communication, building new structures rather than using existing structures, questioning, norms and assumptions in their areas of specialization, being alert to novelty and gaps in knowledge, and using their existing knowledge as a base for new ideas.

Creative teacher should have the following cognitive characteristics.

i. **Good command over the subject matter they teach**

Various studies have revealed that creative teachers have good knowledge of their subject areas. Along with his subject knowledge, the teacher should be hard working and have patience.

They have an unusually intense interest of attraction for a special area (Cropley, 1989). Creative teachers know their subject thoroughly and they keep pace with recent developments in their areas of specialization. During the course of their teaching, they teach what is known and what is not yet known and challenge students to explore and seek the unknown.

ii. **Possess divergent thinking ability**

According to Guilford, 'creative thought means divergent thinking'. Creative teacher is good at divergent and convergent thinking. He recognises the importance of generating a number of ideas or solution. Fluency of thought characterises the creative teacher. Ideas come readily and suddenly to his mind. He evaluates these for quality and logic and selects the best and novel solutions.

iii. **Mastery on basic skills**

It is important for teachers to understand the basic skills which are contained within the innovative elements of a student's work. There is a strong relationship between the mastery of basic academic skills and creativity. Creative behaviour depends upon the mastery of basic skills. Creativity operates when children acquire certain minimum levels of learning.

iv. **Invites unusual and provocative questions of students**

The creative teacher invites the ideas of his students. Creative teacher encourages imagination of students. He enjoys sharing their ideas with their students both in and out of class. They like to pose question and to listen to questions. They encourage students to ask questions.

v. **Senses and identifies problems**

A creative teacher formulates problems in workable, flexible and original ways. He is good in detecting gaps in knowledge and uses principles and skills relevant to the solution of the problem. A creative teacher displays awareness and concern about unsolved problems.

vi. **Encourages different activities to their students**

A creative teacher provides a good number of activities to the students which develop the natural creativity of children and from which they can experience success. There are different kinds of activities that require different solutions by students. Teacher creates situations where students find solutions to the problems. A creative teacher allows students to follow their own styles of work. He readily adapts and if necessary changes his own plans, or mode of teaching to suit to students' need and interests.

Personality and Motivational Characteristics

Creative teacher is endowed with personality and motivational characteristics. The most commonly mentioned personality characteristics include a willingness to face and take risks, perseverance, being open to new experiences, commitment to work, high internal motivation, competence in meeting challenges, reflective, independence of judgement, display of courage, excellent work habits, capacity for sustained effort, persistence, liking to think, manipulation of ideas and a desire to improve upon currently accepted systems. Motivation is an important factor that makes creative effort more possible.

There are some broad set of skills and characteristics associated with teachers who may be described as creative. Some of these characteristics are described as below;

i. **Self-confidence and motivation**

Creative teacher often show their self confidence in different activities they perform. They visualise confidence in their ability and have a strong desire to excel others. They build in their students these qualities and promote their self- concept.

Creative teachers are highly motivated. Motivation is the tendency to move towards goals. It has direction, intensity, and duration. It is a crucial component of all creative productions.

ii. **Independence**

This is a critical trait found in all creative persons. Independence is confidence in action. A creative teacher's independence is seen in situations which are challenging, ambiguous, complex and puzzling. Creative teachers like to think about problems and issues and solve them in individualistic manners. They see themselves as inventive, independent, determined, industrious, enthusiastic, responsible and accountable. Independence is a prime personal disposition of creative teachers and these teachers, therefore, are likely to encourage their students to think independently.

iii. Curiosity

Curiosity is another important quality of a creative teacher. The creative teacher is curious to know more and more about different incidents of his surroundings. Curiosity is associated with exploratory behaviour. There is wide difference among teachers to become curious. Highly curious teachers tend to ask more and better questions in the class, show more persistence in problem solving and be more adventurous in the choice of activities for promoting curiosity of students.

iv. Enthusiasm

Creative teachers are very much enthusiastic. They express their enthusiasm by developing ideas and materials in new ways. Creative teacher tends to be cheerful in the face of adversity and persistent in his efforts. He takes pride in student achievement. He sets well defined goals for himself and his students. Enthusiasm as an important characteristic of creative teachers has also emerged in various research studies.

v. Willingness to face obstacles

Creative teachers are different from others, capable to encounter obstacles. Many times the ideas of creative teachers are not accepted and often they receive unfavourable and discouraging comments. However, the creative teachers are not dragged down by them. They show perseverance.

vi. Openness to experience

Openness to experience has been identified as important characteristics of creative individuals. The creative teacher deliberately opens himself to new experiences. A creative teacher is receptive to what is new and different in the thoughts, actions, and products of oneself and others. A creative teacher is sensitive to details and is willing to act on and react to one's ideas and solutions.

The creative teacher shares information with students and involves them in decision making and problem solving and thus broadens the traditional role of the teacher vis-à-vis student. He never hesitates to be corrected by students and is receptive to the ideas and strategies suggested by colleagues and students. He often evaluates his own efforts. He is willing to tryout strategies and techniques that contribute to quality of teaching and learning.

vii. Task commitment

Creative teachers always try to fulfil their commitment. They tend to spend much time in thinking about their work and that leads to the possibility that something new will develop. Creative teachers display task commitment in whatever activity they undertake. Task commitment refers to the effort brought to bear on a particular task or specific performance areas. Task commitment is often described by using terms like perseverance, endurance, hard work, dedicated practice, self-confidence, and a belief in one's ability to carry out important work. Creative teachers display these qualities.

viii. Intrinsic motivation

Intrinsic motivation is highly required for better achievement. Creative teacher is more inspired by intrinsic motivation. They motivate themselves. Teachers will be more creative when they are intrinsically motivated primarily by the interest, enjoyment, satisfaction and challenge of the work of teaching itself. A teacher's love for his work is primarily related to his creative performance.

ix. Risk taking

To be creative, teachers need to take some risk. Taking into account the nature of problem, sometimes risk may come in the process of creative activity. Fear of taking risk is an obstacle to creative process. A teacher may come up with novel and possibly tangible solution or idea to a problem, but fear of being incorrect stops him from making it public. Teacher should increase capacity for taking risk.

x. Self-concept

Self-concept refers to self-perception. It is concerned with how a person perceives his own self. Teachers who think of themselves as highly capable will try to work hard to match their estimates with their self-perceptions. Self-image of the teacher affects performance "a positive self-image fosters, among other things, willingness to take risks and to engage in self-criticism" (Croply,1989). Teachers who think well about their own abilities tend to do well.

Developing Students' Creativity: A Curriculum Goal for Creative Teachers

Creative teachers, irrespective of the subjects, they lay emphasis on developing and promoting students' creativity. They see creativity as one of the curriculum goals. At the elementary education level, the foundations of creative thinking are to be laid down. The creative teacher searches different alternatives to teach students effectively. Students also love to engage themselves in such explorations and in the process learn and acquire skills, knowledge, and abilities needed for systematic inquiry.

Creativity is not completely spontaneous. The teacher must make conscious and constant effort to produce something creative. It requires understanding, discipline, patience and hard work on the part of the teacher to produce something creative or to make his teaching creative. Creativity does not include any single trait or ability. It involves a number of abilities such as, fluency, flexibility, originality, sensitivity to problems and openness to experience on the part of teacher.

In our classrooms, both teaching and learning are examination oriented. The teacher is anxious to complete the syllabus without bothering to know whether the students are following or not. The society likewise expects the teacher to teach only that which is prescribed and useful to students from the examination point of view. As a result, even if there is a teacher who discourages rote learning and really gets involved in encouraging creative learning by pupils, it never lasts long. Consequently many valuable creative sparks of both teachers and students are lost. Torrance and Myers (1971) observe, "One of the big social dangers today is that people are afraid to become truly involved in anything. It is a natural consequence of a society that encourages a lack of involvement".

Teacher's Creativity and Teaching for Creativity

Teaching for creativity is the need of the hour. Present society needs creative teacher who should encourage creative thinking among students through their teaching. Both teacher's creativity and teaching for creativity are important for bringing about improvement in the quality of school education. For teachers to achieve a high level of effectiveness, there must be transformation of their creativity into a set of values, abilities and skills that will enable them to engage themselves in important, useful, productive and unusual professional work. They have also to impress people in authority by their creative contributions.

It is true that a teacher cannot teach creatively at all times. However, the outcome of a teacher's creativity should be more and better opportunities for students to experience and learn. Creativity in teaching is to be judged by the quality of opportunities actually provided by a teacher to his pupils and the extent to which it resulted in pupil creative productions. Creativity in teaching breeds creativity in learning.

To stimulate creative spark in children, the teacher himself need not be highly creative to begin with. A willingness to welcome, accept and reward or praise students' independent thinking and new ideas are essential. Teachers need to be kind, concerned and courteous. Most of the teachers wish to be considered as possessing all these qualities too, often they miss out simply because they neglect to put them into words. Words of gratitude, praise, sympathy or concern and words of love of joy used by the teachers would enable many a students to progress towards excellence in their own areas of talent. Some teachers find it hard to express words of praise or recognition. Although their heart may swell with pride at their students' achievement they fear that in praising him or her efforts and not try so hard in the future. But surely it is far more likely that it would inspire greater effort and give the added confidence.

Creative teacher concentrate completely with pre-occupied task by using all mental energy. Creative teacher has vision of future problem. He can anticipate the problem which may emerge in future. Teacher should provide ample opportunity for freedom of thought. Teacher should encourage spirit of scientific inquiry among students both inside and outside of classroom. The function of creative mind is to invent ideas and to find out novel solutions to problems.

Teacher should allow the students to express their views with full freedom of expression. Conducive environment is essential for development of teacher's creative activity.

Osborn developed "Brain storming" technique which needs to be used effectively by teacher to develop creative talent of the children. For promotion of creativity among children, teacher must allow them to think as many solutions as possible for a problem that will otherwise encourage divergent thinking of the children.

The teacher must play a crucial and catalytic role not only in recognising the creative potentiality but also in providing adequate facilities for developing the same to the maximum. He knows the environment and the local resources. He has to organise various activities which can provide opportunity for improving the latent potentialities of children. He has to motivate his students and promote his interest and aspirations creatively. The teacher can take up various experiments and innovation according to the students' needs and available resources for developing creativity in children. He is to nourish their natural talent as a true gardener does with the plants.

Strategies for Encouraging Creativity of Teacher

Teachers are the architect of future generations. To develop the creative ability of students, it is highly essential that teachers should develop their creativity. Some suggestions need to be adopted to enhance creative talent of teacher. The suggestions are stated below:

- The teacher to teach creatively, should acquire mastery in various teaching strategies and thorough in core teaching skills, and should adopt innovative approaches suitable to the need of different categories of students.

- The teacher should be a member of key professional organizations relevant to his subject.
- The teacher should keep abreast of subject matter by study of books, periodicals, newspapers and other sources concerning development of his own field and other fields. This will help them to develop their divergent thinking ability.
- Safe, permissive and warm environment need to be provided for development of creative talent of teachers in school.
- Teacher should express his creative talent by publishing various research articles in journals, magazines, books and by engaging him in research and innovation.
- Teachers should cultivate and develop originality, flexibility, fluency, divergent thinking, and self-confidence for improvement of their creative talent.

Creativity develops competency of teachers. It enables the teacher to work in a systematic and planned way, thus reduce stress in life. Every teacher to a certain degree possesses creative abilities but they do not express their talent due to some reasons. Proper stimulation and nourishment are essential in this direction. As creativity is a great resource for teachers' successful teaching, various training programmes need to be organized regularly for teachers to enhance their creative abilities. To keep pace with the knowledge explosion of present society, each and every teacher at different levels of teaching and education must be creative because teacher's creativity begets students' creativity.

Chapter-11

Leadership Role of Teacher

Leadership is a quality of great importance in today's times when there is a hunger for innovation and entrepreneurship. Leaders are the agents of change, they are equipped with skill sets that enable any institution to realize its' goals. As teachers, we are the first leaders in the truest sense that any student sees. As a teacher one has the capability and the capacity to lead students to attain their goals and societal needs. Teachers as leaders are individuals who are able to channelize the teaching-learning process; to make it more meaningful and interesting. They participate in the decision making process, take initiative, organize resources, monitor progress and help others sustain their growth and progress.

Leadership: The Concept

The concept of leadership is a social notion and the functions are formally emphasized with the ability of the leader to influence the people in his organisation in order to achieve the organisational goals. Leadership is the quality to lead others to accomplish the set goals of organisation and who occupies this quality, is a leader.

Leadership is the process of influencing and supporting others to work enthusiastically towards achieving objectives. It is the crucial factor that helps an individual or a group identify its goals and then motivates

and assists in achieving the stated goals. Three major factors that define the leadership concept are:
- Influence/ support
- Voluntary effort
- Goal achievement

Leadership can also be called the catalyst that transforms potential into reality. The concept of leadership in itself covers all interpersonal relationships that influence the working of the institution towards its goals.

It is believed that leadership is a process that is ultimately concerned with fostering change. In contrast to the notion of "management", which suggests preservation or maintenance, "leadership" implies a process where there is movement from wherever we are now to some future place or condition that is different. Leadership also implies internationally, in the sense that the implied change is not random- 'change for change's sake"- but is rather directed toward some future end or condition which is desired or valued. Accordingly, leadership is a purposive process which is inherently value based. In short, our conception of leadership comprises the following basic assumptions:
- Leadership is concerned with fostering change
- Leadership is inherently value based
- All people are potential leaders
- Leadership is a group process
- What are the most effective means of preparing young people for this kind of leadership?

Definition of Leadership

Leadership is defined as an "influencing process" where leaders motivate the members of an organization to get their best efforts and achieve organizational objectives enthusiastically. It is the critical factor that helps an individual or a group to identify its goals and then motivates and assists in achieving the stated goals. There are three important elements in the definition of leadership - influence/support, voluntary effort and goal achievement.

It is defined in different ways by educationists. Hersey and Blanchard (1988) felt three basic competencies necessary for a leader:

a) Ability to interpret and understand the situation
b) Adapting the ability to change behaviour and resources in the light of situation; and
c) Ability to communicate with other members of the organisation to get acceptance and understanding.

Bolman and Deal (1991) suggest that when people are asked "what is leadership", answers seem to fall into one of these categories:

- ability to get others to do what you want (power),
- motivate people to get things done-mostly through persuasion,
- provide a vision,
- leadership is facilitation, and
- empower people to do what they want.

There are problems with all of these but overall they convey the notion that we expect a leader to influence through non-coercive means, to produce some degree of cooperative effort, and to pursue goals that transcend his/her own narrow self-interest.

Types of Leadership

Generally, there are three categories in which leaders

can be grouped viz. laissez-faire, autocratic and democratic. The first category leadership tends to be passive and the influence on each other is causal. Individual initiative is not clear and progress is usually nil. Second, in autocratic leadership there are big status differences between group members and the leader, that's why communication tends to be one way from the leader to group members. Leader's proposal usually accepted without any question. The third category personifies the values and norms of the group. This provides platform for open discussion and judgement is most in the light of suggestions given by the group members. The democratic leader has the ability to perceive the direction in which the group has to move. His foresight, influential power and open-mindedness help the group and this is the reason he is chosen or becomes a leader.

Ingredients of Democratic Leadership

The role of leaders is important in any form of society. Without a body of leaders, there will be no development. Therefore, the role of quality leadership is more important in democracy. Democracy must select its leadership on the basis of character and ability but even character and ability are not enough in the modern India. The leaders of today must have knowledge and enlightenment. Dr. Kalam (2005) said the nation needs young leaders who can command the change for the transformation of India into a developed nation, embedded with knowledge society. The leaders are the creators of new organizations of excellence. Quality leaders are like magnets that will attract the last persons to build the team for the organization and give inspiring leadership even during failures of missions as they are not afraid of risks. Therefore, the mission of dynamic education must be the creation of righteous and creative leaders.

The most important agenda of India must be to usher in a new modern leadership steeped in democratic values that can meet the challenges of globalization, terrorism and corruption. The three essential ingredients of effective democratic leadership: Vision, Dynamism and Integrity (Swamy, 2011). By vision it is meant the ability to take not merely a regional or party view of issues but to look upon them in a national perspective in a vast and varied country, despite that it is inevitable that elected representatives will be committed to certain regional problems and demands. This commitment requires the development of the five dimensions of intelligence namely cognitive, emotional, social, moral and spiritual intelligence.

The second essential ingredient of effective leadership is dynamism, which means the ability to function actively both in the physical and the intellectual sense with the sense of history and thus makes decisions in the national interest by national and calculated risk taking dynamism is essentially thus youthful moral vitality and decisiveness, without ambivalence and procrastination, and with the capacity to take calculated risk placed as we are at a crucial juncture of international history, the emergence of a moral dynamic leadership both at the centre and in the states is a prerequisite for a real breakthrough to progress. Dynamism hence implies the intellectual capacity to think and act in bold terms. The world we live is globalizing at a fast pace. In the last three or four decades science and technology have transferred the face of this planet and today mankind stands at the crossroads in which one path could lead to death and destruction while the other points the way to a possible unprecedented progress and prosperity. At a time like this our political leadership must possess the intellectual equipment and dynamism necessary to grasp the immensity of the challenge and boldly take decisions that are required.

The third ingredient of true leadership is integrity. In one dimension this implies honesty in financial matter. It should be unnecessary to stress this, but corruption at various levels of society continues to be one of the greatest challenges that democracy faces in this country. India is already ranked near the bottom of nations by a corruption index compiled by transparency international. But integrity is also required in a deeper sense is as much as point represents a genuine commitment to ideals and fundamental rights and not merely to the outward forms of democracy.

Characteristics of Democratic Leader

- The democratic leader accepts the basic that leadership is a function of the whole group, not of any one individual.
- A democratic leader is less self-conscious and more group conscious.
- He or she is not always in giving end. He/she believes in give and take process.
- A democratic leader is keen to develop leaders within the group he/she leads, so that if he/she has to leave, the group will not fall apart.
- He/ she never imposes his/her decision on the group rather he/she gives good values to good decisions.

Leadership and Innovation

We are aware of different types of leaderships: social, political, religious and academic. But here we are concerned with academic leadership and how it can help induce innovation in the field of education.

According to Beaudoin (2003), "leadership is a set of attitudes and behaviours that create conditions for innovative change, that enables individuals and organisations to share a vision and move in its direction, and that contribute to the management and operationalization of idea".

To effectively deal with changed demography and value system of learners, a leader has to practice high value system-moral, social and spiritual (Garg, 2011). She must be polite but firm, sympathetic but adhere to rules, supportive but result oriented, transparent but accountable and updated but thorough. In this way, a leader can facilitate development of body, mind and soul. The father of the nation, Mahatma Gandhi used moral and spiritual experiments at the Tolstoy farm to impact the soul of his students. These also led him to have unflinching faith in the virtue of non-violence, which entails self-control and self-suffering. Above all, his words and action were always in unison.

In the current higher education scenario in India, a leader has to strive for financial health of the institution. This perhaps requires innovative and creative thinking.

Innovative leadership must have capacity to:

- Derive the truth forcefully
- Lead a value based life
- Be flexible mentally, emotionally and strategically
- Be creative and think out of the box solutions

Though there are no facile formulae for infallible and innovative leadership, yet vision, clarity, resoluteness, flexibility, accommodation, adaptability, foresightedness, conviction, pragmatism and ability to direct or operationalise concepts are some of the desirable attributes.

Providing intellectual environment for unbiased discussion and setting high performance benchmarks help to manage transformation and facilitate innovations in education. Leadership is not a comfortable position to be in; a leader is continuously challenged to innovate to manage conflicts and contradictions, accommodate different viewpoints, foresee the direction of change and push for development.

By innovatively strategizing priorities, a leader can help foster collaborations and partnerships for more efficient and optimal utilization of resources. Moreover, to provide innovative academic leadership, it is important to be creative, entrepreneurial and above all a good human being. An innovative leader is like a candle which burns to light others. To effectively deal with changed demography and value system of learners, a leader has to practice high value system-moral, social, and spiritual (Garg, 2011).

A leader can create conducive environment for innovation by:

- Identifying "rising stars" and supporting them to achieve desired goals;
- Encouraging altruism, openness and concern for learners;
- Developing tolerance to listen to criticism and keeping critics, rather than sycophants, closer to herself;
- Motivating fellow workers by giving credit to them and owning responsibility for failures; and
- Promoting participative decision making with preference or malice towards none.

Effective Leadership: Qualities and Responsibilities

According to Dr. Kalam (2012), "Leading and

managing are two different ways of organising people. The manager uses a formal, rational method, while the leader uses passion and stirs emotions. A leader is someone whom people naturally follow by choice, whereas a manager must be obeyed. A manager may only have obtained his position of authority through time and loyalty given and not as a result of his leadership qualities. A leader may have no organizational skills, but his vision unites people. An effective leader unites followers in shared vision that will improve an organisation and the society at large. Good leadership must deliver 'true' value. This can happen only through integrity and trust". The hallmarks of a good leader are integrity, equanimity, courage, confidence and impartiality. A leader must be a partner, a teacher as well as a student. He must interact with those under him as a partner, offering constructive criticism (whenever necessary) and generous praise (whenever possible).

Whether it is in business, politics or any other situation, the leader plays a very important role in affecting the fate and welfare of the organization and the people whom he leads. He has to be a person of high moral character and integrity. The leader must be an effective communicator, organizer, monitor and inspirer of men. He must be able to cultivate and develop talents as well as personal relationships. He must be able to make clear, timely and tough (if needed) decisions. Distress come through mouth, when this happens, the smartest thing to do is to admit them. Admitting mistakes and shortfalls do not reflect that the person is weak. It portrays him as a receptive person and his willingness to learn from the wisdom of others.

A leader does not perform the task himself. He gives direction and accepts the responsibility of performing the task. Leadership is a process of developing and coordinating a group's activities towards certain goal accomplishment in a given situation. From this definition, it is clear that the leadership process is dependent on the leader, the followers and the situation. A leader must consider the forces within himself, his followers and in the situation, in order to be effective. Organizations today require leaders whose personal experience is supplemented by an understanding of forces that affect him and the situation in which he is operating. Leader should be the person who culturally binds the organisation. He should bring about more elements and strengthen the culture to ensure that the team members cohesively move in the desired direction for the realization of the organizational objectives.

Success and failure alone cannot be the only test of leadership. For victory and defeat depend upon a number of related factors, that include the ability of the leadership. One of the important attributes of a successful leader is his ability to learn from past mistakes and the willingness to learn from the failures. For a leader the idealistic values of life and selfish values lead to different ways of thinking. If we believe in collective leadership we must pay careful attention to our values of life, to whether our behaviour accords with those values, and to our way of thinking, because the quality of our leadership will have an impact on our field of activity as well as our country. The way we think, our mental attitude, is very important. We have two different sets of values of life. We have to see what we have to adopt for achieving the broad objective of nation building. We have to see that everyone's values of life accord with 'collective leadership'. Which type of leadership is expected for any big accomplishment? Greatness that comes with position is not real greatness. Real greatness does not depend upon position. It depends upon inner values of life. Its basis is the inequality of a person, his work, thoughts and behaviour (Thengdi, 1992).

In the broadest sense, we see the purpose of leadership as encompassing the following values:

- To create a supportive environment where people can grow, thrive and live in peace with one another
- To promote harmony with nature and thereby provide sustainability for future generations and
- To create communities of reciprocal care and shared responsibility where every person matters and each person's welfare and dignity is respected and supported

Values are underlying the leadership process. Leadership is a group process whereby individuals work together to foster change and transformation. Effective leadership necessarily requires: (a) that the group function according to certain principles and values, and (b) that individual members of the group exemplify certain qualities and values that contribute to the effective functioning of the group. These group and individual qualities are summarised below:

Individual	**Group**
Self-knowledge	Collaboration
Authenticity	Shared purpose
Empathy	Division of labour
Commitment	Disagreement with respect
Competence	Learning environment

The aim of leadership is to help the members of group develop a sense of direction and a commitment to that direction. A leader must be able to influence all members of the group. An organization leader ensures that all resources are moving in the direction to achieve the organization's objectives. A leader inspires the organization, develop cohesion and lead the organization to success against hurdles. Leadership believes in co-operation through the communication process. Co-operation needs communication which leads the process of change. The three are so compact that can't be different from one another when practising leadership in modern society. It is true that leadership is the fulcrum on which the demands of the individual and the demands of the organization are balanced.

Characteristics of an Ideal Leader

The following verses from the Bhagavad Gita help us to identify the characteristics of a leader.

Ahimsa satyamakrodhas tyagas shantirapaishunam;

Dayaa bhootteshvaloluptwam maardavam

hreerachaapalam (16.1)

(Fearlessness, purity of heart, steadfastness in knowledge and yoga, alms giving, control of senses, sacrifice, study of scriptures, austerity and straightforwardness)

Tejas kshamaa dhritis shauchamadroho naatimaanitaa;

Bhavani sampadam daiveemabhijaatasya bhaarata (16.2)

(Harmlessness, truth, absence of anger, renunciation, peacefulness, absence of crookedness, compassion towards beings, non-covetousness, gentleness, modesty, absence of fickleness).

Education System and Leadership

Now a key issue facing higher education today is that of leadership. Innovative, flexible and bold leadership qualities are essential to navigate our new complex environment. The obvious dearth of visionary leaders and the consistently increasing calls for effectual and purpose driven leadership in both our private and public national life has made it imperative to groom, prepare coach and mentor the youths so that they shall be adequately equipped to provide the much yearned leadership; since leadership has been described as a set of skills and attitudes that can be learned and practiced. Leadership fosters social change and most of our cultural, social and economic progress is the result of leadership. The youths of today are leaders of tomorrow.

Leaders in the educational system have the ability to transform the system. Generally, leaders in the system can:

- Set the pattern and guide the outcomes of co-operative action
- Guide educational programs, but rely on shared decisions
- Give common understanding to common purposes and goals
- Produce cohesiveness without which co-operation is impossible
- Communicate with all personnel with a sense of mutual understanding and mutual loyalty to the aims of education
- Generate enthusiasm for projects and inspire working towards their completion
- Resolve the differences which frequently arise in growing organizations
- Lead by example and inspiration
- Contribute to the group by advancing useful suggestions

Teacher: A Leader

Teacher as a leader works as a catalyst for cooperation and communication and performs the role of change agent in relation to the members of the organization. Leadership generates course and direction. It is the process of successfully influencing the activities of a group towards the achievement of a common goal. For the purpose a leader has the ability to influence others through qualities such as personal charisma, expertise, command of language, and the creation of mutual respect. He must have humanitarian outlook. He also requires strong communication skills and personal skills, skills of mentoring, decision making, delegation and motivating others.

Teacher as a leader has a multiple role, and therefore, he is looked upon more as one who objectively looks at the issues. He cannot and should not lose temper. His armoury should not be filled with weapons but with patience, empathy and advice. The performance and behaviour of any organization can be greatly affected by the leader. His doors should be opened for anyone coming to seek advice. He should know what attitudes, behaviours and actions are necessary for effective leadership. The leader is judged not by his words alone, but by his behaviour and conduct.

Teacher as an Academic Leader

Teachers are the role model for the students. Every moment the teacher inspires their students. One has to understand how the teacher is a leader. The teacher is considered as a leader from three major fronts.

- Academic leadership
- The leader
- The led

The academic leadership is a broader concept. In this a teacher should be an epitome of knowledge. He /she should always share new area of knowledge to students. The teacher should create the interest among the students that they should always try to gain some knowledge from the teachers. On the other hand, the teacher is a leader. He/she has to lead any event for example - study tours, Industry visit, picnic, any celebrations at college. The students learn from their teacher and follow them. Thirdly, the teacher has to inspire, initiate and motivate others to do the work. The teacher is the real leader.

Sometimes the teachers also represent at many academic platforms, fights for teachers' rights and represent the problem. In that way they show the leadership quality. Teachers are leaders and mentors to take lead in academic leadership.

Parameters for Empowering Teacher as Leader

The parameters of empowerment of teacher as leader are follows:

- Building a positive self-image and self-confidence in learners
- To enhance critical and reflective thinking
- Building social cohesion and fostering creativity, problem solving and reasoning
- Ensuring equal participation in the process of bringing about social change
- Encouraging individual or group action to bring about positive attitudinal change in the society

Activities of Teacher as Leader

As leader teacher should perform the following activities:

(i) **Leadership and communication**

A leader will need to communicate regularly with those for whom he is responsible. The ability to articulate provides an excellent training ground not only for structuring the thoughts and ideas of a person but also for him to learn several other skills that involve organizing, analyzing, evaluating, judging, differentiating and prioritizing. Such skills are needed to put across ideas clearly and convincingly to bosses, colleagues and followers.

An effective communicator is also an intense listener. He would listen carefully as he knows that listening is a way to respecting others. A good leader should be sensitive to the feeling of team he is leading. The day your followers stop bringing you their problems is the day you have stopped leading them.

(ii) **Leader as a follower**

A good leader learns to follow as to lead. Leaders are perceived as consummate learners who attend to the learning. Of both the team and the people they lead-including themselves, of course. No particular style of leadership is effective in all situations and / or with all followers. An effective leader would use a style of leadership that is relevant to the situation as well as meets the needs of his followers. To be effective in a given situation, the leader must be able to adapt his behaviour to the requirements of the situation and his followers. A good leader is also a good follower.

An effective leader should seek to reach out to his followers. He knows that there will always be people who are more intelligent than him. He takes a macro and long-term perspective and is not afraid of criticism. There is a saying about a true leader, "when you are able to know yourself, you are enlightened". In addition, a successful leader keeps himself abreast with the latest information in areas of his responsibility. Information is a tool of updating knowledge. This results in reinforcing his confidence and develops a comprehensive and deep understanding of the objectives.

(iii) **Human development**

Leadership's prime concern and responsibility should be the development of human resources. It is man who imagines, designs, processes, markets and serves the needs of society. The 'management of man' therefore is leader's most critical challenge. It will be appropriate that leadership should concern itself with the organizational and participatory aspects of people-participation in problem solving and decision making. The need of the time is for leaders who can manage man. The "people first" and not the "things first" should be the right approach. Human rather than capital is the key to development.

The leader has a responsibility to help people work cooperatively as a cohesive group. He will also need to set up systems so that he can understand the feelings and reactions of all those for whom he is ultimately responsible. This is a matter of building personal relationships based on trust and confidence as well as inter-group relationships based on cooperation and commitment to organisational goals.

(iv) **Team building**

Organization doesn't really accomplish anything. Plans don't accomplish anything, either. A successful leader has to set new standards, new benchmarks, new ways of doing things and new thinking modes. He should look for intelligence and judgement and most critically, a capacity to anticipate, to see around corners. Also, he should look for loyalty, integrity, a high energy drive, a balanced ego, and the drive to get things done.

(v) **Empowering team**

Empowerment means more than simply "allowing" team members access to decision making. In fact leaders must delegate or share power as well as responsibilities. Thus, it is "transforming followers into leaders". Leaders enable others to become leaders. Empowered team members should be social and political activists who will not allow their work to be co-opted and domesticated by whatever political forces dominate the organisational hierarchy. They recognise their distinctive place in the culture and embrace an emancipate vision and begin to function as transformative leaders. The best leaders are not heroes, they are hero makers. They understand that team members need to be empowered to act to be given the necessary responsibility that releases their potential and makes their actions and decisions count. The leader in the field is most of the time right and one in the rear is wrong, unless proved otherwise.

Maintaining Leadership Skills and Teacher

Leadership skill is a product of knowledge and experience. It has to be acquired, maintained, with vigorous practical training and experience. Functional skill relates to the area of his work, whereas, interpersonal skill is the ability to deal with the people. To be an effective leader, teacher must have at least some managerial skills because teacher must manage resources.

Continuous learning and application of new knowledge becomes an important task of teacher as leader. Learning can also come from exposing oneself to some experience. A successful leader conceptualizes the future. People's motives, tasks ambitions and values keep changing. Therefore, a particular style of leadership will not work for all the occasions. Adaptability with the environment is one of the very critical characteristics of a good leader. The situation dictates which approach best accomplishes the team's mission. Leaders honour their core values, but they are flexible in how they execute them. They understand that leadership techniques are not magic mantras but simply tools to be reached for at the right times. To do all this, leaders will need new energy, a clear sense of direction, to offer effective leadership in this new environment.

Chapter-12

Value-oriented Teacher Education

The present society is passing through a critical stage which is characterised by loss of values in human life. The demon of corruption, violence, indiscipline, and barbarism are spreading all over creating a negative social atmosphere. It is widely accepted that education should be given a value orientation for bringing lasting peace in the world. Presently, it is realized that youth is losing touch with a sense of right and wrong or good and bad. This is because, as a nation, we have failed in our duty to capture the energy of youth and mould it in the right direction. It is high time to prevent our youth from leaving the country or get into violence, and terrorism by providing them better leadership and by strengthening and empowering them. For this, our education system should be restructured with value orientation. The report of Working Group of Modernization of Pre-service Teacher Education Curriculum (1987) emphasized on the value orientation of teacher. According to the report, value education has assumed a special significance in order to enable the child to reconcile the value conflict arising out of tradition and modernity, and it would be possible through proper value-oriented teachers. It is the need of the hour that teacher education should be integrated with value orientation.

Concept of Value

The word value is derived from the Latin word "Valerie" which means "to be strong and vigorous". The dictionary meaning of the term value is 'that which renders anything useful, worthy or estimable'. It refers to the price, worth or importance of a thing.

According to Edgen Brightman, "value means whatever is actually liked, prized, esteemed, desired, approved and enjoyed by any one at any time. It is the actual experience of enjoying a desired object or activity".

Values are socially approved drives and goals that are internalized through the process of conditioning, learning and socialization and that becomes preferences, standards and aspiration of the individual(s) to set a norm in the society. It is difficult to define values because these are as comprehensive in nature as our human life.

Values are considered as the most inevitable components of social living of human beings. It encompasses all the human activities including all pleasures and pains, enjoyment and miseries, appreciation and dislikes. Evaluations or judgements also entail values. Briefly, we cannot understand life without understanding values. Human being starts imbibing values since very early days through surroundings. Values assist individuals to lead their life in a right direction. It helps in taking decisions about when and what actions to be taken, whom to spend time with, and what to do and what not to do. Every task of human being is related to values. A value system is a set of philosophy and beliefs that remains in the mind of every individual while behaving in everyday situations of life. Values in education system make one's own life and the life of his fellow beings lively and meaningful.

The term 'value' covers the entire domain of the development of an integrated personality. There are specific values that an integrated personality reveals through various capacities such as:

- The values of health, strength, stamina and discipline show one's physical capacity.
- The values of courage, confidence, love and dedication show one's emotional capacity.
- The values of clarity, rationality, sobriety and impartiality show one's intellectual capacity.
- The values of honesty, purity, fairness and justice show one's moral and spiritual capacity.
- The values like kindness, politeness, service and fellow-feeling show one's social capacity.

Types of Values

There are various areas of values. The main areas of values are discussed below:

- Social values - Social conformity, discipline, social sensitiveness, altruism, toleration, social adjustment, social loyalty, social justice, social responsibility etc.
- Moral values - Honesty, truthfulness, moral stability, good character etc.
- Cultural values - Faith in God, (Sat-Chit-Ananda i.e. existence, knowledge and bliss) spiritualism, tolerance, simplicity, social service, courtesy and Niskama karma etc.
- Secular Values - Mutual understanding, mutual cooperation, tolerance, appreciation of universal truth, character and humanitarianism.

- Ultimate Values - Truth, beauty, goodness and salvation.
- Aesthetic Values- Beauty, happiness, pleasure, innovative power, creation, art and painting.
- Intellectual values- Critical analytical thinking, understanding, freedom of thought and sound knowledge.
- Democratic Values- Co-operation, mutual understanding, freedom, equality, justice, mutual help, sharing of experiences and taking leadership.
- Universal values- Peaceful co-existence and love for humanity.
- Spiritual values- Oneness with supreme, self-control and meditation.
- Physical values- Good posture, sound health, appropriate eating habits, dignity of labour.

Values in Indian Context

The values enshrined in Indian scriptures are relevant today. In the ancient times, values were reflected in the daily activities of the pupils. Scriptures of India show that the students were educated in their social responsibilities, so that they may perform these in the future, when they take up leadership position in the society. The basic lesson taught them was "Loka Samastha Sukhino Bhavantu" means, 'Let the whole world be Happy'. The students were encouraged to work for social welfare keeping this principle in mind. The Taitariya Upanishad advises the student who is on the threshold of making a career in the society as follows: "Satyam Vada, Dharmam Chara, Matru Devo Bhava, Pitru Devo Bhava, Acharya Devo Bhava,

Atithi Devo Bhava" the meaning of this advice is "Speak the Truth, Perform always the Righteous Action, Worship your Mother, Father, Preceptor and Guest as God". The students and teachers in ancient India were also urged to perform only those acts which satisfy their conscience, thus leading to value based decision-making.

"Sarvey bhabantu sukhinah, survey santu niramayah

Sarvey bhadrani pashyantu, maa kaschit dukhabhag bhabet"

May all live happily, May all see auspiciousness, May none experience distress, May peace prevail everywhere. India is a country that believes in "Basudhaiba Kutumbakam" the whole world is one family.

Erosion of Values and Present Society

At present, there is deterioration of values in all walks of life. The eternal values namely truth, beauty and goodness are disappearing. Religion and ideology are losing their hold; power and knowledge are misused for vested interest. Core human values such as honesty, trustworthiness, ethics and above all humanity are degrading day by day.

Erosion in political values like loss of leadership, political exploitation, lack of code of conduct, lawlessness, scandals and indiscipline are found in the society. There has been erosion in social values like; caste system, social disorganisation, marital disorganisation, malpractices (all types of corruption, bribery etc.) materialistic attitude, social indiscipline, lack of justice and social exploitation etc. Moreover, the growing consumerism has altered our social values and customs. There is also deterioration of economic values such as difference between haves and have-nots, inequality, discrimination, race, BPL, APL etc.

Unfortunately, society today has become self centred.

We perceive ourselves as the focal point of everything and moral progress is often clouded by the shadows of personal gain. We tend to become hypocrite. Glorious customs and traditions have changed. The noble ideas of Indian culture i.e., Dharma, Artha, Karma and Moksha are gradually fading away.

Diverse changes such as advancement in science and technology, knowledge expansion, rapid industrialization, urbanization, privatization and globalization have affected almost every aspect of our society and it has become highly dynamic. Although this process of modernization has made our life easy, several problems have emerged with it such as anxiety and worries in human life. Growing levels of violence, caste and creed discrimination, child labour, gender inequality, physical and mental abuse with women, ill mental health and countless evils of such kind have created value crisis in the society. Immoral and anti-social activities are fast growing in the society which stands as great obstacle in the progress and prosperity of the nation.

Recommendation of Commissions and Committees on Value Education

Realizing the importance of values, different commissions and committees recommended for value orientation in education system. Right from the dawn of independence government of India has appointed various commission and committees to prepare action plans to bring the desired improvement in the existing system of education which include Radhakrishnan Commission (1948-49), Mudaliar Commission (1952-53), Sri Prakash Committee on Moral Education (1959), Ramamurti Committee (1990) etc. The committees and commissions have advocated and underlined the need for value-based education in our educational institutions. Sri Prakash Committee (1959) in this context has rightly observed "the only cure it seems to us is in the deliberate inculcation of moral and spiritual values from the earliest years of our lives".

Indian Education Commission (1964-66) stated, "One of the major crises facing education in India is that of value orientation. It has been usually argued that the main focus during the last three decades has been on quantitative expansion and consequently adequate attention could not be paid to maintain standards and quality of education. The output of the educational system is not only of poor quality but degradation of moral values has also been noticed".

The National Policy on Education (1986) stated that, 'The growing concern over the erosion of essential values and an increasing cynicism in society have brought to focus the need for the readjustments in the curriculums to make education a forceful tool for the cultivation of social and moral values. In our culturally plural society, education should foster universal and eternal values, oriented towards the unity and integration of our people. Such value education should help to eliminate obscurantism, religious fanaticism, violence, superstition and fatalism. Apart from the combative role, value education has a profound positive content, based on our heritage, national and universal goals and perception'. Similarly, the National Curriculum Framework (2005) has proposed inculcation and nurturance of moral, ethical, humanistic and constitutional values.

Attempt of National policy on Education (1986) and Programme of Action (1992) has also emphasized on value education. The then central Ministry of Education formed a working group in this regard under the chairmanship of Sri Kireet Joshi (1983) which, in turn, opined that value determination is the main purpose of education and all teachers should get involved in value development through all activities of school campus. Emphasis was also laid upon including 'value orientation' in teaching -learning of all subjects.

Why do Teachers need Value Orientation?

To conquer the problems of the current technological era, value inculcation and promotion of value education is highly essential. Value education is ingrained in every tradition of Indian culture. In this context, it is essential that education should be value oriented. Only value-oriented education can promote individual and social welfare, love, peace, good will and proper understanding.

Teacher education has now assumed great social importance and has, therefore, been the target of severe criticism. But worse is the fact that it suffers from isolation from society. This isolation makes teacher education incomplete, valueless and worthless in our developing country. This is due to the serious lacunae in terms of values which are missing in teacher education. In the age of scientific materialism, teacher education has also adopted more and more scientific and analytical concepts and has ignored the holistic human values that make a total man.

Unfortunately, today the personality of the teachers has deteriorated. The society now accords a low status to teachers; this profession has been highly depleted and demoralized owing to certain evils that have crept in this noble profession such as political influence, corruption and other unfair practices. Once upon a time, ancient institutions (Gurukul) were highly honoured and considered as temple of learning, but now it has become one of the easiest sources of money making. In certain cases, the personality of the teacher has turned too dubious. They lack moral fiber and spiritual elegance and their behaviour has become highly suspicious, corrupt, degrading and disgusting. Some teachers relentlessly opt for this profession just for the sake of monetary benefits and to gain power and position, rather than for the integrity and sanctity of the profession. We can say that the status of teacher has got devalued due to poor quality of teaching, changing social attitudes or societal response towards teaching profession and professionalism in teaching (Kalita, K., 2015).

The success of any educational system depends on the quality of the teachers which, in turn, depends on the effective teaching-learning process in a class room. Teachers' performance is the most crucial input in the field of education. Therefore, teachers should be aware of the fact that their role is of vital significance for societal development and change. They must make an effort to light a candle instead of cursing the darkness and sow the seeds of value education with a great hope that they would disseminate their fragrance towards the creation of a just and new society as they spurt and blossom (Kalita, K., 2015).

The Report of the Working Group in University Education for the Seventh Five-Year Plan (1985-1990) has emphatically suggested that value orientation in education should constitute a special thrust in the Seventh Plan, teacher education in particular being re-oriented for this purpose.

Emphasising value-orientation in education, our late Prime Minister Indira Gandhi, said, "Our educational system must prepare our young people to be more responsible and resourceful. It must take note of the problems, needs and aspirations of youth as well as the challenges of a changing world. It should teach our young people to see regional problems in the national context and national problems in the international perspective. It should inculcate moral and social values, attitudes of non-violence and tolerance".

Teacher needs value orientation for the following reasons:

i. **Teacher has distinctive position in society**

In Indian culture, the teacher is held in high position and respect. He is considered as a fountain head of all knowledge and a source of great ideals. He is the torchbearer of society. Students look up to him with faith and hope and they seek his advice in important aspects such as human and good social life etc. Hence, if the teacher has a keen sense of values and has faith in the higher purpose of life, he can guide a whole generation through his versatile personality.

ii. **The teacher is the source of knowledge**

That all knowledge comes from the teacher is the belief of students in the class. Since our students are not tuned to independent study from childhood, they believe that whatever their teacher says is the absolute truth and nothing less than the truth. They do not question the authority of the teacher. Hence, if good ideas and values are to be perpetuated and inculcated in the younger generation, they must come from the mouth of the teachers in their classes at all the levels of education. Besides, whatever values the teachers demonstrate in their day-to-day behaviour, their students will imitate and emulate their example in life.

iii. **The teacher has multiple effects**

The influence of the teacher becomes multiple among students who come in contact with him, year after year. If the teacher shares his ideas and values with a few hundred students every year, it means he will have a life-long impact on thousands of them during the period of his service, till he retires.

iv. The teacher has high prestige in society

The whole parent community looks up to the teacher for the welfare and progress of their children. The teacher enjoys tradition and culture, wisdom and knowledge. Hence, the values and ideals of the teacher attain social significance. His life can be a great message to the younger generation for years to come.

v. The teacher is a model for the younger generation

For many children, parents fail to provide guidelines as they are themselves either ignorant or too busy to look after them. It is in school that most students find that their teachers are worthy models. They consciously or unconsciously imitate the values, ideals and habits of their teachers. They even follow their methods, manners and style of speaking that they see in the classroom, day in and day out. Thus, if teachers are committed to certain values in day-to-day behaviour, the children will pick them up soon in their early years.

Hence, it is necessary that teachers under training should be thoroughly exposed to human values in their institution. It presupposes that the teacher educators also have a serious commitment to human values in life. They should be not merely good lecturers of philosophy or sociology or psychology or methodology experts in one method or the other, but they should be oriented towards values.

Integration of Value in Teacher Education

It is often seen that the present-day teachers and

teacher education programmes are not adequately equipped to foster value education in educational institutions. The Education Commission (1966), the National Commission on Teachers (1985) pointed that the state of teacher education in the country is far from satisfactory. Value education is necessary in our teacher education programme, so that it can meet the challenges of value crisis among young generation.

The role of teacher educators is critical as "teachers are the most valuable resource that a nation counts on to mould and nurture its young people" (Idris, Cheong, Nor, Razak & Saad, 2007). Developing values among teacher trainees is significant, because it is not only the aim of national educational goals, but also the goal to prepare students to become responsible citizens.

Development of values has been a major concern to most education system in different countries of the world (UNESCO, 2002). According to UNESCO (2011), pre-service training of teachers needs to focus on values that transform the teacher trainees as individual facilitators in development of values in school pupils. As such, the pre-service training of teachers needs to be transformational by integrating values in the learning process and facilitating values application into contemporary situations. Therefore, teacher educators need skills that enable them to apply participatory methods and reflective pedagogy as they facilitate teacher trainees develop values (UNESCO, 2011).

Following steps should be taken into consideration to integrate value in teacher education:

i. **Objectives**

The objectives of teacher education should be revised in the light of value oriented education. It requires modification of the present syllabus and text books of different subjects. Value-oriented education is meant to:

a) develop awareness in trainees about self and society.
b) inculcate values of truth, honesty, character, self-reliance and self-discipline in life.
c) provide opportunities for a broader personal outlook and positive social attitude.
d) provide awareness about education and its role in national development and international peace.
e) make teachers sensitive to the value needs of children and their full adjustment to the society of the future.

ii.   Courses of study

The present curriculum and textbooks are subject-centred and not value-centred. They need a new orientation in selection of topics, content and follow-up exercises. The courses of study in teacher education should begin with the introduction of values in the list of objectives for each course. Every lesson in the text book should show its application value in life so that trainees grasp the significance and understand the utility of the lesson.

It is worth noting that the NCTE has already suggested a useful paper at all levels of teacher education under the title: Teacher and Education in the Emerging Indian Society. It is relevant for value-oriented education at all the levels, provided the topics are properly selected for that paper and it is taught in that style by the teacher educators. There is no need to have a separate course at present to avoid over-loading of the present curriculum, but the syllabus could be so treated by the teacher educators that the teacher trainees gain an insight into the values of life and be prepared to practise them and teach them to their classes.

iii. Methods of instruction

Before a teacher training programme begins in the institution, there should be an Orientation Programme for trainees during the first week to lead them to higher goals of teacher education than mere job preparation. Besides, every day's work in the colleges should begin with a brief prayer assembly and reading of good thoughts of great scholars, teachers and philosophers. The teacher educators should use progressive methods of teaching which involve trainees in discussions, activities, projects, practicals, independent study, and observation. Exhibition and display of value-oriented writings, pictures and posters should be held regularly in colleges of education. Experts in philosophy, yoga, ethics and moral values should be invited to give lectures to the trainees on values of Truth, Harmony and Beauty (Satyam, Shivam and Sundaram). The teacher educators should demonstrate the human values through their day-to-day dealings with the trainees. They should be models of politeness, and tolerance, love and kindness, discipline and character.

Very little emphasis should be placed on rote memory and recitation work. Field trips and co-curricular activities should occupy important place in the teacher education programme and be frequently organised for trainees to develop their all-round personality. Unless they experience all round development, they cannot help their students in the process of total growth.

iv. **Training for teachers**

It will be fully operative and functional if teachers at all stages receive training in value education either at pre-service or in-service level. There should be adequate provision in teacher training institutions to orient in service teachers through different methods with enriched materials/packages on value education. Proper networking should be established between teacher training institutions like university teaching institutions, CTEs, DIETs etc. for effectiveness of the programme. Teacher trainees should be encouraged to get involved in discussion, activities, projects, practicals and observations relating to values. Varied learning experiences in the class room and out-of-the class in the community should be provided during the training period.

v. **Evaluation**

It is necessary to have a broad based evaluation for value education. Oral test, group discussions, and practical observations by a panel of judges should be made.

Strategies for Imparting Values to Teacher Trainees

Following are the ways by which values can be imbibed among teacher trainees during classroom teaching and learning process:

- Teacher educator must be clear about the values that he wishes to emphasise. A set of universal values will emerge that may include: honesty, peace, humility, freedom, cooperation, care, love, unity, respect, tolerance, courage, friendship, patience, quality and thoughtfulness will be taught to teacher trainees.

- Values cannot be taught in isolation but the teacher educator can provide experiences and situations in which teacher trainees can consider and reflect about values and translate this reflection into action.
- Teacher educator can involve trainees in active games in the classroom to inculcate the values of fair play, honesty, courage, co-operation, respect and love are best learnt through interaction with peers having diverse cultural, ethnic and personality traits among them. Value education should be a process of developing the spirit of rational enquiry and self-discovery.
- Human values need to be cultured for the sake of the mind and the body in the trainees.
- Teacher educators should make teacher trainees need to know human nature. With loving attention and care one can bring out the positive human values in child. In order to create a positive school ethos there must be commitment by the whole staff that value based education is central to the school's mission.
- Value education is most effective when the teacher educator acts as a role model and ensures that it is at the heart of the school's philosophy. Trainees observe the enthusiasm, commitment and "the talk and walk" of teachers which creates the impetus that ensures that values lie at the core of the human existence.
- After the lesson stimulus, whole class discussion allows the value to be explored more deeply. So, teacher educators must encourage healthy discussions and also motivate teacher trainees to

participate and explore themselves.

- Maintaining an ethos in the classroom that is positive and all inclusive, with a feeling of equality, will help teacher trainees' gain most from value lessons. Rajendra Prasad (2005) found that the most preferred terminal values of teacher educators were a world of peace, happiness and self-respect.

To sum up, value oriented education is the need of the hour. The younger generations will be able to face the future squarely, if they are fully equipped by the value committed teachers. To produce such teachers, the teacher education institutions have to strive and work hard for the value-oriented training programmes.

Chapter-13

Integration of Peace in Teacher Education

In the present age, maintaining world-peace is a burning issue. Peace, safety and security are very essential for the growth and development of human culture and civilization. We should respect man as man and not extinguish the spark of humanity that shines in all of us. Peace has its blessing in the form of prosperity, progress, security, love, sympathy and co-existence. Peace allows the growth of culture and civilization. It showers fellow feelings, fraternity and equality among all people. Peace is essential condition to preserve human civilization. For the holistic development of human behaviour, teacher plays a key role. Teacher doesn't only make an individual knowledgeable but also makes him aware of how to communicate with others and live peacefully in the society. So the need of hour is to make younger generation conscious about the importance of peace for the betterment of nation and mankind.

Peace and Peace Education

Peace is the absence of violence and condition of societal friendship and harmony. It means absence of war like situation and freedom from fear of conflict or violence between individuals or different groups of people. Peace is a state of mind with more than just sitting still or silent. R. N. Tagore has rightly said "peace is a condition where the mind is without fear and the head is held high, into the kingdom of freedom". It is a common thinking that peace is an international issue that has nothing to do with our daily life. But promotion of global peace is possible only if every nation is settled in peace. The condition of conflict leads to the mental setup where war is considered the only solution to every problem. In this context, education plays a vital role in the modification of such type of conflict resolution.

Peace education encompasses the key concepts of education and peace. Peace education is to get individuals adopt necessary knowledge, attitude, skills and behaviours for living peacefully, firstly with herself / himself, then with other people. Peace education is a participatory holistic process that includes teaching for and about democracy and human right, non-violence, social and economic justice, gender equality, environment sustainability, peace practices and human security. UNICEF and UNESCO are two international organisations that are particularly active advocates of education for peace. UNICEF describes peace education as follows:

- Act as agent of peace, where children are safe from violence
- Encourage student's basic rights as highlighted in the CRC
- Develop such an institutional environment that models peaceful and respectful behaviour among all members of the institution
- The policies of equality, fraternity and non-discrimination are incorporated in the policies and practices
- Deal with the conflicts in ways where rights and dignity are respected

- Incorporate human rights, social justice, and global issues in the curriculum
- Provide opportunities for discussion of values of peace and social justice
- Encourage the teaching and learning methods that focus on participation, problem-solving and respect for differences

Peace education is the process of acquiring the values, the knowledge and developing the attitudes, skill and behaviours to live in harmony with one self, with others, and the natural environment. During this process, the representatives of different cultures have had to interact with people from different races, ethnicities, religions, sects, dialects and cultures.

In the contemporary world where people from different races, ethnicities, cultures, social classes, and political views live together and it is inevitable; being tolerant is of great importance to create the environment with mutual understanding and respect. It is necessary to create a culture based on freedom, justice, democracy, tolerance and unity to build a peace culture globally (UNESCO, 2005). It is vital to develop peace culture with the help of education. The biggest agent to create peace culture is the human beings themselves, because peaceful relations and structures can be improved through individuals' effort. In order for individuals to place peace loving understanding into their life, they should be trained with peace education from early ages. The quality and the effectiveness of this education are closely related to prevent bullying, creating safe and peaceful culture in schools. To provide this, students should be taught the alternatives of violence and the skills to live in peace.

Definition

There is no universally accepted definition for Peace education. There is good number of definitions available on the basis of different perceptions and approaches.

According to John Dewey, "Peace education is grounded in active citizenship, preparing learners for assiduous participation in a democracy, through problem - posing and problem solving education, and transformative action in our societies".

According to Fan Schmidt and Friedman (1988), "Peace education is holistic. It embraces the physical, emotional, intellectual, and social growth of children within a frame work deeply rooted in traditional human values. It is based on a philosophy that teaches love, compassion, trust, fairness, co-operation and reverence for the human family and all life on our beautiful planet".

UNESCO literature states that peace education is more effective and meaningful when adopted according to the social and cultural context and the needs of a country. It should also be enriched by its cultural and spiritual values together with the universal human values. It should also be globally relevant. Given such a frame work, it is hard to find universally accepted definition.

Education for peace and education about peace are two main approaches to peace education, and all peace education fields can be defined by one or both of these approaches. According to Reardon (1999), "education for peace is an achievement of peace". Education for peace involves developing values, skills and attitudes that are conducive to building peace. According to Reardon (1999), education about peace is "education for the development and practice of institutions and processes that comprise a peaceful social order".

The inclusion of youth in Peace building initiatives brings vibrancy and creativity to peace building efforts. The year 2000 has been declared by the United Nations as the international year for building the culture of peace and it is the first year in the international decade for the culture of peace and non-violence for the children of the world. The United Nations is encouraging young people to participate in the process of building peace. In September 1999, the United Nations Educational Scientific and Cultural Organization (UNESCO) stated, "young people are the present; their involvement is necessary for human development and sustainability".

From the above definition it can be agreed that in the absence of elements such as tolerance, understanding, empathy, cooperation and respect for the difference in others, there cannot be peace. Any strategy or educational system helps to enhance the above said entities among the individuals could be known as peace education. Further, Peace education definitions reveal that it aims at the overall development of the individuals and helps to enhance eternal values in their minds.

Aims of Peace Education

Declaration of the 44th session of the international conference on education held at Geneva in 1994 has listed the following aims of peace education:

- To develop sense of universal values in every individual
- To prepare citizens to cope with difficult and uncertain situations and fitting them for personal autonomy and responsibility

- To educate the individual and develop the ability to recognize and accept the values which exist in the diversity of individuals
- To strengthen peace, friendship and solidarity between individuals and people
- To develop the ability of non-violent conflict resolution among the individuals
- To cultivate the ability to make informed choices, basing their judgments and actions not only on the analysis of present situations and the vision of a preferred future among the individuals
- To teach the citizens to respect the cultural heritage, protect the environment and social harmony
- To cultivate citizens in the line of solidarity feeling and feeling of equity at the national and international levels in perspectives of a balanced and long-term development

Teacher Education and Peace

Teacher educator has an important role in inculcating peace among student teachers. Education for peace and values need to be pursued with will, commitment and the hope for transformation and change. According to Indian tradition and culture teacher has a pivotal role in the process of teaching and learning. The vast majority of teachers strive to teach effectively in order to enhance student learning outcomes, and they draw upon the knowledge and skills acquired throughout their pre-service teacher programme. Similarly, Day (2000) points out that teacher education must concern itself with developing future teachers in a holistic way, allowing the pre-service teacher to reflect on their whole selves. Pre-service teachers must be encouraged to explore their personal values and how these may or may not align with their professional ones. One way in which this exploration could occur is by creating what Gellel (2010) has termed 'communities of practice', connecting pre-service teachers with practising teachers, students and wider school communities. As we know that without peace and human values we can't survive in the world in peaceful manner and we can't enjoy life. In a global scenario of erosion of peace and values, it would be difficult to have individuals in society who would strive to halt the process of peace and value deterioration. It appears that moral and ethical issues, including character education, are great need to become part of the teacher education programs. The professional ethics for teachers is itself a complete programme of peace education for student teachers. In a nutshell it can be concluded that a teacher educator is the teacher of future teachers which means a lot of responsibility. Therefore, for the sustainable human development as well as for the social growth there is a need of peace education.

In the changing global scenario the main aim of teacher education will be to help people to develop themselves as responsible citizens of their immediate society. The focus of teacher education would be to find and evolve ways of inculcating values of peace and harmony based on concepts of right living, mutual respect and trust, cooperation, social justice, open-mindedness and fruitful co-existence. Keeping this in view it is necessary to reorient and restructure teacher education programmes to include the need for this kind of tutoring. Teacher Education for peace is intrinsically linked to the understanding of global world orders and commonalities and at the same time differences of socio-political, economic and legal systems.

Characteristics of Teachers to Instruct Peace Education

- Firstly, teachers who instruct peace education should know about peace, war and violence, their benefits and damages.
- Teacher should know the reasons and results of violence.
- S/he should know the types of violence such as positive violence, negative violence, and psychological violence. Also s/he should know which methods to use to abolish these types of violence.
- Prospective teachers who emphasized peace education should, firstly, be at peace with him/ her and the society.
- The personal qualities of the teachers who instruct peace education should have, being respectful, understanding, patient, tolerant, forgiving, equalitarian, self-confident, fair, cooperative, innovator, and solution oriented, integrative, empathetic, and unprejudiced.
- Prospective teachers should have some skills for peace education. The most important skills of the teachers who instruct peace education should have self-knowledge, empathy, effective communication and effective listening, managing diversities, and peace building.
- Other skills that prospective teachers emphasized are peace-making, living together, problem solving and conflict resolution, emotions and anger control, leadership, entrepreneurship, reflective thinking, critical thinking and creative thinking.

Teacher Education Programmes for Facilitating Peace

The ultimate aim of teacher education in nowadays is to inculcate peace among pre-service teachers. Teacher education plays a very crucial role as it prepares the quality teachers who have the responsibility on their pupil teachers to make our students good citizens of the country. A teacher should have clear understanding of his vocations, demands and realization of his serious responsibility towards society and nation. Is he/she only a transaction machine of instruction or having a sensible attitude by which he/she can impart peace education through his effective pedagogy and integration of peace with different subjects? Unless a teacher possesses a peaceful heart, peace cannot be reflected in his student. Students are the mirror image of teachers with respect to behavioural tendencies and attitude. So teachers should have a clear vision, motivation, skills and awareness for the success of the initiative for education for peace and values (NCF-2005). Education for peace states that teacher education institutions, in this context, have a very vital role to play as they are the centres that mould the teaching fraternity of the country through their pre-service and in-service teacher programmes. It also states that the teacher education curriculum frameworks of 1978,1988 and 1998 emphasized the role of teachers as catalyst in promoting social sensitivity, tolerance, co-operation, democratic and secular values, national integration, international understanding etc. through inclusion of relevant themes in the "foundation course" and school experience programmes. So it is essential to reconsider the teacher education programmes in order to build peaceful and value laden teachers both through pre-service and in-service teacher education.

Peace Education in Teacher Education

Teaching is known as the mother of all professions. This is a profession which creates all other professions. Teacher education refers to the different policies, procedures and programmes designed to equip the prospective teachers with proper knowledge, attitude, behaviour and skills which are required to perform their tasks effectively in the classroom, school, college and in other communities. In past few years, India had witnessed multifarious changes in its teacher education programme. A number of teacher education programmes have been mushrooming in different parts of the country. Varieties of subjects have been included in the teacher education programme. In this time of proliferated globalization and modernization what we really lack in the society is peaceful coexistence and harmony among the people belonging to different cultures and regions of the world. So the teacher education programme must be equipped with such plans, policies and courses of studies which can be able to build an intellectual group of teachers who can further train, teach and create a peaceful and harmonious society.

The rationale behind including peace education in teacher education curriculum is given below. The prospective teachers will acquire knowledge of peace education and they can further teach their students about the importance of peace and harmony. The teachers are considered as the role models for their students. So, if they act as the pioneer of peace and harmony, students will follow them and thus we can expect a peaceful society for today's generation.

The teachers are involved in the plan and policy making committees. It is very important for the teaching professionals to be aware of the importance of peace and harmony education, so that they can make proper plans and policies of education which can help in establishing peace and harmony. In teacher education programme, the teachers are trained to adopt certain teaching methods in classroom which promotes participatory learning, co-operation and tolerance among the students. In physical education, the student teachers are taught some practice relaxation exercises and meditation for building peace of mind.

Need of Teaching Peace in Professional Institutions

An educational process that develops individuals to acquire special competencies for professional practice is known as professional education. So by acquiring certain professional education, a person can step into that particular profession. They are the nation builders and together they constitute a whole of the responsible citizens of the country. So introducing peace and harmony education in every professional course is of immense importance. It can help to grow the sense of peaceful coexistence in the minds of the people belonging to different professions. A mass of intellectual being will be created who can lead the generations towards a peaceful and harmonic world. In the words of MalalaYousafzai, "With gun you can kill a terrorist; with EDUCATION you can kill terrorism".

So if we want to build a terror free, nonviolent, peaceful and tolerant nation, we need to impart education and create huge educated and intellectual mass instead of making plans to kill the terrorists. Because if you kill one terrorist, two more will be created. So we need to uproot the terrorism and for that we need to educate the citizens properly. Through education only, the value of peace and harmony can be realised. We must not forget that maximum intellectual mass are created in professional institutions. That is why peace and harmony education should be made an integral part of every professional course. In the present scenario, the need of peace education is very essential and vital for peace of mind, peace in the family, peace in society, peace between nations and peace in the universe for progress of nations. So the seed of peace and harmony should be inculcated inside every human being from very beginning. And it is the responsibility of the teachers to make students aware of the importance of peace and harmony at a very tender age. That is why the first and foremost profession which need to be trained and taught about peace education is the teaching profession. All the teacher education institutions should try to strengthen the teaching of peace education in their institutions so that the emerging teachers and teacher educators can know and be aware of their duties and responsibilities towards making the nation terror free and more tolerant with peaceful coexistence and proper harmony among the people.

Role of Teacher in Peace Education

The teacher plays a prominent role in the process of peace building. Teacher must understand that the problems of multicultural, multiethnic and multi religious nature need not be dealt with in isolation rather all these problems are interconnected and must be addressed as a whole with all other problems of peace and violence. The different roles that the teacher plays in peace building are discussed below.

Peace education embodies students and teachers in a process which is change oriented; also it contributes to them to behave peacefully. This contribution continues even after education has finished, so it makes solution-oriented environments, where no elements of violence exist or where conflicts are resolved functionally, and this is quite important for educational processes, development and quality of life.

Peace education is taken into consideration with peaceful pedagogy, and the content of this pedagogy is made up of cooperative learning, democratic society, moral sensitivity, critical thinking, and tolerance. Thus, peace education is seen as one of the most effective ways to create positive, peace culture oriented societies.

Teacher's Role as Agent of Democratisation through Peace

Teachers and the education system must play the role of agents of democratisation. They must seek to uphold cultures of peace by respecting the diversities prevalent in the societies. The role of teacher is to develop critical abilities among the learners and at the same time they must be informed about the multiple contested positions in the society. Some teachers see peace education as the process of acquiring knowledge about political institutions and civic rules whereas others see it as nurturing principles of participation and engagement (Schulz et al., 2010). Citizenship and history curricula at international levels have acquired the philosophy of cultivating democratic skills, shared values, the human rights, respect for diversity and civic responsibilities (Davies, 2004). Teachers must use their teaching skills to teach the learner to participate in peaceful questioning, criticising injustice and the ways to arrive at peaceful solutions (Davies, 2011). Teachers are expected to facilitate 'deliberative' democratic processes in the classroom (Davies, 2004). An important role of teacher in encouraging peace among its learners is to create a type of environment where the democratic values are not only taught but reinforced and modelled in the entire education structure. It has been argued by many thinkers that schools that model democratic practice are the most effective in promoting civic engagement, sense of political efficacy and future political participation among the students.

Strategies

Following strategies may help for promotion of peace among teacher trainees:

- Teacher trainees should be trained in alternative pedagogical skills which may help in resolving conflicts in order to promote culture of peace
- Be appreciative of our composite culture and national identity from an international perspective
- Teacher's perceptions of caste, religion, class, gender and other cultures should be based on constitutional values and empirical evidence
- Be aware of the factors that make peace unstable such as gender disparity, prejudice, ideologies of conflict, violence, harassment, in classroom and between our neighbours
- Be committed to the professional ethics of the teacher' profession
- Emphasis should be on fostering civic values by working collaboratively through dialogue, debates, workshops and different healthy competitive situations
- Development of warm and co-operative relationships with students, realizing that they are shouldering a serious responsibility of building the future of the nation and the world
- Co-operative learning techniques can be used

beneficially in internship programme of pre-service teacher education programme
- Based on content and pedagogy, in-service teacher training programmes should be organized separately on a regular basis
- Peace education should be both in pre-service and in-service teacher training programmes in order to make the trainees realize the importance of peace for the individual and for the nation

Teacher Education institutions play significant role in the promotion of peace education among student teachers. As an integral part of education system, teacher education is intimately related to the society. As we know that teachers are very important in the overall development of any nation through their impact in the educational system, in this regard teacher educators play a vital role for inculcation of peace among pre-service teachers to be good human beings. A peace and value based approach must form the backbone of educational system and also the teacher education system. Inculcation of peace and value based education approach offer a new way of thinking about education and how children can be supported to develop to become successful and happy members of the global society. It encourages reflective and inspirational attributes and attitudes. Teacher trainees can be nurtured to help people, discover the very best of themselves which enables them to be good global citizens and prepare them for their working life. Education for peace aims at promoting broader capabilities, attitudes and skills that matter not just in schools but also life beyond schools, making the world a better place not just for themselves but also for their family, friends, colleagues and others.

Chapter-14

Stress Management and Teacher

Stress is an unavoidable characteristic of life and work. It is often described as a psychological condition and body discomfort. Every individual experiences stress at some time or other. When a person experiences a constraint inhibiting the accomplishment of desire and demand for accomplishments, it leads to potential stress. Organizations create stress in the individuals. Everyone has different stress triggers. Work stress tops the list, according to surveys, forty percent of U.S workers admit to experiencing office stress and one quarter say work is the biggest source of stress in their lives. Why one should be concerned about stress? The reason is that the stress has more negative consequences than positive. According to Fred Luthans, "stress is defined as an adaptive response to an external situation that results in physical, psychological, and/or behavioural deviation for organisational participants".

Stress: The Concept

The word 'stress' is derived from the Latin word 'stringi' which means 'to be drawn tight'. When we say, 'I am stressed' or 'I am under stress', we mean, the way stress is felt, experienced and affected by our body and mind. Stress may be understood at both physiological and psychological level. Stress reaction may occur either to internal or external stimulus. Thus stress means tension, worry, grief, anxiety, depression, restlessness, headache, irritation, threat etc. Stress is a psychological condition occurs due to a 'perceived threat'. Anything that cause stress to the individual is called stressor.

Stress is the body's natural defence against predators and danger. It flushes the body with hormones to prepare systems to erode or confront danger. This is known as the "Fight-or flight" mechanism. When we are faced with a challenge, part of our response is physical. The body activates resources to protect us by preparing us either to stay and fight or to get away as fast as possible.

The body produces larger quantities of the chemical cortisol, adrenaline and noradrenaline. These trigger an increased heart rate, heightened muscle preparedness, sweating, and alertness. All these factors improve the ability to respond to a hazardous or challenging situation.

Stress refers to a response of the organism to a noxious or threatening condition (Pearlin et al. 1981). According to Selye (1993) Stress is the non-specific (i.e. common) result of any demand upon the body, be the effect mental or somatic. Harm (1993) defined, "Stress is whatever stresses people". Lovallo (1997) defined, "stress is experienced in the condition in which person-environment transactions lead to perceived discrepancy between the physical or psychological demands of a situation and the resources of the individual's biological, psychological, or social systems".

Bengt Arnetz et al., (1987) conducted a study of the effects of psychological stress on the body's ability to fight disease. Similarly Kie-colt-Glaser (1987) of Ohio University College of medicine compared the immune system functioning of married and divorced women. On several measures, the immune systems of recently divorced women functioned less well than married women. These studies offer amazing evidence for the intimate relationship between our psychological and physical selves. Leading causes of death and disability such as heart disease and stroke are almost certainly linked to stress and immunity to infection is greatly affected by stress (Cohen Williamson, 1991). It is even probable that the link between stress and immunity extends to susceptibility to cancer (O'Leary, 1990; Taylor, 1986)

Features

Following are the features of stress:

- Stress is both psychological and physical aspect
- It is common to both the genders
- It results from the deviation of expectations from actual situation
- It is symptomatic. Potential stress appears with the symptoms. If the potential stress is ignored it leads to actual stress
- Stress is treated to be negative. Nevertheless, it has positive consequences. This is called as eustress
- Stress is related to the attitude of the person. It does not occur when the person is having an indifferent attitude to the opportunity
- Stress is associated with certain common biological disorders such as heart attack, stroke, diabetic, blood pressure, neurological disorders etc.

Causes of Stress

Individuals play multiple roles in their personal life and organisations. In their personal life, they play the roles of family head, husband, father, brother and son. In social life they play the roles of club members, informal community group members, members of recreation groups, religious groups, and a number of other social groups. While playing their role in different situations, if they confront any adverse situation these create stress among them.

Stress is a psychological response to events that upset our personal balance. The potential causes are numerous. These may be linked to outside factors such as the state of the world, environment in which one lives or works or the family. It may come from one's own irresponsible behaviour, negative attitude or feeling or unrealistic expectation. The causes of stress are highly individualistic. A range of physical to emotional factors causes stress. These include threat, fear, uncertainty, frustrations, conflicts, pressures, environment, fatigue and over work.

A perceived threat will lead a person to feel stressed. This can include physical threats, social threats. A threat may lead to stress. Threat can also lead fear which again leads to stress. When there is a gap between what one does and what one thinks, there is cognitive dissonance and one feel stressed. There are many causes of stress in life like fear of death, ill health, being victim of a crime, self-abuse, family change, sexual problems, argument, physical changes, moving to new locations, financial crisis, environment and increase of responsibilities. Following aspects cause stress in the individual:

- **Frustration:** comes from obstacles that prevent from meeting one's needs or achieving personal goals. These may be internal or external.
- **Conflicts:** involving two or more incompatible needs or goals, the choice between two desirable options or decision involving disagreeable alterations.
- **Pressures:** stress can stem from expectations from others or demands placed on one.
- **Environment:** It is a response to things around us like noise, crowd, and pressure of work that causes stress.
- **Fatigue and overwork:** This kind of stress builds up over a long time and takes a hard toll. It can be caused by working too much or too hard at jobs and at home. It can also be caused by not knowing how to manage the time well and taking time for rest and relaxation.

Symptoms of Stress

Different types of symptoms occur in stress. These are as follows:

- Everyone reacts to stress differently. But there are some common symptoms of stress. One may shake uncontrollably, breathe faster, deeper than normal or even vomit. Stress can even trigger an asthma attack.
- Intellectual symptoms include mental problem, difficulty in taking decision, confusion, poor judgement, and lack of concentration.
- Physical Symptoms include digestive problem, sleep disturbance, fatigue, high blood pressure, weight gain or loss, skin problems, asthma, shortness of

breath, decreased sex drive and heart palpitations.
- Emotional symptoms are becoming moody and hyper sensitive, restlessness and anxiety, depression, anger and resentment, irritation, lack of confidence, apathy and urge to laugh or cry at inappropriate times.
- Behavioural symptoms are eating more or less, sleeplessness, isolation, neglecting responsibilities, increased alcohol, drug use, nervous habits, teeth grinding or jaw clenching, overdoing activities such as exercising or shopping, losing temper and over reacting to unexpected problems.

Factors Responsible for Creating Stress

There are three basic sources from which Individual experiences stress. These are mainly Individual factors, environmental factors and organisational factors.

i.   Individual Factors
- *Personality and individual differences*: Individual's basic dispositions are the main reasons for potential stress. Introversion, extroversion, masculinity, rigidity, locus of control, personal life, demographic differences such as age, health, education and occupation are some of the reasons causing stress in individuals.
- *Family Problems*: Family issues influence the personal life of individuals. Poor marital relationships, nagging wife, family separations, extra marital relationships, disturbing children, poor settlement of family members, aging parents, dual working couple, parenting or childcare challenges, death of spouse or other close family members are some of the reasons for greater stress in the individuals.

- *Economic Problems*: Economic difficulties are the main cause of stress. Poor management of personal finances, heavy family expenditure and constant demand for money, poor earning capacity and slow financial growth in the job are some of the economic reasons responsible for greater stress.
- *Lifestyles*: Lifestyles of individuals can cause stress. The following situations of lifestyle cause stress;
    - Sedentary lifestyles cause greater stress
    - Life trauma is potential reason for stress
- *Physiological Stressors*: Physiological stressors are situations and circumstances that affect our body. Examples of physiological stressors include rapid growth of adolescence, menopause, illness, ageing, giving birth, accidents, lack of exercise, poor nutrition and sleep disturbances.
- *Thoughts*: Thoughts play important role in causing stress. Our brain interprets and perceives situations as stressful, difficult, painful or pleasant. Some situations in life are stress provoking, but it is our thoughts that determine whether these are problem for us or not.

ii. **Environmental Factors**

The environment can bombard us with intense and competing demands to adjust. Examples of environmental stressors include weather, noise, crowding, pollution, traffic, unsafe and substandard housing and crime.

iii. **Organisational Factors**

An organisation is a combination of resources, goals, strategies and policies. In order to make people to work, organisations create structure, process and working conditions. In modern organisations, number of factors creates an environment of stress. The changing environmental dynamics, globalisation, organisational adjustment leads to stress among employees. In addition, a number of internal organisational factors cause employee stress. Organisational stressors are as follows:

- *Working conditions:* Working conditions and stress are inversely related. Employees working with poor working conditions are subject to greater stress. The factors that lead to more stress are crowded work areas, dust, heat, noise, polluted air, strong odour due to toxic chemicals, radiation, poor ventilation, unsafe and dangerous conditions, lack of privacy, etc.

- *Organisational tasks*: Organisational tasks are designed to meet the objectives and goals. Poorly designed tasks lead to greater stress. Task autonomy, task inter-dependency, task demands, task overload is some of the potential reasons for stress in organisations. Lack of adjustment and poor tolerance to others lead to greater degree of stress.

- *Administrative policies and strategies*: Employees stress is related to certain administrative strategies followed by the organisations. Downsizing, competing pressure, unfair pay structures, rigidity in rules, job rotation and ambiguous policies are some of the reasons for stress in the organisations.

- *Organisational structure and design*: As pointed out earlier organisational structure is designed to facilitate individual's interaction in the realisation of organisational goals. Certain aspects of design like specialisation, centralisation, line and staff relationships, span of control and organisational communication can severely create stress in organisations.

- *Organisation process and styles*: a number of organisational processes are designed for meeting organisational goals. Communication process, control process, decision making process, promotion process, performance appraisal process, etc. are designed for realising organisational objectives. These processes limit the scope of functioning of employees.

- *Organisational life cycle*: Every organisation moves through four phases of organisational life cycle. They are birth, growth, maturity and decline. In each of these stages the structure and the design of organisation undergoes frequent changes. In addition, human beings are subject to adapt to the stages in the life cycle. In this case employees are subject to job stress.

- *Group dynamics*: Groups are Omnipresent in organisations. Groups arise out of inherent desire of human beings and spontaneous reactions of people. In organisations both formal groups exist. Groups have a number of functional and dysfunctional consequences. They provide social support and satisfaction, which is helpful in relieving stress. At the same time, they become the source of stress also. Lack of cohesiveness, lack of social support, lack of recognition by the group and incompatible goals cause stress.

- *Workplace stressors*: Stress is created in workplace through different situations; like conflict among co-workers, unexpected/ unwanted transfer of work, location, lack of mobility/ transport of high risk patients for health facility, poor communication with co-workers, lack of support from authority, no forum to express work concerns and issues and lack of resources for doing work effectively.

Causes of Stress for Teacher

When a teacher confronts some unpleasant situations, negative emotions such as anger, anxiety, tension, frustration or depression from some aspect of his work creates stress.

Following situations are responsible for creating stress among teachers:

- Poor common room condition (small room, many individuals)
- Lack of adequate instructional materials and teaching resources
- Lack of proper facilities within a school (health, cooling, lighting, media facilities, etc.)
- Job insecurity
- Decreased job mobility
- Low salaries
- Little opportunities for promotions
- Interruptions during teaching time
- Conflict between amount of time to teach and curriculum
- Heavy workload gives teachers no time relax within a day

Effects of Stress on Teacher

Stress has many adverse impacts on teacher.

Prolonged stress has many physiological effects. These include hair loss, eating disorders, tense, muscle ache and pain, palpitations and chest discomfort, fainting, choking, indigestion and nausea, diarrhoea and frequent urination, breathlessness and hyperventilation and tension, headaches. Prolonged stress has cognitive, emotional and behavioural effects also. These are lack of concentration/ability to think rationally, being easily distracted, reduced memory, increased errors, organization and planning, deterioration, increased tension, change in personality, irritable/aggressive, depression/isolation, reduced self-esteem, speech problems, less enthusiasm, lower energy levels/sleeplessness, absenteeism and burnout, loss of interest in work, lack of motivation in teaching and learning, poor teacher-taught relationship.

Stress Management Strategies

Stress has direct or indirect relation with health. Health is associated with capacity to work, and work is associated with production. When productivity of life is lessened, one needs to manage and control stress, so that one can work efficiently and live fruitfully. The current texture of society compels us to become aware of stress and stress management.

Stress management does not imply complete elimination of stress from life. It involves removing excessive strain, that one can get rid of undesirable effects of it on mind and body. There are number of ways by which we can manage our stress. Some ways help us get immediate relief from stress; a few others make us resistance against stress by way of psychological and physical distress.

Stress management strategies that address the symptoms of stress are typically relaxation strategies.

Relaxation strategies help to reverse the stimulation caused by the stress response. Therefore, they can reduce the risk of stress related health problems. It is important to note that relaxation strategies can be useful for managing stress in the short term, but because they do not remove the root cause of stress (danger), they are not useful at managing stress in the long term.

Different stress management strategies may be adopted to remain free from stress. These are enumerated below:

- **Breathing exercises**

Breathing exercises have been scientifically shown to induce relaxation. There are several ways to perform breathing exercises. There is a method called "relaxing breath" originated from yoga.

- **Healthy living**

Adopting health enhancing behaviours can help us be less vulnerable to stress and make us better able to manage it when it arises. Health is our greatest resource and this resource will help us to manage stress. Beyond having a positive impact on stress, these behaviours are also associated with many other benefits such as reduced risk of physical and mental illness and an enhanced sense of wellbeing.

Taking healthy diet regularly also help individuals to maintain stress free life. A healthy diet should consists of plant based food items such as fruits, vegetables, grains, beans, nuts and seeds. It should be low in overall fat, saturated fat, sodium and sugar.

- **Regular physical activity**

Regular physical activity is associated with many health benefits including a significant reduction in the risk of heart disease, high blood pressure, diabetes, cancer, stroke, depression and other illness. At least 150 minutes of moderate to vigorous physical activity should be done every week.

Moderate activity includes bicycling, low impact aerobics, dancing, shovelling snow and badminton. Vigorous activities include jogging, high-impact aerobics, most competitive sports and swimming, steady- paced laps. Other forms of physical activity include stretching, yoga and weight lifting.

During physical exercise, the body releases a hormone called adrenaline. During exercise adrenaline serves a purpose as it is needed to get the body moving and keep it moving. In times of stress, the hormone is secreted but there is no physical action (running, jumping etc.) so the body stays in this stimulated state. Research reveals that a relax state usually occurs after physical activity. A few types of exercises including yoga have additional benefits as they promote body awareness and breathe control. If we are feeling stressed, we should go out for a brisk walk, play a sport with some friends or do any kind of physical activity that we enjoy. The benefits of physical activity especially regular physical activity extend well beyond stress management.

- **Stop use of tobacco**

We should quit smoking and use of tobacco to manage stress. Majority of people continue to use tobacco as they are addicted to nicotine. Nicotine stimulates the pleasure centre of the brain. When the brain of smoker is deprived of nicotine, he or she experiences negative emotions, which makes one feel stressed. Tobacco does not relieve stress in fact it causes it. Although it is difficult to quit but with one's will power one can do it.

- **Sound sleep**

    Lack of sound sleep negatively affects our health. It reduces level of energy; decreases ability to think clearly and solving problems. It also negatively affects mood and weakens immune systems.

- **Maintain healthy relationship**

    The people in our life are extremely important resources for stress management. They can provide help as well as emotional support. Although, Face book and other social networking sites are a convenient way to communicate with people, but they are not the basis of mutually beneficial, health enhancing relationships. However, we should always try to keep good relationship with other people.

- **Meditation**

    There are different methods of practicing meditation. Typically, it begins by assuming a comfortable posture such as sitting on cushion or a chair. Then by gently closing eyes one can begin to relax muscles.

- **Hobby**

    Anyone who spends time doing a hobby knows that it can also be relaxing. A hobby that is too demanding, time – consuming or expensive, however, will probably add to stress.

- **Time management**

    To be effective, we must manage our time properly. Here are some suggestions on how to reclaim our time. This includes eliminating time wasting activities, other unnecessary distractions, such as use of face book, playing computer game, and watching television etc. One should make a daily and weekly plan to long term goals and to meet personal needs. One can also break up a large project into smaller, more manageable part, set deadlines for completion of each part. Recognize that you do not have to say "yes" to every request that other make.

Teacher may adopt the following Stress Managements strategies to manage the stress in life. To deal effectively with stressful situation 'four A's need to be adopted:

Change the situation
(i) Avoid the stressor

(ii) Alter the stressor

Change your reaction
(iii) Adopt to the stressor

(iv) Accept the stressor

The above 'four A's are discussed below:

(i) **Avoid unnecessary stress**
- Not all stress can be avoided, and it is not healthy to avoid a situation that needs to be addressed.
- Learn how to say "no". Know your limits and stick to them. Whether in your personal or professional life, refuse to accept added responsibilities when you are closed to reaching them.
- Avoid the people who stress you out.
- Take control of your environment.

(ii) **Alter the situation**
- If you can't avoid a stressful situation, try to alter it. Figure out what you can do to change things so the problem doesn't present itself in future.

- Express your feelings instead of batting them up. If something or someone is bothering you, communicate your concerns in an open and respectful way.
- Be willing to compromise. When you ask someone to change their behaviour, be willing to do the same.
- Be more assertive. Do not take a backseat in own life. Deal with problems head on, doing your best to anticipate and prevent them.
- Manage your time better. Poor time management can cause a lot of stress.

(iii) **Adopt to the stressor**

If you can't change the stressor, change yourself. For this you can:

- Reframe problems
- Adjust your standards
- Look at the big picture
- Focus on the positive

(iv) **Accept the things you can't change**

Some sources of stress are unavoidable. You can't prevent or change stressor such as death of a loved one, a serious illness or many other things. In such cases, the best way to cope with stress is to accept things as they are.

- Don't try to control the uncontrollable
- Share your feelings
- Learn to forgive
- Make time for fun and relaxation

Teacher should do the following activities in professional life to manage the stress:

- Prioritise activities and tasks
- Develop self-confidence in him
- Accept challenges
- Ready to experiment
- Ability to take decision
- Ability to negotiate
- Ability to accept constructive criticism
- Be democratic in action and decision
- Accept change as integral part of life
- Adapt to innovations

At present, stress is a common phenomenon and has become a way of life. The cause and effect relationship in stress is difficult to obtain because it is a psychological phenomena. Stress of teachers can be reduced by identifying the stressors. Changes in life style and other small strategies can help to deal with stress effectively. Learning to be assertive, taking regular exercise, avoiding alcohol and drug can reduce stress. Time management, sharing thoughts, listening music or relaxation strategies are some of the simple ways to manage stress. Stress management is highly essential on the part of teacher. Development of education, student and institution largely depend on teacher. So, teachers' good health is the first essential. Teacher plays a vital role in building the character and personality of students. Teacher has a unique position in the society. If teacher remains stressful, it has adverse impact on teaching-learning process, personality development of students' and above all institutional development. So, the teacher should always be free from stress.

Chapter-15

Views of Great Educationists for Teacher

Teacher plays the most influential role in student's life. They are good role models, trusted friends and even confidants for their students. A successful teacher develops an affinity with, an understanding of and a harmonious relationship with his/her pupils. They modifies behaviour, transmit knowledge and skills, ignite the mind, enlightened the personality of the students. Several prominent educational thinkers and philosophers of India and west recognised the superior and prominent role of the teacher in the educational endeavour.

Swami Dayananda

Swami Dayananda was born in an orthodox Brahmin family in 1824 in Kathiawar of Gujarat. Creation of ideal man was his aim of education. Swami Dayananda supported the ancient Indian education i.e., Dharma, Artha, Kama and Moksha.

Swami Dayananda emphasized that there should be an intimate relationship between the 'Acharya' (preceptor) and the 'Antebasi' (disciple). He says education cannot be a one-way process. It is a bi-polar process, where the teacher and the child learn. He gave a code of conduct for the students and the teachers. A teacher should have a high moral character. He should have a good academic background and should treat all the students equally. He should help the students to lead a simple life like the students of the 'Gurukulas'. Students should study regularly and lead a life of celibacy. Teachers should be parents' substitute. Their relationship should be like the relationship between the parents and children. The teacher should be a strict disciplinarian. He should control the students through the instrument of love and affection.

Rabindranath Tagore

Rabindranath Tagore, the brilliant poet of India and the founder of Visva-bharati was born in Calcutta on 7th May 1861. He was a great educational practitioner. Tagore was fully traditional as far as teacher is concerned. In his view, the teacher should be fully learned, celibate, men of high character, ideal conduct, patient and devoted to the children. He expected of the teacher to understand individual differences of the students, to arrange proper education for them, and behave with them with love and sympathy. He termed despotic teachers as jail wardens. Tagore supported nationalism and international goodwill. Teachers alone can develop nationalism and internationalism in the children. For this all, he considered the need of teacher training.

Tagore was against the mechanical and parrot like repetition used by our teachers. He was an ardent lover of the children. He had an implicit faith in the child's inborn potentialities. So, he wanted to give the child an opportunity for full development of his potentialities. For the expression of his potentialities, Tagore felt that the environment is more important than the formal rules and methods, techniques and text-books, buildings and equipment. He was concerned with the association of body and mind to establish a harmony.

Tagore tried to recreate our traditional intimacy between the teacher and the student. In this process, both the students and the teachers lived together in natural surroundings leading the discipline life of celibacy (Brahamacharya). The minds of the teacher and students are awakened through the process. They come close to learn from each other. The teacher has to create a creative atmosphere in the Ashram. Tagore says, "they only deserve to be teachers who are patient and tolerant". A teacher should be prepared to accept his students as his friends. On ideal teacher, Tagore says, "only he can teach, who can love. The greatest teachers of men have been lovers of men. The teaching is a gift. It is a sacrifice. It is not a manufactured article of routine work, and because it is a living thing, it is the fulfilment of knowledge of the teacher himself". Further, Tagore says, 'Teacher is like a lamp lighting other lamps. But a lamp cannot put light into other lamps if it does not itself burn and shed light."

Swami Vivekananda

Swami Vivekananda, the patriot saint of India, was born in Calcutta in a Bengali Kayasta family on 12th January, 1863. Vivekananda laid great emphasis on the personal contact of the pupil with the teacher-"Guru grihavasa". One should live from his very boyhood with one whose character is like blazing fire and should have before him a living example of the highest teaching. Without the personal life of a teacher there would be no education. The teacher should be a Tyagi (man of renunciation). He should act as a friend and guide of the child. He should consider teaching as worship to God. Every soul is the soul of God and every child is a God. Hence the teacher should serve children in the spirit of service to God.

Swami Vivekananda believes that all teaching is a process of giving and taking: the teacher gives and the students receive. Therefore, effective participation of the students and teachers is essential in the educative process. Swamiji rightly says, "The true teacher is he who can immediately come down to the level of the student and transfer his soul to the student's soul and see through and understand through his mind. Such a teacher can really teach and no one else".

Swami Vivekananda rightly stated that, "we want that education by which character is formed, strength of mind is increased, intellect is expanded by which one can stand on one's own feet. The ideal of all education, all training should be man making. The work of man making is done by the ideal teacher".

Swamiji advocates that the nature of the human mind is such that "no one ever really taught by another, each of us has to be teacher himself". The work of the external teacher is only to give suggestion and the rest is to be done by the internal teacher himself, the mind within. The external teacher should act like a doctor, who understands the nature of the child and must know the proper method to tackle him in the best manner possible. A modern teacher imparts bookish knowledge simply to prepare them for an examination. Swamiji does not accept this modern attitude. He wants that a teacher should be like a father, who will give the students their spiritual birth and show them the way to eternal life. He should initiate the students to practise the essential virtues of Brahamcharya and Shradha.

Mahatma Gandhi

Mahatma Gandhi, the father of the nation, the apostle of truth and non-violence was born in Gujarat on 2nd October, 1869. He was a great educationist and has contributed a lot to the field of education. He has given his views on teacher.

Gandhiji said the teacher should be an ideal person, torch of knowledge and man of good conduct. In his view, a person taking this profession as a mere profession cannot become an ideal teacher. A teacher can become an ideal teacher only when he accepts this profession as an act of social service. He has to function in several forms, as father, friend, assistant and guide to the students, so he should be forbearing, liberal and patient. The teacher must have those qualities which he wants to promote in children. Gandhiji believed that students learnt more from the personality of a teacher than from books and lectures. In the words of Gandhi, "it is possible for a teacher situated miles away to affect the spirit of the pupils by his way of living".

Gandhi advocates devotion to the teacher (Guru-Bhakti), He says "education of the heart could only be done through the living touch of the teacher". Education becomes effective and fruitful only to the extent to which there is personal touch between the teacher and the taught. A flower is blossomed is loved by all and in this lies its glory. Similarly man may be viewed as having achieved everything in life when he becomes perfect in character. Teacher should develop good character which will help them to elicit devotion from the students. It will be very difficult to achieve character building in the absence of devotion to the teacher. Gandhi anticipated a non-violent personality of the teacher. He should have devotion to duty, to the students and to God. He is to play the role of a mother. Therefore, Gandhiji in his book 'My views on Education' says "One who can not take the place of a mother cannot be a teacher". So, throughout his book he has used the word mother teacher instead of teacher. Because the teacher must really be a mother of the children, the child should never feel that he is being taught. Let her simply keep her eye upon him and guide him.

Sri Aurobindo

Sri Aurobindo was a great leader of India. He was a saint, patriot, philosopher, poet, political leader and educationist. Teaching in Integral system of education is considered as a "Sacred Trust". The teacher occupies a very important place in this system. He should have a high level of personality. He should develop traits like self-control, absence of superiority and spiritual equality of man. He should be free from egoism. About the quality of the teacher, Sri Aurobindo says, "He is a man helping his brothers, a child leading children, a light kindling other lights, an awakened soul awakening other souls, at highest a power." The Guru (Teacher) should have three instruments- teaching, examples and influence to make his teaching lively and effective. A good company or "satsanga" is another important quality for a teacher. The mother on teacher says, "One must be a saint, and a hero to be good teacher. One must become a great 'yogi' to be a good teacher". The teacher should have close contact with the students. Knowledge of psychology is also recommended for the teacher in Aurobindo school. He assumed the role of the teacher as friend, philosopher, guide and helper.

The teacher is not an instructor or task-master; he is a helper and guide. His business is to suggest and not to impose. He does not actually train the pupil's mind, he only shows him how to perfect his instruments of knowledge and helps and encourages him in the process. He does not impart knowledge to him; he shows him how to acquire knowledge for himself. He does not call forth the knowledge for himself. He does not call forth the knowledge that is within. He only shows him where it lies and how it can be habituated to rise to the surface.

In brief, the teacher should be an integral yogi. He should be to eliminate his ego, master his mind, develop an insight into human nature and to progress in impersonalisation. He should be absolutely disciplined and having an integrated personality.

Gopabandhu Das

Utkalmani Pandit Gopabandhu Das was born on 9th October in 1877 in a small village Suando, near Sahkigopal of Puri district. He founded a garden school in Sakhigopal which was known as "Satyabadi Vanavidyalay" or the School in the Grove". It had great impact on the national life of Odisha.

Gopabandhu's Satyabadi system of education was built in the ideals of ancient Gurukula system. Satyabadi School was started with highly educated teachers like Pandit Nilakantha Dash, Pandit Godabarisha Mishra, Krupasindhu Mishra, Acharya Harihara, Pandit Basudev Mohapatra who worked on small pittances, sacrificing lucrative jobs. Teachers were talented and dedicated to the all-round development of students and institution. The teacher had a very great role to accomplish in all the activities. They remained exemplary for the students and for the society as a whole. Teachers were ideal and living a very simple life. There was close relationship between teacher and student. For this, Gopabandhu has aptly said, "A school does not consist of only buildings, chairs and tables; there must be educated, sincere and idealistic teachers"(Das, 1976). Teachers bore high morale and were versatile geniuses spreading their fragrance all over Odisha. They were never perturbed by the questions of students, but considered it as their pious duty to get their doubts clarified. They were the real friend, philosopher and guide of the students. Besides the regular class room teaching, every teacher had some extra duty to be accomplished. These include, looking after hostel, student discipline, debate and discussion, excursion and field trip, morning assembly and prayer, distribution of reliefs to the marooned people at the time of flood etc.

Sarvepalli Radhakrishnan

Sarvepalli Radhakrishnan, was an Indian philosopher and statesman.He says, "The end-product of education should be a free creative man, who can battle against historical circumstances and adversities of nature".

Sarvepalli Radhakrishnan rightly opines, 'the teacher's place in society is of vital importance. He acts as the pivot for the transmission of intellectual tradition and technical skills from generation to generation and helps to keep the lamp of civilization burning. He not only guides the individual, but also so to say, the destiny of the nation. Teachers are removers of spiritual blindness. 'Andhakaranirodhata gurur ityabhidhyate'. 'Andhakar' is not merely intellectual ignorance but spiritual blindness. He who can remove that kind of spiritual blindness is called a 'guru'. He must be an example of 'sadachar' or good conduct. He must inspire the pupils who are entrusted to his care with love of virtue and goodness and abhorrence of cruelty and violence. Our teachers are the reservoirs of this new spirit, the new spirit of adventure in intellectual, social matters and political matters. If you do not have that spirit, you cannot communicate that spirit to the youth, who are entrusted to your care. Radhakrishanan rightly says, "Teachers, according to our tradition, have sovereign over themselves and servants of people. They maintain absolute control over their own feelings and try to help humanity to the extent possible. That has been the tradition. The greatest teachers of our country have been those who have made over civilization live". Therefore, he says, "The teacher's place in society is of vital importance. He acts as the pivot for the transmission of intellectual traditions and technical skills from generation to generation and helps to keep the lamp of civilization burning".

APJ Abdul Kalam

Dr. A.P.J. Abdul Kalam is known as missile man in the World. He was scientist and become 11th president of India. But as he writes, he wanted to be known as teacher. Dr. Kalam writes that if people remember me as a good teacher it will be the biggest honour for me. When he became the president in 2002, he made no compromise on his pen chart for teaching. To him, teaching is a very noble profession that shapes the character, caliber and future of an individual.

According to Kalam, "Better than a thousand days of diligent study is one day with a great teacher". "Your heart is slightly larger than the average human heart, but that's because you're a teacher". "Teachers can change lives with the right mix of chalk and challenges". "Teaching is the greatest act of optimism".

The teacher provides knowledge and facilitates shaping the student's with great dreams and aims. The teacher creates self-confidence in the students and helps them inculcate the idea "I can do it" spirit through the process of education and learning. The teacher does not create "parrots". Learning needs freedom to think and freedom to imagine. The purpose of teaching is to create nation building capabilities in the students. Dr. Abdul Kalam says, "I believe there is no other profession in the world that is more important in society than that of a teacher". He also says, "Teachers are the backbone of any country, the pillar upon which the aspirations of students are reconverted into realities. The teachers must be perpetual seekers of intellectual integrity and universal compassion".

Jiddu Krishnamurti

Jiddu Krishnamurti, an eminent educationist, has a lot of contribution to the field of education. According to him, the educator has to be careful, thoughtful and affectionate in the creation of the right environment for the development of understanding to enable the child to deal intelligently with human problems. In order to achieve all this, the educator needs to understand himself, instead of relying on ideologies, systems and beliefs. Let the educator not be concerned in terms of principles and ideals, but be concerned with things as they are. The teacher will not depend upon a method, but will study each individual pupil. In his relationship with young pupils and children, the teacher is dealing not with mechanical devices, but with human beings who are impressionable, volatile, sensitive, afraid and affectionate. In order to deal with them, a great of patience and understanding are needed.

Teachers try to shape the pupils ways of thinking and feeling and mould them in accordance with their own cravings and intentions. Many parents and teachers often seek to fulfil themselves in their children, and build walls around them, conditioning them by their own beliefs and ideologies, fears and hopes. But the right kind of teacher helps each individual pupil to become aware of himself and the influence around him. If the teacher is merely an instrument for imparting knowledge, there can be no respect for him from his pupils. In order to obtain respect from his pupils, he must respect his pupils first, and treat them as intelligent beings otherwise he can only get indifference or even disrespect from them.

The best teachers are those who become teachers by their own choice, and not by persuasion or selection by others. Dedication and vitality are needed in all teachers. The teacher should discuss matters relating to the classroom and well-being of the students with them. The teacher should encourage students to be considerate and to understand the moods and peculiarities of their classmates, and to be helpful, kind, thoughtful and patient in their relationships with their classmates and other schoolmates. Discouraging pupils from merely accepting statements from books, and formulae, and exercising their critical thinking and judgment, questioning and skepticism need to be part of the educative process in the classroom. Creative intelligence is thereby being encouraged by the teacher.

The teacher will not guide the student to any particular vocational goal, because that impairs creativity. He can help the student to discover what he is most interested in, so that he may be able ultimately to find his own vocation. An educator is not merely a giver of information; he is the one who points the way for his students to attain wisdom and truth, because he does not teach pupils what to think, but how to think. The true educator is inwardly rich and should be given the highest place in an enlightened society.

In the opinion of J. Krishnamurti, the teacher himself should be a total human being and an integrated man, only in such a situation he can transform children as total human beings and integrated men. He has emphasized on these two facts; first, the teacher should love the children and treat them affectionately; and second, he should only help the children in learning, they will learn of their own.

Dr. Zakir Husain

In view of Dr. Zakir Husain, teacher is the custodian of the highest values. What type of man is the good teacher? Human types have been characterised by Dr. Zakir Husain based on some dominating principles. "The highest principle of theoretical man is Truth, that of the imaginative man Beauty, that of the economic man Gain, that of the religious man Salvation, that of the political man Power, that of the social man Love. Pure types are, of course, rare but some principle predominates. The good teacher, as I see him, is predominantly a character of the social type". The dominating note in the social type to which the teacher belongs is love for other fellowmen, a sense of solidarity with them, an urge to help them and belong to them and to experience joy in giving oneself up for them. The teacher is not to dictate or dominate, he is to help and serve, to mould and shape in faith and love. He has to transmit these values to his pupils through the magic of his own personality. He can only do this if he has himself experienced these values.

Friedrich August Froebel

Friedrich August Froebel, a German was born in the village of Oberweisbach on April 21, 1782. He was the originator of the kindergarten system and one of the outstanding educationists during the last century. He is famous in the history of education and an ardent lover of childhood, and an apostle of play in education. The philosophy of education, which he inherited about the nature of the child, is proved from his famous saying, "come, let us live for our children".

Froebel started the employment of women as teacher in nursery schools. According to him, women can work as the substitute of the mother for the children. They can act as mothers and can live for the children. They are more sympathetic and patient than men. Their function is to look after the young plants (small children) grow according to their own natural course of development under their care. In his words, "the tree germ bears within itself the nature of the whole tree", "the development and formation of the whole future life of each being is contained in the beginning of its existence. The teacher being a gardener, in the kindergarten (children's garden) cannot remain entirely passive. He should provide them with necessary guidance at the time of need". For instance, when the children are offered gifts, it is the duty of the teacher to suggest them the occupations connected with these gifts. He is required to sing songs connected with these gifts also. Thus, under the guidance of the teacher, the children can develop correct ideas. Froebel's education is a controlled development. Hence, it is the function of the teacher to control the process of education. As a result of which the children can attain self-development through self-activities under the guidance of the teacher.

John Dewey

John Dewey, a great educationist was born in Burlington in the year 1859. He is one of the most productive and influential philosophers that the world has ever produced. The educational ideas and ideals of John Dewey though revolutionary in character, were founded on sound logic.

According to Dewey,"The teacher is a guide and director; he steers the boat, but the energy that propels it must come from those who are learning. The more a teacher is aware of the past experiences of students, of their hopes, desires, chief interests, the better will he understand the forces at work that need to be directed and utilized for the formation of reflective habits".

Teacher is considered as the prophet of the true God."The teacher is engaged, not simply in the training of individuals, but in the formation of the proper social life". Every teacher should realize the dignity of his calling; that he is a social servant set apart for the maintenance of proper social order and the securing of the right social growth. In this way the teacher always is the prophet of the true God and the usher of the true kingdom of God.

Dewey supported democratic ideology. He respected the individuality of man, so while looking at the teacher with respect; he did not allow him to impose his ideals on the students. He took the teacher as a social worker. He said that the function of the teacher is to create such an environment that the children become able to find solutions to their problems by taking part in it and develop interest and skill for the execution of required activities as needed in the practical life. He termed it as social efficiency. Thus, Dewey accepted the teacher as the planner of proper environment and guide to the children.

Dewey has given sufficient freedom to the teacher to frame curriculum and carry on the administration of his ideal school. He cannot impose his will on the pupils, first, he should plan the environment and through it to guide the experiences of the children. The inspector of school cannot criticise the activities of the teachers. They will simply give sympathetic suggestions and advice to create a healthy learning situation.

Maria Montessori

Maria Montessori, the originator of the Montessori Method was born in Italy in 1870. She worked with feeble minded children at the psychiatric clinic of Rome University. From her experience of dealing with these children, she concluded that feeble-mindedness is after due to the dullness of the senses. She diagnosed sense training for them and found marvellous results. She became one of the greatest thinkers of education of the present century.

Dr. Montessori says that "education is the active help given to the normal expansion of the life of the child". The child is potential being and education should aim at its full development. Nothing is to be added to the child to what he already is. It is only unfolding and developing what already exists. In her words, "If any educational act is to be efficacious it will be only that which tends to help towards the complete unfolding of the child's individuality, the child has a body which grows and a soul which develops". "The broader the teacher's scientific culture and practice in experimental psychology, the sooner would come for her the marvel of unfolding life, and her interest in it". "The more fully the teacher is acquainted with the methods of experimental psychology, the better will she understand how to give a lesson". Thus, according to Montessori, education should be considered as development from within and not from without. Individual attention should be paid to each child. Education should guide the process of unfolding of the latent powers of the child-the sheds of what he is destined to become by nature.

Montessori treats each child as an individual. The

teachers are not teachers in Montessori Schools, because they do not teach the children. They are nothing but directors as they simply direct and guide the movements of children. The teacher studies the child as a psychologist, a scientist and a doctor.

In the Montessori system, the most important function of teacher is to observe the psychological and individual development of the child and to develop his psychic activity. The teacher is an active observer, a guide. He is to provide the required environment and material at the right moment. Thus, he helps the child in his auto-development. That is why Montessori prefers to call a "directress" about whom it has been well pointed out: "Instead of felicity of speech she has to acquire the power of silence; instead of teaching she has to observe; Instead of the proud dignity of and when claims to be infallible she assumes the vesture of humility".

Montessori thinks that a teacher should care for the child like a gardener who cares for the plant so that the natural growth of the child is properly guided and aided in the process of unfolding itself. She should allow the child to grow according to his own inner law. Her business is to provide for suitable environments to children with suitable opportunities to think for themselves. In the words of Montessori, the Directress should be partly doctor, partly scientist and completely religious. Like a doctor she should avoid scolding or suppressing the patient in order to avoid worst situations. Like a scientist she should wait patiently for the results and should conduct experiments with her material. Like a religious lady she should be there to serve the child.

Chapter-16

Teacher Education for Sustainable Development

The concept of sustainable development emerged as a response to a growing concern about human society's impact on the natural environment. In 1987, Brundtland Commission defined sustainable development as, "development that meets the needs of the present without compromising the ability of future generations to meet their own needs". Sustainable development is thought to have three components: Environment, Society and Economy. The wellbeing of three areas is intertwined and not separate. For example, a healthy, prosperous society relies on a healthy environment to provide food and resources, safe drinking water, and clean air for its citizens. Sustainable development may also be defined as a vision of development that encompasses population, animal and plant species, ecosystems, natural resources, water, air, energy and that integrates concerns such as the fight against poverty, gender equality, human rights, education for all, health, human security, inter-cultural dialogue etc. The Sustainable Development Goals (SDGs) address the shortcomings and challenges of the UN's Millennium Development Goals (MDGs) and promise to provide the foundation for a global green economy. The growth of any country into a great nation is only possible if there are skilled and enthusiastic teachers to inculcate the appropriate knowledge, aptitude and skills. The education of teacher must be given by the government through appropriate and efficient teacher education programme. Teacher provides the necessary competency, skills, knowledge and ideas that would convert the individual into efficient and useful member of the community he belongs to.

Sustainable development is described by the United Nations Economic Commission for Europe (UNECE): Strategy for Education for Sustainable Development as being underpinned by an ethic of solidarity, equality and mutual respect among people, countries, cultures and generations: it is development in harmony with nature, meeting the needs of the present generation without compromising the ability of future. Sustainable development requires:

- Balancing environmental, social, and economic considerations in the pursuit of development and an improved quality of life
- Promoting the ideals of gender equity, just and peaceful societies, human rights, environmental preservation and restoration, cultural diversity and poverty alleviation.

Principles of Sustainable Development

The Rio Declaration on Environment and Development fleshes out the definition by listing eighteen principles of sustainability. These are stated below:

- People are entitled to a healthy and productive life in harmony with nature.
- Development of today must not undermine the development and environment needs of present and future generations.

- Nations have the sovereign right to exploit their own resources, but without causing environmental damage beyond their borders.
- Nations shall develop international laws to provide compensation for damage that activities under their control cause to areas beyond their borders.
- Nations shall use the precautionary approach to protect the environment. Where there are threats of serious or irreversible damage, scientific uncertainty shall not be used to postpone cost effective measures to prevent environmental degradation.
- In order to achieve sustainable development, environmental protection shall constitute an integral part of the development process, and cannot be considered in isolation from it.
- Eradicating poverty and reducing disparities in living standards in different parts of the world are essential to achieve sustainable development and meet the needs of the majority of people.
- Nations shall cooperate to conserve, protect and restore the health and integrity of the Earth's eco system. The developed countries need to acknowledge the responsibility that they bear in the international pursuit of sustainable development in view of the pressures their societies place on the global environment and of the technologies and financial resources they command.
- Nations should reduce and eliminate unsustainable patterns of production and consumption, and promote appropriate demographic policies.
- Environmental issues can best be handled with the participation of all concerned citizens. Nations

shall facilitate and encourage public awareness and participation by making environmental information widely available.

- Nations shall enact effective environmental laws, and develop national law regarding liability for the victims of pollution and other environmental damage. Where they have authority, nations shall assess the environmental impact of proposed activities that are likely to have a significant adverse impact.
- Nations should cooperate to promote an open international economic system that will lead to economic growth and sustainable development in all countries. Environmental Policies should not be used as an unjustifiable means of restricting international trade.
- The polluter should, in principle must bear the cost of pollution.
- Nations shall warn one another of national disasters or activities that may have harmful trans-boundary impacts.
- Sustainable development requires better scientific understanding of the problems. Nations should share knowledge and innovative technologies to achieve the goal of sustainability.
- The full participation of women is essential to achieve sustainable development. The creativity, ideals and courage of youth and the knowledge of indigenous people are needed too. Nations should recognize and support the identity, culture and interests of indigenous people.
- Welfare is inherently destructive of sustainable devel-

opment, and Nations shall respect international laws protecting the environment in times of armed conflict, and shall cooperate in their further establishment.

- Press, development and environmental protection are interdependent and indivisible.

Education for Sustainable Development (ESD)

Education for sustainable development allows every human being to acquire the knowledge, skills, attitudes and values necessary to shape a sustainable future. Education for sustainable development means including key sustainable development issues into teaching and learning; for example, climate change, disaster risk reduction, biodiversity, poverty reduction and sustainable consumption. It also requires participatory teaching and learning methods that motivate and empower learners to change their behaviour and take action for sustainable development. Education for sustainable Development consequently promotes competencies like critical thinking, imagining future scenarios and making decisions in a collaborative way. Education for Sustainable Development requires far-reaching changes in the way education is often practised today. UNESCO is the lead agency for the UN Decade of Education for Sustainable Development (2005-2014).

Societies generally expect educational systems to prepare young people for their future professional life and/or continued studies. The educational system is seen as having a socialising role and is expected to contribute to preparing young people to take up their responsibilities in helping to shape the complex society in which we all now live. There are different problems in education. The introduction of issues of sustainable development in the curriculum of both primary and secondary education is therefore strongly recommended by several international organisations, such as UNESCO and UNECE. Above we described issues of sustainable development as complex because of the tight connections between social, economic and ecological aspects, but also because many proposed solutions, may lead to new (global) risks. This implies that education for sustainable development requires at least a holistic approach, rather than the reductionist approach which is common in traditional educational systems. Indeed, a reductionist approach can often be the origin of these problems. It follows that, if we desire a consensus rather than a compromise, then sustainability challenges need to be approached at a systemic level.

Education increases human welfare, and is a decisive factor in enabling people to become productive and responsible members of the society. A fundamental prerequisite for sustainable development is an adequately financed effective educational system at all levels of education. The levels of education are accessible to all and that augments both human capacity and well-being. The core themes of education for sustainability include lifelong learning, interdisciplinary education, partnerships, multicultural education and empowerment. Special attention should also be paid to the training of teachers, youth leaders and other educators. There is a need to reorient education, create awareness and organise training so as to promote widespread public understanding, critical analysis and support for sustainable development.

For sustainable development education should develop:
- The competence to understand and to change his / her own living conditions

- Competence to participate in collective decision making
- Competence to show solidarity with those who are unable to control their living conditions because of a diversity of reasons

Educating for sustainable future is a formidable challenge. What is to be sustained? What is to be developed? Who are the key assets to development? What kind of world do we want for the future? The new vision of education for sustainable development places education at the heart of the quest to solve the problems threatening our future. Education- in all its forms and at all levels- is seen not only as an end in itself but also as one of the most powerful instruments for bringing about the changes required to achieve sustainable development. Teachers, of course, are vital actors in this process and consequently have been given special attention.

Education has an important role in enabling people to live together in ways that contribute to sustainable development. Education and training should contribute to all three areas of sustainable development, namely:

- The Social perspective- education and training strengthen social cohesion by investment in human capital;
- The Economic Perspective- education and training contribute to building a knowledge society based on sustainable economic growth; and
- The Environmental perspective- Education and training are crucial for changes in citizens' behaviour on issues such as: consumption, transport, use of sustainable energies, etc.

According to Scott (2002), Education for Sustainable

Development (ESD) should encourage schools to stimulate their pupils to reflect on their own lifestyle regarding sustainability issues. It implies that they should be able to reflect on the concept of sustainable development with respect to decisions they take in the context of their own life. Lijmbach (2000) considers the role of education as an instrument for the development of automatically thinking persons. They strongly emphasize, together with other researchers (Rauch, 2004) a critical reflection of the different visions on sustainable development and even on the desirability of sustainable development.

The paramount importance of education in effecting social change is recognised. Mainstreaming education must now be realigned to promote awareness, attitudes, concerns and skills that will lead to sustainable development. Basic education which promotes awareness, attitudes, concerns and skills that will lead to sustainable development. Basic education which promotes functional literacy, livelihood skills, understanding of the immediate environment and values of responsible citizenship is a precondition for sustainable development. Such education must be available to every child as fundamental right irrespective of their economic class, geographical location and cultural disparity. Adequate resource and support for education for sustainable development are essential.

Teacher Education and Sustainable Development

During the 1990's UNESCO acknowledged teacher education institutions and teacher educators as main elements in reorienting education to address sustainability. Later, in 1998 the United Nations Commission on sustainable development called for UNESCO to build up guidelines for reorienting teacher training to address sustainability.

Teacher education is a priority for UNESCO and, indeed, for the international community as a whole. Within its special work programme on education, the United Nations Commissions on sustainable development invited UNESCO to make a significant effort to help teachers worldwide not only to understand sustainable development concepts and issues but also to learn how to cope with interdisciplinary, value-laden subjects in established curricula.

UN World Summit in Johannesburg in 2002 accentuated reorientation of education system for sustainable development.Education for sustainable development promotes the progress of knowledge, skill, understanding, values and action which are essential for creating a sustainable world. The Organization of Economic Cooperation and Development also suggested higher educational institutions have vital role in practicing on campus water and energy efficiency practice, green campus and eco-friendly way of life. So, teachers of all levels of educational institutions have the responsibility for creating sustainable future.

For promotion of equitable and sustainable development of all sections of society, the young generations to be educated through perspectives of gender equity, values for peace, respect for the rights of all and respect to the value of work. Extreme commercialisation and competitive life style of people has brought ecological crisis. Children should be aware of the harm of exploiting natural resources and learn to conserve it, change their attitude towards pattern of consumption. Increasing violence among the people has brought stress in the society. Teacher education has a crucial role to play in promoting values of peace based on equal respect of self and others. NCF-2005 states, teacher education as a whole needs urgent and comprehensive reform to meet the need of the present scenario for sustainable development.

Sustainable Development Programmes for Teacher

Teacher education includes both pre-service and in-service programmes. Both aim to prepare prospective teachers for sustaining the future of the nation. Following activities will help the teachers towards sustainable development.

i. **Professional development programme**

Professional development initiative is a central aspect for improving the competencies and empowering teacher and teacher educators. The prospective teachers should be given training to develop their competencies to adapt themselves to the new challenges and changing nature of the society. They need to be well trained in reflective practices.

A Chinese proverb states, 'If you give people fish, they can eat for a day, but if you teach them to catch fish, they can eat for a lifetime'. In this context, it can be suggested that pre-service teachers should be taught how to catch fish for themselves, that is, to take ownership of their learning. This reveals that there is a close association between teachings for the short term needs of pre-service teachers and teaching for their long term needs. UNESCO recommends three principles of professional development, academic rigour, experimental learning and reflection.

- **Academic rigour:** It demands from the teacher educators and student teachers the up to date knowledge about key issues related to global realities and sustainable development themes from many disciplines.

- **Experimental learning:** Education for a sustainable future must be based upon an experimental learning process that invites teachers to analyse and interpret information in a variety of forms (e.g., ext, tables, diagrams, computer games and linked WWW-sites);review new knowledge in the light of current understandings; reflect upon and generalize from learning experiences, develop skills in a wide variety of teaching and learning strategies; and adapt and apply new ideas and skills to practical educational tasks. The student teachers need to be provided with a lot of 'experiences' which help them to convey the ideas of the teacher educator.
- **Reflection:** Reflection is integral to the professional development experiences in education for a sustainable future.
- **Mentoring:** Through mentoring the teacher educators is to provide pre-service teachers with classroom opportunities that serve as a basis both for the learning of curriculum and assessment and for issues of teaching particular concepts and of assessing students. Teacher educators should redesign their course in a way that modelled the development of the classroom atmosphere and approaches to teaching and assessing that meets individual needs. He should create a safe and inviting place for them to post questions and write about how they are making sense of the issues of teaching and learning in which they are engaged.

ii. **Curriculum development**

The review of curriculum documents needs competencies. Different approaches to educational practice have been suggested for educators to develop competencies. For practice of competencies they should be supported by a curriculum which reflects various educational approaches. Text book and other materials should be reviewed to determine whether they reflect educational approaches for development of competencies. Materials need to be developed to further ESD. According to a report of UNESCO, competencies for teacher educators includes following four broad categories:

- Learning to know
- Learning to do
- Learning to live together
- Learning to be

These four categories include some common features of ESD namely: a. A holistic approach, which seeks integrative thinking and practice; b. Envisioning change, which explores alternative futures, learns from the past and inspires engagement in the present; and c. Achieving transformation, which serves to change in the way people learn and in the systems that support learning.

The UNECEF Strategy for ESD and the UNESCO international Implementation Scheme for the United Nations Decade for Education for Sustainable Development (2005-2014) suggest a broad range of concepts and topics that can serve as entry points, including peace studies; ethics and philosophy; citizenship; democracy and governance; human rights; poverty alleviation; cultural diversity; biological and landscape diversity; environmental protection; ecological principles and an ecosystem approach, natural resource management; climate change, personal and family health (e.g., HIV/AIDS, drug abuse); environmental health (e.g. food, water pollution) corporate social responsibility; indigenous knowledge; corporate social responsibility; indigenous knowledge; production and/or consumption patterns; economics; rural/ urban development; environmental technology; and sustainability assessment.

iii. Monitoring and assessment

Audit, assessment as well as monitoring systems for educational institutions should be developed in order to assess contribution of institution towards sustainable development. Educational institutions should operate according to sustainable development principles as a contribution to ESD and create an enabling environment for the development and practice of competencies.

iv. Governing and managing institutions

The management and governance of the institution should be supportive to sustainable development. Governance should also ensure transparency and accountability in its functioning. This will ensure legitimacy of ESD practices, as well as improve and further develop the competencies. It is essential that management should use evaluation as an important learning tool that plays an integral part in strategic planning.

Sustainable Pedagogy

Understanding of sustainable development and environmental awareness is a burning issue these days therefore it should be the first lesson for the child. Environmental education should be an important part of the curriculum at the entire levels. i.e., primary to higher education. The central aim of environment and sustainable development must include helping students learn how to identify elements of unsustainable development. It has become very essential on the part of the teacher to explore sustainable pedagogies in a way to bring home strategies that imparts love and concerns for nature and issues concerning the environment.

Sustainable pedagogies may be considered as instructional strategies that reflect the philosophy of sustainability which comprises of values based on simplicity, conservation, preservation and harmony with nature. Sustainable pedagogies may be considered as falling in line with the view that education as sustainability, or sustainable education, is holistic where learning is approached as change, requiring the engagement of the whole person and institution (Sterling, 2001).

Sustainable pedagogies are the way of teaching that advocate sustainable practice to save energy. Saving energy is not in the physical sense but in the process of teaching that can go a long way in bringing in the right changes. Increasing teaching efficiency by choosing the right strategy for a topic and matching a topic area to appropriate strategy also renders teaching sustainable. For example, the abstract concepts relating to environment, the teacher should teach students by doing practical and by demonstration in the classroom.

Pedagogical practices incorporate sustainable practices entails the use of appropriate instructional strategies that foster creativity, problem solving, project execution and implementation, communication and collaboration. As the environment is primary concern of sustainable development so any instructional strategy that gives opportunities to interact with the environment need to be encouraged. Teaching strategies should include the advocacy enquiry, involving investigation of differing viewpoints, debate and discussions all of which would enable students to develop, express and justify their own views about sustainability issues (Huckle, 2005, & UNESCO, 2005). Sustainable teaching has key features which nurtures a shift from knowledge sharing to transforming learners just as in the 'education as sustainability' point of view (Cotton & Winter, 2010).

Sustainable instructional practices promote participatory learning activities where there is no role and scope for social hierarchies and learning hierarchies. Learning happens together through mutual give and take and sharing of ideas. Sustainability tends to simplify issues and encourages simplicity in living and thinking. Sustainable pedagogies highlight simplicity in teaching by making the activities simple and learning tasks feasible and comprehensible.

Instructional strategies that minimize wastage of resources are sustainable as there is less wastage of learning resources like paper note books, writing materials etc. Technology empowered classrooms and techno pedagogies are sustainable. It also embodies the principle of reuse and recycle.

Role of Teacher for Sustainable Development

For sustainable development of the nation teacher has a vital role. The teacher has to deal with sustainable issues in the classroom that needs specific knowledge, skills and competencies.

The environmental education should be an important part of the curriculum at all levels i.e., primary to higher education. Teacher should take a foremost role in pursuing the action on sustainable development and environment education, whether acting as individuals infusing environmental perspectives into their classes or cooperatively fostering environmental education through their educational institutions i.e., through more outdoor activity. It is not only concerned with social science or science teachers but it is the ethical duty for all types of teachers who are involved in inculcating education.

Sustainable teacher also advocates for objective teaching wherein factual information is conveyed and subjective opinions, personal interpretations, biases and prejudices are avoided. Teachers need to indulge in critical reflection and ongoing discovery for re-examining judgements, interpretations, assumptions and expectations (Chappel 2007, Henn & Andrews 1997, McAlpine & Weston 2000).

Sustainable practice by the teacher in the classroom provides an excellent route to transfer skills for sustainability to the learners. The teacher continues to be a rich source of information and stimulator of ideas. The teacher very often kindles the flame of imagination and contributes to fostering of inspiring teachers who can influence and nurture innovative thinking among learners.

Teacher will introduce nature in the classroom, develop insight to environment, help to foster sustainable concept among the learners. Topics like growth mechanism, life cycle, population are closely related to the issues connected with sustainability and closely connected to the real world lives. Outdoor teaching and learning paves the way for sustainable practice. Learner and teacher get opportunities to interact and observe nature. Online learning and tutoring are considered as zero energy balance as there is no wastage of paper, stationery and assessments. The role of teacher is to tap the hidden curriculum through nature of content delivery. The teacher to a large extent orients the future citizens to realize the vision, mission, and target of the sustainable development goals.

Teaching and Learning for a Sustainable Future

is a UNESCO programme for the United Nations Decade of Education for Sustainable Development. It provides professional development for student teachers, curriculum developers, education policy makers, and authors of educational materials. Teacher educators should be trained on sustainable pedagogies. Those pedagogies should be based on the values of simplicity, conservation, preservation and harmony with nature. Instructional strategies on sustainable practice must encourage creativity, problem solving, project execution and communication.

Teacher education programme leads to development of teacher's efficiency and competency that would enable and empower the teacher to meet the requirements of the profession and face the challenges therein. Present structure of teacher education programme should undergo changes according to the changing needs of the society. Changes should be brought in approaches to teaching for improvement of teacher's competencies, innovative strategies to be followed for professional development of teacher, topics related to sustainability need to be incorporated in the teacher education curriculum. More specifically pre-service teacher education programme should be organised in such a way that will provide an opportunity for developing teachers' competence and confidence in implementing whole school approaches to sustainability. Enrichment of pre-service education in particular and teacher education in general must lead to a sustainable development. It is high time to bring balance between theory and practice in teaching and to redesign teacher education curricula for meeting the needs of pre-service teachers better. Content and pedagogical reforms need to be recommended to address sustainable future.

Chapter-17

Role of Teacher for Future of the Nation

Teacher is the real social architect who can really shape the destiny of India by imparting need based education for the future generation of the society. In the era of knowledge explosion all countries virtually try to impart quality education which is highly essential for the emergence of a learning society. Teacher not only disseminates knowledge but also creates and generates new knowledge. This is the new role of the teacher. In this context, the National Council of Teacher Education (NCTE,1998) in its document has emphasized that teachers are the torchbearers in creating social cohesion and national integration by revealing and elaborating the secrets of attaining higher values in life. The teachers having a futuristic vision can only lead the society towards an egalitarian one.

Challenges and Future Teachers

The challenges that the education system and society facing today and the role of future teachers' are discussed below:

A critical challenge facing teacher educators in today's global society is how to effectively prepare future teachers for educating a diverse student population. A classroom is diverse in many ways; ethnically, culturally, socio-economically as well as other forms of diversity. This raises concerns about who will teach our children and how will the quality of education they would receive. To create capable citizenship of high quality, we need high quality education.

Now people and parents are far more alert and interactive. They demand not only education but good quality education. They are not satisfied with what is being offered; they demand to know how it shall contribute proper settlement of the learner in life. Teachers of tomorrow shall have to remain alert to the fact that the new advances in ICT attract young children and they acquire proficiency more swiftly than their elders. The 'Reciprocal Learning' shall create its own space in future deliberations between the teachers and taught. In this age of globalization teachers everywhere ought to acculturate, transcreate and modernize themselves because present day students are starving and striving for that. The future teachers need to be very efficient and should play multifarious roles for all-round development of students and nation.

Every year, thousands of bright students go abroad in search of latest knowledge and nearly half of them do not return. In this way, 'brain drain' takes place to foreign country. Unless quality of education is first improved, industrial and economic development can't be possible. Brain drains also will continue. In this context teacher's role is very important.

Present society needs professionally competent teachers. Improving competency of teachers has become essential to create a brave new India for today and tomorrow. Globally competent leaders for various professions and for politics of tomorrow are produced today in classrooms. Hence, world ranking of universities has assumed great significance. Many Indian universities and colleges are therefore making efforts to come up in top 100. Many of them have five star infrastructures, far more physical and financial resources. Yet they do not rank high in the world list. It is mainly because these institutions lack professors with excellence.

Following questions need to be asked to nurture teachers of excellence:

- As teachers are they thinking in global terms?
- Are they globally competent?
- Are they think great, dream big, and show commitment?
- Are they educating students with global perspectives?
- Are they nurturing students to become globally competent leaders?

No people can rise above the level of its teachers (NEP,1986). This statement may not be valid for today and tomorrow. There shall be no place for those 'teachers' who are not attuned to new knowledge and skill that is raining incessantly from all sides. Teachers of tomorrow shall derive respect from their students only if they remain conscious of the fact that their initial education, training and skill acquisition shall not help them lifelong. Only a lightened lamp can ignite others. Future teachers shall have to be conscious of changes in subject content on one hand, and the pedagogy on the other. In higher education, awareness of new advances, researches and innovations shall have to become part of the curriculum and examination. Teacher training institutions must include this in their activities for the benefit of both pre-service and in-service education. Teachers are the backbone of educational institutions.It is they who take the institutions to greater heights. If we enable teachers in the institutions to be innovative, creative and competitive by world standard, then we do not need to do anything else to win the world. Thus, the role of the teachers is very important in making the nation. If the teachers are excellent the nation will have excellent citizens.

In India practically every teacher teaches in a multi religious class and knows how important it is to let every child know how precious he/she is to him. Only the teacher can particularly in the initial stages show the seeds of the beauty that emerges out of 'unity in diversity'. Schools would, thus become the centres of social cohesion, religious amity and value nurturance. Teachers can transform uninitiated, innocent individuals into great performers and achievers. The task before future teachers, and education, at this juncture of history is indeed, stupendous. Education is the ray of hope for one and all, most particularly to those who are still not out of misery, poverty, ill-health and other socio-economic deprivation. Every teacher, therefore, has to acquire mastery over the skill of discrimination that alone would guide the learner on the right path. This is the greatest challenge before the teachers of today and tomorrow.

The teacher's role has changed in recent years. There has been a paradigm shift from instructional techniques to developing learning techniques. The teachers, henceforth, need to keep themselves updated along with understanding of the urgency of motivating themselves so that they can successfully discharge their responsibilities.

Teachers form the nucleus of any system of education. They are one of the main pillars of the society, responsible for educating young people for future careers for different walks of life. An educational institution should not be just confined to teaching and learning but it should be considered as a place where consciousness is aroused and illumined; soul is purified and strengthened. It is the place where the seeds of discipline, devotion and commitment are planted and fostered with deliberate efforts. A constructive companionship between teachers and students must develop.

Teachers are undoubtedly the most important group of professionals for our nation's future. A teacher's job is to help student to expand horizons of their awareness, and to facilitate them into taking responsibility for their own actions, behaviour, attitude and learning. Teacher's role is to increase students' motivation and develop the skills or strategies that make the students more competent and to structure the learning environment so that students are able to take responsibility of their own learning. It is believed that a teacher builds the interest of the students in education, a committed teacher can turn back a drifted away student; a good teacher is a psychologist of his student who can read student's mind and aptitude.

The personality traits, academic achievement and professional efficiency determine his image as a teacher. The secret of his success lies in his love for his work and love for the students. K.G. Saiyidain points out love as the secret of his personality. He says, "Love that unlocks all doors and conquers all obstacles. With affection he will gain confidence of the child, wins into his heart and releases his dormant force and energy. Sacrifice and dedication to his service enables character and humanitarian qualities of love, sympathy, compassion, affection and so on are more important than his intellectual achievements".

Dr. S. Radhakrishnan says, "Education is a universal right and not a class privilege". Our achievements in education deserve to be judged on this parameter. No system of education, particularly of school education, can flourish without the active and adequate presence of fully equipped, professionally competent, motivated and inspired teachers who are individually convinced that they are preparing not only the future generations but also the future of their country.

The emerging role, responsibility and performance levels of future teachers succinctly summarized in the Delors Commission report "Learning the Treasure Within" in 1996 by UNESCO. The importance of the role of teacher as an agent of change, promoting understanding and tolerance, has never been more obvious than today. It is likely to become even more critical in the 21st century. The need for change, from narrow nationalism to universalism, from ethnic and cultural prejudice to tolerance, understanding and pluralism, from autocracy to democracy in its various manifestations, and from a technologically divided world where high technology is the privilege of the few to a technologically united world, places enormous responsibilities on teachers who participate in the moulding of the characters and minds of the new generation.

Role of Future Teachers

The future teacher needs to play the following roles to meet various demands and challenges of the students and society.

I. Teacher will acquire mastery in soft skills

Education is for life and not for mere living. It is a transformative process that is designed to bring about desired change in the personality and behaviour of the learner. As a sociological term, soft skills may be considered as the cluster of personality traits, social graces, communication, personal habits, friendliness, and optimism that characterize relationships with other people. Soft skills incorporate all aspects of generic skills that include the cognitive elements associated with non-academic skills. These skills are identified and recognised to be the most relevant and important critical skills in this fast-moving technological era.Future Teachers are required to develop soft skills to meet the future challenges.

Domains of soft skills

- *Relationship management skills*

This skill is the prerequisite for the success. It is the ability to work with people from different socio-cultural background to achieve a common goal. Teachers must be trained to recognise and respect others attitude, behaviour and beliefs and contribute to the groups plan and co-ordinate the group's decision. If the future human capital can attain these skills, then the coming generation will collaborate, innovative ideas and cooperate as a taskforce towards the well-being of the nation as a whole.

- *Communication and Presentation Skills*

Most of the time, it is observed, students will forget what the books taught. But they will never forget what the teacher said.Thus, teacher plays significant role in students' life.The most important key to successful teaching is the communication skill. Good communication skill is a prerequisite for those in teaching profession. Effective communication is essential for a well-run-classroom. A teacher, who is able to communicate well with students, can inspire them to learn and participate in class and encourage them to come forth with their views thus creating a proper rapport. Good communication skill is invaluable asset since the teacher is entrusted with the task of creating a shared environment in the classroom.

As a teacher, he communicates ideas, information, views and expectations in various forms-through written words, gestures, body language, voice and presentations. How efficiently as a teacher he is appreciated, is directly proportionate to how well he communicates with his students. A skilful and efficient communicator opens the door to effective conversation. Communication has various dimensions and meanings. Some refers it as the process of sending and receiving information. Communication skills and the ability to build rapport are essential ingredients for creating conducive environment in a classroom. Richard Cullen (1988) provides useful ideas on features of teacher talk, which can help foster communication with students. His initial list includes; use of referential questions (rather than display questions), content feedback (rather than form focused feedback), use of speech modification such as rephrasing and attempts to negotiate meaning. He suggests the following activity list which is desirable in a classroom:

- Questioning/eliciting
- Responding to students' contributions
- Presenting/ explaining
- Organising/giving instructions
- Evaluating/correcting
- Sociating /establishing and maintaining classroom rapport

Teachers should be aware of the importance of these skills in teaching. It is only through communication skills that a teacher can introduce creative and effective solution to the problems of the students. Thus a teacher can enhance the learning process if he/ she has a repertoire of effective communication skill.The absence of good communicative skill leads to the poor presentation of the views and decisions. Communicative skills must be the integral part of every educational system and every teacher is expected to have good and effective command over the communication skills.

II. Teacher must fulfil students' expectations

UNESCO has classified the purpose of learning in to four dimensions. They are (i) Learning to Know, (ii) Learning to Do, (iii) Learning to live together, and Learning to Be. It is important for every educational institution and the teachers to introspect whether the four dimensions as mentioned are actually happening in the respective institutions.Every student expects the teacher to be very good in the subject taught. The expectation is that he can take the students beyond the syllabus. If a teacher is not able to live up to the expectations of the students, they may not attend the lectures. Besides the subject knowledge, students expect the teacher to have good general and interdisciplinary knowledge. Subjects versatility is an important quality expected from a good teacher.

III. Teacher must be technology friendly

We are living in the age of technology. In the digital age teacher ought to be a techno pedagogue. The teacher should learn the latest technology. He ought to be interested in technology, value technology and have favourable attitude towards technology. At the same time the technology ought to be Teacher Friendly. All forms of technology, such as, lap-tops, LCD projectors, Radio, TV, Computers, Internet iPad, Mobile web 2.0, e-Book and e-reader should be accessible and intelligible to the teachers. Teacher should be fully proficient in applying the principles of techno-pedagogy, such as, Media Message Compatibility, Proximity of Message Forms, Integration of Message, Media and Modes, Media Language Proficiency, Message Authenticity and Media Fidelity. But, technology finds more of integration in other fields than in education.

IV. Teacher will build a humane and caring society

One of the eminent educationists and great philosophers Dr. S.Radhakrishnan considers the teacher's place in society is of vital importance. Teacher acts as the source of the transmission of intellectual traditions and technical skill from generation to generation and helps to keep the lamp of civilization burning. If the teacher does not care, he can not expect his students to care either. The role of the teacher is to enable the student to become a responsible democratic citizen.

V. Teacher will act as an agent of change

It is teacher who interacts with students of different ages and frames of thought to ensure that wide-ranging educational objectives are achieved without brain-washing or propaganda. As an agent of change he himself has to be flexible and ready to change. J. Krishnamurti rightly says, the right kind of teacher is not satisfied with preparing of students for examination. The teacher's role is to understand the child and not insisting his ideals. He should develop among the students the spirit of individual freedom; make them to think critically and rationally. He must create a new ideal society and new social order.

VI. Teacher will promote kinship with environment

Naturalistic philosophy grants to the teacher the place of the friend and the observer, not of the information monger or dictator. Teacher is not to interfere with the child's activities or influence him. The teacher provides the educative material, creates the opportunities for learning, makes the ideal environment and thus contributes the natural and progressive development of child's innate potentialities.

The teacher must take a lead in promoting kinship with environment. Good environment, whether human or physical, has a humanizing element. Without having to incur any major expenditure, simple initiatives on the part of the teacher will enable each institution to present a much clearer and more beautiful look as a place of learning.

Role of Teacher Education Institutions and Programmes for Teacher

We require improving the quality of teacher education and developing educational standards that include local and national issues. Teacher education institutions must take the lead to prepare humane and professional teachers that need to be wholistic. The teacher education programmes need to integrate innumerous skills and competencies in teacher education curriculum. Along with content and methodology there is a need to integrate emotional competencies, such as, self-awareness and self-management, social sensitivity and social management. There is need to integrate life skills, info-savvy skills, such as asking, accessing, analyzing, applying and assessing. It is also essential to integrate techno-pedagogic skills and spiritual intelligence dimensions such as spirituality, self-awareness, quest for life values, convention,leadership, commitment and character.

As an integral part of education system, teacher education is intimately related to society.The need of the hour is to have competent, committed and professionally qualified teachers who can meet the demands and challenges of the society. Therefore, the role of teacher is of paramount importance. They lay the educational foundation for the children, and build the nation by developing its human resources in the best way possible. Future teachers need to be enlightened, emancipated and empowered to lead communities and nations in their march towards better and higher quality of life.

References

Acharyulu, S.T.V.G.(1995). Becoming Creative Teachers, in Gulati, S. (Edited) *Education for Creativity- A Resource Book for Teacher Educators*. New Delhi, NCERT.

Agarwal, S.K. (1998). *Population and Environment:Environmental Issues and Researches in India.* Udaipur, Himansu Publications.

Aggarwal, J.C. (1990). *Indian Education in the Emerging Society.* New Delhi,Vikas Publication.

Aggarwal, J.C.(2009). *Landmarks in the History of Modern Indian Education.* New Delhi, Vikash Publishing House Pvt.Ltd.

Ainscow,M.(1997). Towards Inclusive Schooling, *British Journal of Special Education,* 24(1), 3-6.

Akoojee, S., & Nikomo, M.(2007). Access and Quality in South African Higher Education: The Twin Challenges of Transformation, *South African Journal of Higher Education,* 27(3), 385-399.

Ametz, B.B. & Others. (1987). Immune Function in Unemployed Women, *Psychosomatic Medicine,* 49(1), 3-12.

Antonovsky, A. (1979). *Health, Stress and Coping.* San Francisco, Jossey-Bass.

Argyris, C., & Schon, D. (1974). *Theory in Practice: Increasing Professional Effectiveness.* San Francisco CA, Jossey-Bass.

Armstrong, D., Armstrong, A.C & Spandagou, I. (2011). Inclusion: By Choice or by Chance, *International Journal of Inclusive Education,* Vol. 15(1), 29-39.

Ayala, F. (2014). Evolution and Value – Expositions.*Online Journals,* University of California, Irvine, 50-58.

Bajapai, A. (1991). *Fifth Survey of Educational Research*1988-92, M.B. Buch, Volume, 2 NCERT, Sri Aurobindo Marg, New Delhi.

Ball, S. J.(2006). *Education Policy and Social Class: The Selected Works of Stephen J Ball*. London, Routledge.

Bateman, T.S., & Scott, A.S. (1999). *Management: Building a Competitive Advantage*. Boston, McGraw-Hill.

Beck, U. (1992). *Risk Society: Towards a New Modernity*. London, Sage Publication.

Benakanal, U.A. & Sahoo, P.K.(1994). Faculty Development and Academic Staff Colleges,*University News*, Dec.19, 8-14.

Bhardwaj, J. (2005). Value Oriented Education, *Journal of Value Education*, New Delhi, NCERT.

Bhatia, K.K. (1989). *Principles of Education*. New Delhi, Kalyani Publications.

Black-Hawkins, K., Florian, L., & Rouse, M. (2007). *Achievement and Inclusion in schools*. London.

Bower, J. E., & Segerstrom, S.C.(2004).Stress Management, Finding Benefit, and Immunefunction: Positive Mechanisms for Intervention Effects on Physiology, *Journal of Psychomatic Research*, 56(1) 9-11.

Brophy, J. (2001). Genetic Aspect of Effective Teaching, In Wang, M.C. and Walberg, H.J. *Tomorrow's Teachers*. MC Cutchan Publishing Company.

Chakrabarti, M. (1997). *Value Education: Changing Perspectives*. New Delhi, Kanishka Publishers.

Chakraborty,A.K.(2008).*Education in Emerging Indian Society*. R. Lall Book Depot, Meerut.

Chauhan, S.S. (2008). *Innovations in Teaching-Learning Process*. New Delhi, Vikash Publishing House Pvt. Ltd.

Christman, D. (2001).21stcentury Leadership: the Broadened Attributes of a Soldier, in Kolenda, C. (Ed), *leadership: The warrior's Art*.Carlisle,PA, Army War College Foundation Press.

Clarke, A. (1995). Professional Development in Practicum Settings: Reflective Practice under Scrutiny. *Teaching and Teacher Education*, 11(13), 243-261.

Cohen, Sheldon, Williamson & Gail, M. (1991).Stress and Infectious Disease in Human, *Psychological Bulletin*, 109(1), 5-24.

Coolahan, J.(2002). *Teacher Education and the Teaching Career in an Era of Life Long Learning*. OECD Education Working Papers, (2), OECD Publishing.

Cropely, A. J. (1989). Gifted and Talented: Provision of Education. In T. Husen and T.N. Postlethwaite edited the *International Encyclopaedia of Education* (Suppl. Vol.1), N.C. New York,Pergamon Press.

Crosby, P. B. (1979).*Quality is free*. New York, McGraw Hill.

Cullen, R. (1998). Teacher Talk & Classroom Context, *ELT Journal* 52(3).

Czubaj, C.A. (1996). Maintaining Teacher Motivation, *Education*, 116(3), 372-376.

Das, B.C.,& Pathak, U.N. (1977). Orientation Programme and the Professional Awareness of Teachers. *University News*, 35(51), 3-6.

Das, G. (1976). *Gopabandhu Rachanabali, Part-I*. Cuttack, Gopabandhu Sahitya Mandir.

Dash, B.N. (2014).*Trends & Issues in Indian Education*. New Delhi, Dominant Publishers.

Dash, S. C. (1964). *Pandit Gopabandhu- A Biography*. Cuttack, Gopabandhu Sahitya Mandir.

Dave, R.H. (2003). *Teacher Commitment*. New Delhi,NCERT.

Davidson, J.(1998). *The Complete Idiot's Guide to Managing Stress*. New Delhi, Prentice Hall of India.

Davis, M., Robbins Eschelman, E., & McKey, M. (1995). *The Relaxation & Stress Reduction Workbook(4th ed.)*. Oakland, CA,New Harbinger Publication.

Day, C. (2004). *A Passion for Teaching*. London, Routledge Falmer.

Delors, J .(1996). *Learning : The treasure Within*. Report of the International Commission on Education for Twenty-first century.Paris, UNESCO.

Deming, W.E. (1986). *Out of crisis*. Cambridge, Cambridge University Press.

Dernbach, J.C. (1998).Sustainable Development as a Framework for National Governance. Case Western Reserve Law Review.

Dewey, J. (1933). *How We Think: A Restatement of the Relation of Reflective Thinking to the Educative Process*. Boston M.A, Houghton Mifflin Publications.

Dienye, V.U. (2011). Education for Value Orientation in a Multicultural Society: The Case of Nigeria, *African Journal of Education and Technology*, 1(3).

Dindigul. (14th Aug. 2012). Life Skill Training for Teachers to Help Students. The Hindu, www.thehindu.com.cities. Madurai. Retrieved on 20th July, 2013.

Dingus, J. (2003). Making and Breaking Ethnic Masks. In G.Gay (Ed.), *Becoming Multicultural Educators: Personal Journey toward Professional Agency*. San Francisco, Jossey-Bass.

Ebmeier, H., & Nikolas, J. (1999). The Impact of Collaborative Supervision on Teacher's Trust, Commitment, Desire for Collaboration and Efficacy, *Journal of Curriculum and Supervision*, 14(4), 351-369.

Ekman, P., & Friesen,W.V.(1969). The Repertoire of Non-verbal Behaviour: Categories, Origins, Usage and Coding, *Semiotica,* 1, 49-98.

Ellins, J & Porter, J. (2005). Departmental Differences in Attitudes to Special Educational Needs in the Secondary School. *British Journal of Special Education,* 32 (4), 188-195.

Elliot, B. & Crosswell, L. (2001). Commitment to Teaching: Australian Perspectives on the Interplays of the Professional and the Personal in Teachers Lives. Paper presented at the *International Symposium on Teacher Commitment at the European Conference on Educational Research.* Little France.

Elliott, J.A. (2006). *An Introduction to Sustainable Development.* London,Rutledge Publisher.

Farrell, T.S. C. (2007). *Reflective Language Teaching: From Research to Practice.* London, Continuum press.

Florian, L. (2007). Reimagining Special Education. in L. Florian (ed.) *The Sage Handbook of Special Education.* London, Sage Publications.

Florian, L., & Rouse, M. (2001). Inclusive Practice in English Secondary Schools: Lessons learned, *Cambridge Journal of Education.*31(3), 399-412.

Fontana, D.(1981).*Psychology for Teachers.* London, British Psychological Society and MacMillan Publishers.

Forlin, C. (2001). Inclusion: Identifying Potential Stressors for Regular Class Teachers, *Educational Research,* 43 (3),235-245.

Forlin, C. (2004). Promoting Inclusivity in Western Australian Schools, *International Journal of inclusive Education,*8, 183-200.

Fredrikson, U. (2004).*Quality Education: the Teacher's Key Role.* Education International Working Papers. (14) Brussels.

Fullan, M. & Steigelbauer, S. (1991). *The New Meaning of Educational Change.* New York, Teachers' College Press.

Gaible, E & Burns, M. (2005). Using technology to Train Teachers: Appropriate Uses of ICT for Teachers' Professional Development in Developing Countries. Washington DC, infoDev/World Bank. Available at:http://www.infodev.org/en/publication.13html.

Gandhi, M.M. (2014). Value Orientation in Higher Education–Challenges and Role of Universities and Colleges: Retrospect and Future Options, *International Journal of Education and Psychological Research*, Vol.3, No.1.

Garg, S. (2011). Scholarship, Sustainability and Ethics in Open Learning: Some Reflection, *Indian Journal of open Learning*.

Garland, T. (1999). Life Skills Education: Perceived Effectiveness of a 4-H Out-of-School Program. Retrieved from www.eric.ed.gov.

Gay, G. (2000). *Culturally Responsive Teaching: Theory, Research and Practice*. New York, Teachers College Press.

Gilborn, D. & Youdell, D. (2000). *Rationing Education: Policy, Practice, Reform and Equity*. Buckingham, Open University Press.

GoI. Ministry of Education. (1953). *Report of the Secondary Education Commission*(1952-53), New Delhi.

GoI, Ministry of Education. (1964-66). *Kothari Commission-1964-66*. New Delhi.

GoI. (1985). *Challenges of Education*. New Delhi.

GoI. (1986). *National Policy on Education*, MHRD, New Delhi.

GoI. (1993). *Yash Pal Committee Report- Learning Without Burden*. MHRD, New Delhi.

GoI.(2007).*National Knowledge Commission Report to the Nation*, New Delhi.

Greenberger, D., & Padeshy, C. (1995). *Mind Over Mood: Change How You Feel by Changing the Way You Think*. New York, Guilford Publication.

Grubb, W. N. & Lazerson, M. (2004). *The Educational Gospel: The Economic Power of Schooling*.Cambridge MA, Harvard University Press.

Gulati, G. (2009). Empowering Teachers and Children through Life Skills Training. Retrieved from http://www.unicef.org/india/education 1878.htm.

Hemchand, T.K. (2008). *Problems of Teacher Education*. Delhi, Crescent Publishing Corporation.

Jenkins, A., & Ornelles, C. (2009). Determining Professional Development needs of General Educators in Teaching Students with Disabilities in Hawaii, *Professional Development in Education*, 35 (4), 635-654.

Joshi, H. (2014).Value Education, *International Journal of Research and Analytical Reviews*, 1(4).

Kalam, A.P.J. (2005). Education Systems for Developing the Capabilities of the Leaders, the Decennial Celebration Address of the NAAC on 5th Nov. 2004, New Delhi, *University News*, 43(6), 16-18.

Kates, W.R.,et al. (2005). Sustainable Development: Environment. *Science and Policy for Sustainable Development,* 47(3), 8-21.

Kauffman, J.M.,et al. (2005).Diverse Knowledge and Skills require a Diversity of Instructional Groups: A Position Statement, *Remedial Special Education*, 26 (1), 2-6.

Keay,J.,& Lioyd,C.(2009). Determining Professional Development in Physical Education: The Role of a Subject Association. *Professional Development in Education*, 35(4), 655-676.

Khublkar, R.(2008). *Know Your Stress. Manage Your Stress*. Hyderabad, Neelkamal Publications Pvt. Ltd.

Kiecolt-Glaser J.K., et al.(1987). Marital Quality, Marital Disruption and Immune Function, *Psychosom Media*, 49(1) 13-24.

Ladson-Billings, G.(2001).*Crossing Over to Canaan: The Journey of New Teachers in Diverse Classrooms.* San Francisco, Jossey-Bass.

Lal & Malhotra.(2008).*Education in the Emerging Indian Society.* Meerut, R. Lall Book Depot.

Lambe, J. (2011). Pre-service Education and Attitudes towards Inclusion: The Role of the Teacher Educator within a Permeated Teaching Model. *International journal of Inclusive Education*, 159(9), 975-999.

Lovallo,W.R. (1997). *Stress and Health: Biological and Psychological Interactions.* Thousand Oaks,Sage Publications.

Mangrulkar L. & Others. (2000). Life Skills Approach to Child and Adolescent Healthy Human Development. Pan American Health Organization.

McLaughlin, M., & Rouse, M. (2000). *Special Education School Reform in the United States and Britain.* London, Routledge.

Ministry of Education. (1948-49). Report of *Radhakrishan Commission* (1948-49).

Mishra, C. (2010). *Satyavadire Satabarsha.* Cuttack, Kataka Students' Store.

Mishra, D. (2009). *Shahebarshara Satyavadi Bana Vidyalaya.* Cuttack, Basant Publication.

Mohanty, J. (2003). *Teacher Education.* New Delhi, Deep & Deep Publications Pvt. Ltd.

Mukherjee,S. (2007).*Contemporary Issues inModern Indian Education.* Authors Press, New Delhi.

Mukhopadhya, M. (2005).*Total Quality Management in Education.* New Delhi, Sage Publications.

NCERT. (2005). *National Curriculum Framework-2005*, New Delhi.

NCTE. (1998) *Curriculum Framework for Quality Teacher Education*, New Delhi.

NCTE. (2003) *Secondary Teacher Education Programme (Pre-Service)*. Draft Approach Paper, New Delhi.

NCTE. (2009). *National Curriculum Framework for Teacher Education: Towards Preparing Professional and Humane Teacher*. NCTE, New Delhi.

NCTE. (2009). *Report of National Council for Teacher Education*, New Delhi.

Nias, J. (1981). Commitment and Motivation in primary School Teachers, *Educational Review*, 33(3), 181-190.

Oleary. (1990). Stress, Emotion and Human Immune Function, *Psychological Bulletin*.

Pal, R. (1996). Academic Orientation of University Teachers-A Qualitative Inquiry,*University News*, Dec. 16, 5-8.

Pasha, P.M. (2007). Accreditation in Higher Education: A Restatement, *University News*, 45 (32) 6-12.

Pathania, K.S. & Sharma, R.K. (2005). Role of Academic Staff Colleges in the Professional Development of Teachers,*University News*,43(16), 8-11.

Pearlin, L.I., & Others. (1981). The Stress Process, *Journal of Health and Social Behaviour*, Nov.22, 337-356.

Phillips, D. Walters, S., & Roger, G. (1995). *Teaching Practice: A Handbook for Teachers in Training.*New York, Macmillan Publications.

Rai, R. (2014). Inculcation of values: A Necessity Today. *International Journal of Research and Technology*, 5(1), 30-32.

Rajsekhar, H.M. & Chandar, K.M. (2002). Usefulness of Refresher Courses in Professional Development,*University news*, 40(5), 1-3.

Rath, R. (1999). *Satyasandha*. Cuttack, Gopabandhu Sahitya Mandir.

Resnick, L.B. (2005). Teaching Teachers: Professional Development to improve Student Achievement, *Research Points*, 3(1), 12-18.

Ross, J.A.(1994). The Impact of an In-service to Promote Cooperative Learning on the Stability of Teacher Efficacy. *Teaching and Teacher Education*, 10, 381-384.

Rouse, M. (2007). Enhancing Effective Inclusive Practice: Knowing, Doing and Believing, *Kairaranga*. Wellington, New Zealand Ministry of Education.

Rouse, M., & Florian, L. (1997). Inclusive Education in the Market Place, *International Journal of Inclusive Education*, 1(4), 323-336.

Rushdy, S. (2005). Value-based Teacher Training at New Era Development Institute, *Journal of Value Education*, New Delhi, NCERT.

Satapathy, M.K. (2007). *Education, Environment and Sustainable Development*. New Delhi, Shipra Publications.

Schank, R.C. (1988).Creativity as a Mechanical Process. In R.J. Sternberg (edited) *The Nature of Creativity*. Cambridge University Press.

Schon, D.A.(1983).*The Reflective Practitioner: How Professionals Think in Action*. New York, Basic Books.

Schon, D.A. (1987). *Educating the Reflective Practitioner: Towards a New Design for Teaching and Learning in the Profession*. San Francisco, CA, Jossey-Bass.

Selye, H. (1993). History of the Stress Concept, In L. Goldberger and S.breznitz (eds.).*Handbook of stress: Theoretical and Clinical Aspects*. New York, Free Press.

Seshadri, C. (2005). An Approach to Value Orientation of Teacher Education,*Journal of Value Education,* New Delhi, NCERT.

Seymour, D. (1992). *On Q: Causing Quality in Higher Education*. American Council on Education, New York, Macmilan Publishing Company.

Sharma, R.N., & Sharma, R.K. (1996).*Problems of Education in India*. New Delhi,Atlantic Publishers and Distributors.

Sharma,S.(2009). *Teacher Education-Principles, Theories and Practices*. New Delhi, Kanishka Publishers.

Sharma, S. P. (2003). *Education of Teachers*. Jaipur, Mangal Deep Publications.

Shulman, L.S. (2004). *The Wisdom of Practice: Essays on Teaching, Learning, and Learning to Teach*. San Francisco, Jossy-Bass.

Siddique, M.A., Sharma, A.K., & Arora, G.L. (2009).*Teacher Education: Reflections towards Policy Formulation*. New Delhi,NCERT.

Singhal, R.A. (2003). *In Search of Teacher Commitment*. NCERT, New Delhi.

Singh, P. (2004). Towards Value Based Education, *University News*, 42 (45) 11-12.

Sui, D. Z., & Bednarz, R.S. (1999). The Message is the Medium: Geographic Education in the Age of the Internet, *Journal of Geography*, 98(3), 96.

Swamy, S. (2011). An Agenda for Indian Youth facing Globalization, *Organizer*. Republic Day Special, 16-19.

Taylor, S.E. (1986).*Health Psychology*. New York, Random House.

The Hindu, "Life Skills Training for Teachers to Help Students, (2012). Retrieved from http:// www.thehindu.com/ news/cities/Madurai/life-skilltraining-for-teachers-to-helpstudenty article3765693.ece UNESCO | Education - What are the "skills" Referred to in this Approach? http://portal.

Tilburg, D., & Cooke, K. (2005). A National Review of Environmental Education and its Contribution to Sustainability in Australia: Frameworks for Sustainability, Canberra: Australian Government Department of Environment and Heritage and Australian Research Institute in Education for Sustainability.

Torrance, E. P., & Mayers, R.E. (1971). *Creative Learning and Teaching.* New York, Dodd Mead & Co.

Travers, J.F. (1982).*Educational Psychology.* N. Y., Harper & Row.

UNESCO. (2004). UN Decade in Education for Sustainable Development; International Implementation Scheme, UNESCO, Retrived, http://www.heacademy.ac.uk/assets/York/documents/ourwork/tla/sustainability/EmployableGraduates2008.pdf.

UNESCO .(2005). *Children out of School: Measuring Exclusion from Primary Education.* Montreal UNESCO Institute for Statistics.

UNICEF. (2006). *Empowering Teachers and Children through Life Skills Training.* website: www.unicef.org/India/edcuation-1878.htm. Retrieved on 20th July 2013.

Venkaiah, N. (1998). *Value Education.* New Delhi, APH Publishing Corporation.

Walia, K. (2003). *Perception of Teacher Commitment.* New Delhi, NCERT.

Weinstein, C., Curran, M., & Tomlinson-Clarke, S .(2003). Culturally Responsive Classroom Managemet: Awareness into action. *Theory into Practice, 42(3), 269-276.*

WHO .(1997). Life Skill Education in School, Program on Mental Health, Division of Mental Health and Prevention of Substance Abuse, Geneva.

WHO. (1999).WHO Information Series on School Health

Preventing HIV/AIDS/STI and Related Discrimination: An Important Responsibility of Health Promoting Schools, WHO/HPR/HEP/98.6. Geneva.

Willian, W.K. (1995).The Evolution of Values from Instinct,*The Philosophical Review*, 24 (2).

Yadav, P & Iqbal, N. (2009). Impact of Life Skill Training on Self-esteem, Adjustment and Empathy among Adolescents. *Journal of the Indian Academy of Applied Psychology.* (35) Special Issue, 61-70. Retrieved from http://medind.nic.in/jak/t09/s1/jakt09s1p61.pdf.

Yu,J., Yang, H.,Kuo, L., & Yang, H.(2012). Teachers' Professional Development in Free Software for Education in Taiwan. *International Journal of Computers and communications,* 6(1), 51-59.

Zeichner, K., & Liston, O. (1996). *Reflective Teaching*. Mahwah, NJ, Lawrence Erlbaum.

Black Eagle Books

www.blackeaglebooks.org
info@blackeaglebooks.org

Black Eagle Books, an independent publisher, was founded as a nonprofit organization in April, 2019. It is our mission to connect and engage the Indian diaspora and the world at large with the best of works of world literature published on a collaborative platform, with special emphasis on foregrounding Contemporary Classics and New Writing.

www.ingramcontent.com/pod-product-compliance
Lightning Source LLC
Chambersburg PA
CBHW020517080526
44583CB00013B/631